Oxford Studies in European Law

General Editors: Paul Craig and Gráinne de Búrca

Conflicts of Rights in the European Union

A Theory of Supranational Adjudication

AIDA TORRES PÉREZ

OXFORD
UNIVERSITY PRESS

Great Clarendon Street, Oxford OX2 6DP

Oxford University Press is a department of the University of Oxford.
It furthers the University's objective of excellence in research, scholarship,
and education by publishing worldwide in

Oxford New York

Auckland Cape Town Dar es Salaam Hong Kong Karachi
Kuala Lumpur Madrid Melbourne Mexico City Nairobi
New Delhi Shanghai Taipei Toronto

With offices in

Argentina Austria Brazil Chile Czech Republic France Greece
Guatemala Hungary Italy Japan Poland Portugal Singapore
South Korea Switzerland Thailand Turkey Ukraine Vietnam

Oxford is a registered trade mark of Oxford University Press
in the UK and in certain other countries

Published in the United States
by Oxford University Press Inc., New York

British Library Cataloguing in Publication Data

Data available

Library of Congress Cataloging in Publication Data
Torres Perez, Aida.
Conflicts of rights in the European Union : a theory of supranational
adjudication / Aida Torres Perez.
p. cm.
Based on the author's thesis (doctoral)—Yale Law School, 2006.
ISBN 978-0-19-956871-0
1. International and municipal law—European Union countries.
2. Judicial review—European Union countries. I. Title.
KJE969.T67 2009
341.242'2—dc22   2009024661

Typeset by Newgen Imaging Systems (P) Ltd., Chennai, India
Printed in Great Britain
on acid-free paper by the
MPG Books Group, Bodmin and King's Lynn

ISBN 978-0-19-956871-0

1 3 5 7 9 10 8 6 4 2

GENERAL EDITORS' PREFACE

This book engages with two important and persistent themes which are closely related in European Union law and scholarship. The first concerns the proper role of the European Union and the EU judiciary in the field of human rights protection, while the second concerns the nature of the authority-relationship between EU and national law in this field.

These two themes engage many interesting and difficult questions which have attracted the attention not only of academics and lawyers, but also of many other ordinary citizens. They have increasingly been the subject of public discussion at times of proposed treaty reform, including most recently during the debates on the EU Constitutional Treaty and the Lisbon Treaty, when the motto 'unity in diversity' was popularized and promoted. The combined effect of the ECJ's long-asserted claim to the supremacy of EC law over national law with the growing engagement of the EU with human rights matters has sharpened the controversy over the legitimacy of the ECJ's role in cases where human rights protected under national law are implicated.

Aida Torres Pérez, in this book, develops an account of how the ECJ's role in these sensitive and difficult fields, which are regularly characterized by interpretative disagreement and contestation of authority, might be legitimated by relying on the idea of dialogue. Adding to the rich literature which has developed in recent years on constitutional pluralism in the EU, her analysis seeks to develop a theory to justify a non-hierarchical and dialogic interaction between national courts and the ECJ in the field of human rights adjudication. She presents a theoretically informed and lucid account of the value of dialogue between courts as a way of developing collective deliberation, achieving better-reasoned outcomes for society as a whole, and ultimately for building a common identity within a broadly pluralist framework. Further, she presents and defends a comparative methodology for the ECJ to adopt, premised on a policy of deference to national courts.

This book presents a thoughtful and interesting argument on a set of familiar debates and controversies of continued salience. The author draws on debates within legal and political theory, and on comparative law, pointing in particular to relevant parallels within the US experience in the field of human rights. Her argument constitutes a valuable and distinctive contribution to the rich and growing literature on constitutional pluralism and judicial legitimacy in the EU, and it should be of interest to all those concerned with the unique and fascinating interaction of legal orders in Europe.

Paul Craig and Gráinne de Búrca

To my parents, Juan and Rosa María
and to my brother, Josep

ACKNOWLEDGEMENTS

This book is based on my doctoral dissertation completed at the Yale Law School. In the course of writing the dissertation, I was extremely fortunate to have the generous support of outstanding professors, colleagues, and friends. Without them, the dissertation would have not seen the light of day. I owe my deepest and sincerest debt of gratitude to Owen Fiss, who supervised the dissertation. His academic excellence and devotion to the law were a continuous source of inspiration. His illuminating insights and in-depth critical remarks offered invaluable help. Working under his supervision was a truly challenging and fulfilling experience. I am also grateful to Bruce Ackerman and Paul Kahn for their sharp and provocative comments. My friends and colleagues at Yale, a bright and cheerful group of people, greatly contributed to the success of this endeavour, both academically and personally. Jon Taylor made my life in New Haven happy. He was more helpful than he can imagine. I am deeply grateful for financial support from: La Caixa, Caja Madrid, AGAUR (Generalitat de Catalunya), and the Lillian Goldman Scholarship. Without their support I would have not been able to pursue my doctoral studies abroad.

Thanks are also due to those who were there even before I started this project and who then supported me throughout. Marc Carrillo always encouraged my work with enthusiasm. His academic and personal faith in me allowed me to pursue my academic career with freedom and confidence. For her contagious passion, brightness, and provocative thoughts, I want to thank Neus Torbisco. Her generosity as an academic and a friend has no boundaries. I am forever indebted to Victor Ferreres. Not only did he play a significant role in my decision to pursue my doctoral studies at Yale, but more importantly he always offered his irreplaceable advice and generous support. Our ongoing discussions, each time I was back to Barcelona or he was in the US, contributed considerably to my understanding of my dissertation topic. I profoundly admire his clear and free thinking, academic brilliance, and intellectual rigour and passion.

In the process of reviewing the manuscript for publication, I need to thank the two anonymous reviewers for their comments and criticisms which helped me to clarify and refine my arguments. I also thank Chris Champion and Alex Flach for their kind support and remarkable efficiency. My thanks go to Maribel González Pascual, Marisa Iglesias, Nico Krisch, Hèctor

López Bofill, Pau Luque, Alejandro Saiz Arnaiz, and Daniel Sarmiento for illuminating conversations and insights. Finally, special thanks to my friends, Raquel Anna and Serna Roy, who have always been and will always be there.

My parents and brother patiently suffered my extended absence. Their love and care gave me confidence and courage despite the distance between us. This book is as much their achievement as mine.

CONTENTS

TABLE OF CASES

Introduction

Should member states of the European Union (EU) be free to pass affirmative action measures to advance the position of women in the work-place? Or does the equality principle prevent them from doing so? Should an environmentalist demonstration be banned because it hinders free movement of goods? Or should the right to free speech and assembly prevail? May the commercialization of a magazine in another member state be banned to protect press diversity? Or should free speech and free move-ment of goods be secured? Should human dignity disallow the exploitation of a laser game involving the simulation of killing people? Or should the freedom to provide services prevail? All these questions have been the sub-ject of cases decided by the European Court of Justice (ECJ), the highest court within the EU legal system.[1] As is well known, even though the EU was not originally designed as a system to protect fundamental rights, the ECJ developed a whole bill of rights through its vigorous case law. EU fundamental rights were not only enforced against EU institutions, but also against state action. Consequently, the scope of application of consti-tutional and EU fundamental rights might overlap, and their respective interpretations might diverge. To some extent, state courts are asked to replace the constitutional standard of protection with the standard defined by the ECJ. In this vein, the ECJ claims authority for adjudicating funda-mental rights norms that will be applied to review state action, sometimes in opposition to the constitutional interpretation of parallel rights. This claim of authority needs to be justified.

At the outset, the first part of the book will identify the object of the inquiry and place this project in the context of the plurality of systems protecting fundamental rights in Europe. In the aftermath of the Second

[1] *Katarina Abrahamsson and Leif Anderson v Elisabet Fogelqvist*, C-407/98; *Eugen Schmidberger, Internationale Transporte und Planzüge v Austria*, C-112/00; *Vereinigte Familiapress Zeitungsver-lags- und Vertriebs GmbH v Heinrich Bauer Verlag*, C-368/95; *Omega Spielhallen- und Automat-enayfstellungs GmbH v Oberbürgermeisterin der Bundesstadt Bonn*, C-36/02.

World War, a widespread consensus began to call for developing international institutions and forms of co-operation that would constrain the excesses of state sovereignty. Although the EU emerged as an economic project integrating the three foundational Communities,[2] the integration process ultimately sought to weaken state sovereignty in favour of supranational governance.[3] Sovereign powers previously reserved to the states were transferred to a supranational organization capable of enacting binding norms wihtin the state territory. In the long run, it was thought, economic interaction would further political integration.[4] Indeed, as a result of successive Treaty amendments, the powers of the EU expanded quantitatively and qualitatively. The Maastricht Treaty (1992) is regarded as a turning point on the path to greater political integration.[5] At the same time, the number of member states has been steadily increasing from the six original founders[6] to the current twenty-seven member states.[7] The foundational Treaties did not include any written catalogue of rights. As a consequence, the question arose as how to ensure that laws coming from a supranational source would not violate fundamental rights. Over time, the ECJ created a set of rights through its case law. Yet, there was no guarantee that standards of constitutional protection would not be lowered. Moreover, the ECJ incorporated these judicially-made rights to the states, creating areas of overlap between the scope of application of constitutional and EU fundamental rights. Overlapping scopes of application

---

[2] The European Coal and Steel Community (ECSC 1951), the European Atomic Energy Community (EURATOM 1957), and the European Economic Community (EEC 1957).

[3] Manfred Zuleeg, *A Community of Law: Legal Cohesion in the European Union*, 40 FORDHAM INTERNATIONAL LAW JOURNAL 623, 623 (1997); JOSEPH H. H. WEILER, THE CONSTITUTION OF EUROPE 341 (Cambridge University Press 1999); ERNST B. HAAS, BEYOND THE NATION-STATES. FUNCTIONALISM AND INTERNATIONAL ORGANIZATION 452 (Stanford University Press 1964).

[4] As Ernst B. Haas, *Technocracy, Pluralism and the New Europe*, in INTERNATIONAL REGIONALISM 152 (Joseph Nye ed. 1968), remarked: 'The supranational style stresses the indirect penetration of the political by way of the economic because the "purely" economic decisions always acquire political significance in the minds of the participants'; Ernst B. Haas, *International Integration: The European and the Universal Process*, 15 INTERNATIONAL ORGANIZATION 366, 366 (1961).

[5] This Treaty created the European Union, which encapsulated the three European Communities and was complemented by the policies and forms of co-operation in the fields of 'common foreign and security policy' and 'justice and home affairs', the so-called second and third pillars.

[6] Belgium, Germany, France, Italy, Luxembourg, and the Netherlands.

[7] In addition to the six founders, Denmark, Ireland, and the United Kingdom (1973), Greece (1981), Spain and Portugal (1986), Austria, Finland, and Sweden (1995), Cyprus, Czech Republic, Estonia, Hungary, Latvia, Lithuania, Malta, Poland, Slovakia, and Slovenia (2004), Bulgaria and Romania (2007).

bring about potential conflicts when the respective interpretations of parallel rights diverge (Chapter 1). From the constitutional standpoint, state courts have the obligation to ensure respect of state constitutional rights. From the European standpoint, state courts must follow EU rights, even if the interpretation given by the ECJ differs from the constitutional one. Yet, why should the ECJ have the last word regarding fundamental rights' interpretation as opposed to state constitutional courts? The main purpose of this book will be to explore the grounds for the legitimacy of the ECJ's claim to authority in adjudicating fundamental rights.

In Europe, the mass violations of human rights committed during the Second World War exposed the potential dangers of unchecked, even democratic, state sovereignty. The European Convention for the Protection of Human Rights and Fundamental Freedoms (ECHR) was aimed at constraining state action to secure the fundamental rights of individuals.[8] The Convention was drafted in the framework of the Council of Europe, an international organization founded in 1949 to promote human rights. Signed in 1950, the European Convention set up the European Court of Human Rights (ECtHR) to interpret and protect the newly instituted bill of rights. Since then, the ECtHR has created a quasi-constitutional order of human rights in Europe. Currently, forty-seven European states are parties to the European Convention, including every member state of the EU. Hence, in Europe, there are at least three spheres of rights protection: national, supranational, and international. Each of these systems includes a bill of rights and a specific court with the supreme authority to interpret them: state constitutional or supreme courts, the ECJ, and the ECtHR. This triangular interaction will be reflected upon (Chapter 2). Although this work will focus on the interplay between state courts and the ECJ, the existence of the European Convention and its Court should not be ignored for a complete picture of the multilevel system of rights protection in Europe.

The second part of this book will advance the adoption of a pluralist framework for the interplay of fundamental rights law in the EU. Current institutional models addressing rights' conflicts in the EU will be critically analysed (Chapter 3). Much of the academic debate has focused on whether

---

[8] As was expressed during the drafting debates, see Council of Europe, Collected Edition of the Travaux Préparatoires 40, 140 (1975): 'Behind the State, whatever its form, were it even democratic, there ever lurks a permanent temptation.... Even parliamentary majorities are in fact sometimes tempted to abuse their powers. Even in our democratic countries we must be on guard against this temptation of succumbing to reasons of States.... No one can say that he is, in the future, protected from the totalitarian danger.'

state constitutions or EU Treaties should be regarded as the supreme law of the land; and whether constitutional courts or the ECJ should have the final say in case of conflict. This chapter seeks to demonstrate the short-comings of hierarchical models relying on supremacy as the principle struc-turing interaction between norms protecting rights. On the one hand, the claim for constitutional supremacy fails to acknowledge the transformations brought about by European integration. On the other hand, recognizing a measure of autonomy to the EU legal order does not imply admitting the unlimited supremacy of EU law over state constitutions. In addition, this chapter will show that specific proposals formulated from non-hierarchical approaches are unsatisfactory as well. Even though these specific proposals are not embraced, a pluralist framework regarding the structure of power in the EU will be advanced. According to this framework, the foundation-al-constitutional norms of the interacting legal systems are not hierarch-ically ordered. A pluralist model not only provides a better account of the European reality, but should be normatively embraced as well. This chapter draws from the ideas advanced by Neil MacCormick[9] and Neil Walker[10] on constitutional pluralism, and posits the principle of institutional balance as its main benefit. As such, a pluralist model furthers the opportunity to over-come the dangers of exacerbated state sovereignty by fragmenting public power among several institutions beyond the state. At the same time, a plur-alist model limits the excesses of concentrating power at the supranational level by establishing mutual checks and balances between the national and supranational orders—national and supranational courts in this case. Thus, any theoretical approach to constitutional rights' conflicts needs to acknow-ledge this underlying pluralist political structure.

Next, the implications of this pluralist framework for the system of rights protection in the EU will be examined (Chapter 4). The tensions between uniformity and diversity regarding the meaning of fundamental rights are endemic to any system in which political power is allocated among multiple spheres. In the US, there is a vast literature converging on federalism and rights, which may well provide valuable insights for EU dilemmas, without

---

[9] Neil MacCormick, *Risking Constitutional Collision in Europe?*, 18 OXFORD JOURNAL OF LEGAL STUDIES 517 (1998); NEIL MACCORMICK, QUESTIONING SOVEREIGNTY. LAW, STATE AND NATION IN THE EUROPEAN COMMONWEALTH (Oxford University Press 1999).

[10] Neil Walker, *Flexibility within a Metaconstitutional Frame: Reflections on the Future of Legal Authority in Europe*, in CONSTITUTIONAL CHANGE IN THE EU. FROM UNIFORMITY TO FLEXIBILITY? 9 (Gráinne de Búrca & Joanne Scott eds. 2000); Neil Walker, *The Idea of Constitu-tional Pluralism*, 65 THE MODERN LAW REVIEW 317 (2002).

suggesting that the EU should reproduce American answers. This chapter will be devoted to discussing the arguments underpinning state diversity and supranational uniformity regarding fundamental rights' interpretation. This debate has not yet been thoroughly examined in the EU. In many cases, the arguments for state diversity do not go beyond state sovereignty, which is no longer adequate given the EU pluralist structure. At the same time, the virtues of supranational uniformity tend to be assumed, without questioning the reasons underpinning this claim. It will be concluded that the ECJ should not impose uniformity for its own sake. The values underlying state autonomy justify accommodating a certain degree of diversity and a measure of deference to state courts.

The third part contains the core of the book. It spells out the proposed theory of supranational adjudication in the EU. This work seeks to demonstrate that dialogue may provide the conceptual model for the ECJ's legitimacy in adjudicating fundamental rights (Chapter 5). Rather than investigating whether the ECJ is actually obeyed or not, this inquiry takes a normative standpoint towards the notions of legitimacy and authority. In the last few decades, constitutional and democratic theories have increasingly explored a dialogic ideal as the source of law's legitimacy. The present inquiry draws from Habermas's insights,[11] and yet the turn to dialogue as a source of legitimacy is associated with the particular pluralist institutional structure of the EU. In the EU academic literature, the term dialogue and a variety of close notions are commonly employed. As such, the words' specific definitions and connotations have become muddled. Despite multiple and varied references to dialogue in the literature, mostly from a descriptive standpoint, there has been no thorough and rigorous account establishing its legitimating potential regarding the ECJ's adjudication of fundamental rights norms. This book will offer such a theoretical account of how the legitimacy of ECJ adjudicative decisions regarding fundamental rights might be grounded in the ideal of dialogue. Such a theory of supranational adjudication would serve as a normative model to critically assess the activity of the ECJ and to improve current institutional practices. According to this view, the meaning of fundamental rights should be constructed through an ongoing dialogue between the ECJ and state courts. Dialogue, understood as argumentative communication based on the exchange of reasons, contributes to reaching better-reasoned outcomes for the community as a whole. Also, dialogue enhances participation in the interpretive process in such a

---

[11] Jürgen Habermas, Between Facts and Norms (MIT Press 1998).

way that the outcome might be regarded as a shared product of collective deliberation. Additionally, dialogue benefits the building of a common identity; and ultimately, this is the most consistent form of interaction within a pluralist framework. Each of these arguments will be fully developed. This chapter will also explore the prerequisites that need to be fulfilled for an effective judicial dialogue to develop with the capacity to ground the normative legitimacy of the ECJ's authority. Basically, dialogue obtains when there are competing viewpoints about the meaning of law, and at the same time there is common ground for mutual understanding. For dialogue to develop, neither of the interacting courts should have ultimate authority; and at the same time they should mutually recognize each other as part of a common enterprise. Finally, all courts should have equal opportunity to participate in dialogue evolving over time. As will be demonstrated, these prerequisites are met in the EU or, at least, the political structure of the EU allows for them to be met. Then this chapter will go on to address some objections to the possibility of developing a model of dialogue among courts. Finally, the implications of judicial dialogue for the mode of judicial reasoning in interpreting fundamental rights will be analysed (Chapter 6). In particular, this chapter will explore the comparative method and deference as mechanisms contributing to the ECJ's authority-building. These mechanisms are consistent with the ideal of dialogue within a pluralist framework, but they are highly contested in the literature. Thus, this chapter will articulate a normative justification of the comparative method. In addition, it will expand on how the ECJ should operationalize this method, coupled with a reflection on a policy of deference to state courts.

Hence, this book revolves around two main themes: constitutional pluralism, as the framework of institutional interaction in the EU; and dialogue, as the source of the ECJ's legitimacy in adjudicating fundamental rights. If eventually ratified, the Lisbon Treaty would recognize the legally binding force of the European Charter of Fundamental Rights. According to the pluralist framework, however, there is no hierarchical relationship between the rights enshrined in this Charter and constitutional rights. Thus, potential conflicts of rights in the EU might become even more visible, and the question about the source of the ECJ's legitimacy in adjudicating fundamental rights even more relevant.

PART I

Rights in Europe

Fundamental Rights Conflicts in the European Union

1 Fundamental rights in the European Union

At the outset, a terminological clarification is needed as to the meaning of 'fundamental rights'.[1] This work does not offer a substantive definition or list of rights that should be considered to be fundamental. Rather, rights are regarded as fundamental when they are recognized as such by the respective legal systems. In general, this recognition implies that these rights are hierarchically supreme norms, judicially protected against encroachment by public authorities, including the legislature. These rights reveal the essential values of a given polity and receive the highest level of protection. In state legal systems, these rights tend to be included in the constitution and protected by constitutional courts. In the European Union (EU), the foundational Treaties did not include a catalogue of rights, but they were the outcome of a creative European Court of Justice (ECJ) case law. The story of the judicial creation of a set of EU fundamental rights has been recounted on many ocasions, and there is no need to go over it again.[2] Case

[1] For a reflection of the use of the term 'fundamental rights' by the ECJ, see Bruno de Witte, *The Past and Future of the European Court of Justice in the Protection of Human Rights*, in THE EU AND HUMAN RIGHTS 859, 860–863 (Philip Alston ed. 1999).

[2] For instance, Joseph H. H. Weiler, *Eurocracy and Distrust: Some Questions Concerning the Role of the European Court of Justice in the Protection of Fundamental Rights within the Legal Order on the European Communities*, 61 WASHINGTON LAW REVIEW 1103 (1986); TREVOR C. HARTLEY, THE FOUNDATIONS OF EUROPEAN COMMUNITY LAW 130–142 (Oxford University Press 1998); TAKIS TRIDIMAS, THE GENERAL PRINCIPLES OF EC LAW 202–243 (Oxford University Press 1999); Alejandro Saiz Arnaiz, *El Tribunal de Justicia, los Tribunales Constitucionales y la Tutela de los Derechos Fundamentales en la Unión Europea: entre el (Potencial) Conflicto y la (Deseable) Armonización. De los Principios no escritos al Catálogo Constitucional, de la Autoridad judicial a la Normativa*, in

by case, the ECJ gave recognition to rights such as free speech, property, non-discrimination on grounds of sex, good administration, or the right to a fair trial. In 1999, the Cologne European Council launched the drafting of a Charter of Fundamental Rights for the European Union. The main goal of writing down a catalogue of rights was to make these rights more visible to the citizens, rather than to create new rights for the EU. In the Nice European Council (2000), the Charter was jointly approved by the European institutions—Council, Commission, and Parliament. Nonetheless, the member states did not agree to include the Charter in the text of the EU Treaty. Hence, the Charter was not granted legally binding force. The project for a European Constitution (signed by the heads of state and government in October 2004) incorporated this Charter within its text. As is well known, however, the process of ratification failed after the negative outcome of the referenda held in France and the Netherlands.[3] As a consequence, the status of the Charter remained that of an institutional declaration without binding force.[4] The Lisbon Treaty, signed in December 2007 and currently under ratification, grants legal binding force to the Charter. Article 6.1 reads: 'The Union recognises the rights, freedoms and principles set out in the Charter of Fundamental Rights of the European Union of 7 December 2000, as adapted at Strasbourg, on 12 December 2007, which shall have the same legal value as the Treaties.' Thus, the Lisbon Treaty would give the Charter the same legal value as the Treaties, but without including the Charter's text. This odd formulation might be explained within the context of seeking to downplay the constitutional implications of the integration process after the failure of the constitutional project.[5] The negative outcome of the Irish refrerendum (June 2008) has cast a shadow over the success of the ratificacion process and thus over the future

CONSTITUCIÓN EUROPEA Y CONSTITUCIONES NACIONALES 531, 542–583 (Marta Cartabia, Bruno de Witte & Pablo Pérez Tremps eds. 2005).

[3] Respectively, 19 May and 1 June 2005.

[4] It should be kept in mind that, although the Charter as such does not have legal binding force, it is a relevant document. The Charter constitutes a political declaration adopted by the main European institutions listing the rights they are committed to respect. In addition, most of the rights included in the Charter are already protected by the ECJ case law. Hence, as some claim, the Charter might be used as reference to guide the action of political and judicial institutions, and to identify and interpret EU fundamental rights.

[5] The European Council's mandate to the Intergovernmental Conference in charge of amending the Treaties expressly stated: 'The TEU and the Treaty on the Functioning of the Union will not have a constitutional character. The terminology used throughout the Treaties will reflect this change' (*Presidency Conclusions*, Brussels, 21/22 June 2007).

of the Charter.[6] In any event, the Charter tends to include rights already protected by the ECJ case law or EU legislation, such as the respect for private and family life (art. 7), the right to the protection of personal data (art. 8), the right to freedom of expression and information (art. 11), the right to equality before the law (art. 20), the right to vote and to stand as a candidate at elections to the European Parliament (art. 39), and right to an effective remedy and to a fair trial (art. 47).[7]

Different legal systems might consider different rights to be 'fundamental'. The determination of which rights are given this recognition depends on the historical and political circumstances of time and place in which the respective constitutions were drafted. Thus, rights protected by state constitutions and the ECJ as fundamental rights are not necessarily the same ones. In practice, however, there is substantial coincidence between the rights regarded as fundamental within the European and constitutional legal systems, such as the right to life, free speech, privacy, non-discrimination, a fair hearing, etc. Indeed, as the ECJ has repeatedly declared, one of the main sources for interpreting EU rights is the constitutional traditions common to the member states. Nevertheless, even when there is agreement on the rights to be protected, this does not mean there is agreement on the scope of protection in the particular instances of application. Since these rights are interpreted by different institutions constituting different spheres, their meanings might vary. Generally, the meaning of fundamental rights is subject to a pervasive disagreement. Given the typical, indeterminate language of fundamental rights clauses, they admit several interpretations.[8] Moreover, fundamental rights embrace basic values for individuals and societies so that their meanings tend to be

---

[6] In the Brussels European Council (December 2008), it was agreed that Ireland would convoke a second referendum before November 2009.

[7] In some occasions, the Charter expressly expands the scope of specific rights to adapt them to social changes, such as article 3.2, including 'the prohibition of eugenic practices, in particular those aiming at the selection of persons' and 'the prohibition of the reproductive cloning of human beings'; or article 5.3, banning the 'trafficking in human beings'. Probably, the major innovation consists of the inclusion in Title IV of a set of social rights. Nevertheless, the constant references to EU law and national legislation and practices downplay the efficacy of their recognition as fundamental rights. Additionally, *Protocol 30 on the Application of the Charter of Fundamental Rights of the European Union to Poland and to the United Kingdom* expressly declares that 'nothing in Title IV of the Charter creates justiciable rights applicable to Poland or the United Kingdom, except in so far as Poland or the United Kingdom has provided for such rights in its national law'.

[8] ROBERT ALEXY, A THEORY OF CONSTITUTIONAL RIGHTS 2 (Oxford University Press 2002), asserts that the problem of the interpretation of constitutional rights resides in the fact that they

contested.[9] Hence, the members of a community might reasonably disagree regarding fundamental rights' interpretation.[10] These disagreements have received great attention within political philosophy and constitutional theory. Instead of focusing on disagreements within national communities, this book considers disagreements between legal systems in the framework of a supranational community, namely, the EU.

Divergences in the scope of protection of parallel rights between member states and the EU, as well as among several member states, may have different origins. First, one of the legal systems may not recognize a specific right at all, or it may simply understand that right differently. For example, the Irish Constitution recognizes the right to life of the unborn, whereas other state constitutions do not explicitly list it. Secondly, divergences between systems might be a result of the different ways in which to strike a balance between conflicting rights within each system. Different legal orders might recognize the same two rights as fundamental, but the balance between these rights might lead to different outcomes. For instance, the balance between free speech and privacy might be resolved differently in different systems. Thirdly, fundamental rights might clash with other social values or general interests. Both systems may protect a certain right, but, in one system, this right might clash with a social value or general interest that does not have the same relevance in the other. For example, both states and the EU protect the right to property. However, in some cases, the general EU interest in the success of the common market might require limiting this right. Also, the effectiveness of EU basic freedoms of movement of goods, services, people, and capital might clash with state constitutional rights.

It is important to emphasize that diverging interpretations of rights, by themselves, do not necessarily amount to conflicts. The fact that different states interpret the same rights in different ways does not necessarily create a conflict because these interpretations may be applied within different polities. In Europe, however, as a consequence of the development of

---

regulate 'in a highly open manner what are in part deeply controversial questions about the basic normative structure of state and society'.

   [9] See Jeremy Waldron, *Vagueness in Law and Language: Some Philosophical Issues*, 82 CALIFORNIA LAW REVIEW 509, 526–540 (1994), describing the notion of 'essentially contested concepts'. This author defines 'contestability' stating that 'a phrase becomes contestable when it is clear that it embodies a normative standard, but different users disagree about the detailed contents of that normative standard'. 'Essential contestability' may indicate that 'the disagreement is in some sense indispensable to the usefulness of the term'.

   [10] JEREMY WALDRON, LAW AND DISAGREEMENT (Oxford University Press 1999).

a supranational system including fundamental rights, the spheres of application of EU and constitutional fundamental rights might overlap. In this context, state authorities might be bound concurrently by constitutional and EU rights. Thus conflicts might occur when the scopes of application of EU and constitutional rights overlap, and these rights are interpreted differently by the respective courts. In these circumstances, deciding the case at hand according to the constitutional or the ECJ interpretation would lead to different outcomes.

A different concern is the aspiration for uniformity in the meaning of fundamental rights. From this perspective, divergences are seen as problematic, even if there is no actual conflict of application in specific cases. Behind the idea of fundamental rights, or more generally human rights, lies an aspiration for universality. Arguably, these are rights that all human beings should enjoy, simply because of their humanity. Also, the universality of human rights incorporates the ideal of equality: all human beings deserve to be treated equally regarding the enjoyment of basic rights. In the face of reasonable disagreement regarding the content of these rights, however, other values, such as democratic self-government or political and cultural identity, might justify the validity of diverse interpretations within different polities. In addition, imposing supranational uniformity for its own sake does not secure the most adequate level of rights protection and might bring about unwelcome homogenization. The tension between imposing homogeneity or recognizing a certain degree of diversity regarding the meanings of rights will have to be addressed by any model that seeks to give an account of rights conflicts in Europe.[11] This confrontation constitutes yet another facet of the pervasive tension between the drive toward uniformity encapsulated in the ideal of fundamental rights and the particularities of their application within specific polities.

2 Overlapping constitutional and EU fundamental rights

Given the lack of a written EU bill of rights, after the ECJ's proclamation of the supremacy of EU law over state law, including constitutional law,

---

[11] Kalypso Nicolaidis & Robert Howse, *'This is my EUtopia...': Narrative as Power*, 40 JOURNAL OF COMMON MARKET STUDIES 767, 784 (2002): 'The tension between unity and diversity is at the core of the post-national paradigm.'

it was soon realized that EU institutions were not bound by fundamental rights. Initially, the ECJ's case law protecting fundamental rights did not trigger any opposition among state actors or in the academic literature. To the contrary, given the absence of a written catalogue of rights in the EU, the ECJ case law protecting fundamental rights was rather welcomed. This lack of resistance to a clear form of (supranational) judicial activism might be attributed to several reasons.[12] First, the process of European integration was market driven, and, in this context, fundamental rights protection was not a main concern.[13] The main goal of the three foundational European Communities was economic integration in specific fields. Secondly, EU rights, at the beginning, were not incorporated against the states but were only binding on EU institutions. Indeed, because these rights provided an instrument to constrain the action of European public authorities, they contributed to the legitimacy of the EU legal system. Furthermore, the common objection to judicial review based on its counter-majoritarian nature did not arise because EU legislation was not regarded as expressing the popular will.[14] The main law-making bodies, namely, the Council and the Commission, do not directly represent the people, while the European Parliament does not play a central role in the legislative process. Therefore, the review of EU legislation by the ECJ did not seem to impinge upon the values of democratic self-government. Lastly, there had not been clear instances of dispute regarding levels of protection between constitutional and EU fundamental rights.

Over time, however, the ECJ rights discourse raised increasing uneasiness. The furtherance of the integration process brought its controversial features to the foreground, as European integration moved beyond the purely economic into the political. As a result of successive Treaty amendments, EU powers expanded. Thus, EU powers were no longer limited to economic matters but went far beyond, covering subjects that affected individuals as human beings and not just as economic actors. In addition, by the end of the 1980s, EU fundamental rights were incorporated to the states.[15]

---

[12] See Weiler, *supra* n 2, at 1116–1117 (1986); Joseph H. H. Weiler, *Methods of Protection: Towards a Second and Third Generation of Protection, in* II Human Rights and the European Community: Methods of Protection 555, 577–581 (Antonio Cassese, Andrew Clapham & Joseph H. H. Weiler eds. 1991).

[13] For these purposes, the European Convention on Human Rights had already been signed in 1950.

[14] Weiler, *supra* n 2, at 1115–1117.

[15] *Hubert Wachauf v Bundesamt für Ernährung und Forstwirtschaft,* C-5/88; *Elliniki Radiophonia Tileorassi AE v Dimotiki Etairia Pliroforissis and Sotirios Kouvelas,* C-260/89.

As EU rights were enforced against state action, including legislative acts, a democratic concern emerged because laws enacted by national parliaments were subject to rights interpreted by a supranational court, sometimes in opposition to the constitutional interpretation of parallel rights. Judicial review of legislation always poses a counter-majoritarian difficulty since the decisions of the body representing the people are struck down by judges lacking public accountability. At the national level, this difficulty might be counteracted through different mechanisms, since the judiciary is part of a broader institutional system of checks and balances. For example, the design of a 'centralized model' of judicial review was aimed at responding to this democratic concern by creating a specific constitutional court that would be exclusively in charge of reviewing legislation.[16] Usually, a special institutional relationship between parliament and the constitutional court is established, regarding, for instance, the selection of judges.[17] Additionally, parliament has the ability to react to constitutional court decisions promoting a constitutional amendment.[18] Thus, broadly speaking, national parliaments have a certain capacity in which they may interact with constitutional courts. At the same time, the EU Parliament neither participates in the selection of ECJ judges nor plays a role in the process of Treaty amendment.[19] In this context, democratic concerns arise not only because the ECJ is an unelected institution but, even more exacerbating, because the ECJ belongs to a supranational system of governance. Moreover, after the incorporation of EU rights to the states, the ECJ rights discourse could be regarded as a tool to monitor state action and expand the EU influence in areas of state powers. Some argued that the ECJ was making an 'offensive' use of fundamental rights in order to 'extend its jurisdiction into areas previously reserved to member states' courts'.[20] The ECJ was accused of

---

[16] Most European countries have adopted a centralized model of judicial review. See Víctor Ferreres, *The European Model of Constitutional Review of Legislation: Toward Decentralization?*, 2 INTERNATIONAL JOURNAL OF CONSTITUTIONAL LAW 461, 461–463 (2004). For a thorough analysis of this model see VÍCTOR FERRERES, CONSTITUTIONAL COURTS AND DEMOCRATIC VALUES. A EUROPEAN PERSPECTIVE (Yale University Press 2009).

[17] Ferreres, *The European Model*, at 468–470.

[18] Víctor Ferreres, *Souveraineté Nationale et Intégration Européenne dans le Droit Constitutionnel Espagnol*, 9 LES CAHIERS DU CONSEIL CONSTITUTIONNEL 106, 111 (2000).

[19] *Id.* at 111–112. Ferreres argued that the increasing importance of fundamental rights in the ECJ's case law, not only as limits to the action of European institutions but also as limits to state legislation, would make it necessary to establish new bases securing the democratic legitimacy of the ECJ's work and impact.

[20] Jason Coppel & Aidan O'Neill, *The European Court of Justice: Taking Rights Seriously?*, 29 COMMON MARKET LAW REVIEW 669, 669–670 (1992). Opposing this view see Joseph H. H. Weiler

using fundamental rights instrumentally to foster integration. In addition, the potential for conflict between standards of protection was realized concerning sensitive issues such as abortion[21] and affirmative action.[22]

On the whole, the areas of potential overlap and conflict between constitutional and EU rights are those in which the ECJ has incorporated EU rights to the states. EU rights have been incorporated to the states when they act 'within the field of application of EU law', which is an elusive formulation. According to ECJ case law, this formula includes two types of situations: (i) state acts implementing EU law, and (ii) state acts derogating from the EU basic freedoms of movement. In practice, the ECJ has tended to monitor state compliance with EU fundamental rights when state authorities broadly act within the field of EU law, as will be discussed next.

2.1 *State acts implementing EU law*

The term 'implementing' is itself rather vague.[23] State acts applying regulations[24] and transposing directives[25] have been regarded as instances of implementation. In this context, conflicts might arise, for example, when the standard of protection given to a constitutional right is higher than the standard of protection given to a parallel right under EU law.[26] If national courts reviewed state acts implementing EU law under more protective constitutional rights and struck these state measures down, the efficacy and uniformity of EU law within that state territory might be undermined. For example, in a series of cases known as the 'banana saga', German courts and the ECJ entered into conflict regarding the scope of protection of the right to property and the freedom to pursue a professional or trade activity.[27] The EU had adopted a regulation establishing quotas and tariffs

& Nicolas Lockhart, '*Taking Rights Seriously' Seriously: The European Court and its Fundamental Rights Jurisprudence*, 32 COMMON MARKET LAW REVIEW 51 (1995).

[21] *The Society for the Protection of Unborn Children Ireland Ltd v Stephen Grogan and others*, C-159/90.

[22] *Eckhard Kalanke v Freie Hansestadt Bremen*, C-450/93; *Katarina Abrahamsson and Leif Anderson v Elisabet Fogelqvist*, C-407/98.

[23] See Piet Eeckhout, *The EU Charter of Fundamental Rights and the Federal Question*, 39 COMMON MARKET LAW REVIEW 945, 958–969 (2002).

[24] *Hubert Wachauf v Bundesamt für Ernährung und Forstwirtschaft*, C-5/88, para. 19.

[25] *Booker Aquaculture and Hydro Seafood v The Scottish Ministers*, C-20/00, para. 88.

[26] *Hubert Wachauf v Bundesamt für Ernährung und Forstwirtschaft*, C-5/88.

[27] See Norbert Reich, *Judge-made 'Europe à la carte:' Some Remarks on Recent Conflicts between European and German Constitutional Law Provoked by the Banana Litigation*, 7 EUROPEAN JOURNAL OF INTERNATIONAL LAW 103 (1996); Christoph U. Schmid, *All Bark and No Bite: Notes on the*

for third-country bananas in order to restrict their importation. These provisions had a particularly harsh effect upon German importers, some of whom were put at risk of bankruptcy. Against the claims of the German government and the resistance of German courts, the ECJ ruled that, in the pursuit of the general interest, the EC regulation did not disproportionately impair substantive fundamental rights.[28] In turn, the German Constitutional Court instructed lower courts to grant effective legal protection of a provisional nature to individuals, particularly if they were in danger of bankruptcy.[29] In other words, the Constitutional Court allowed lower courts to suspend temporarily the efficacy of the EC regulation. The reaction of the ECJ in the next case that reached this court was twofold.[30] The ECJ opposed the jurisdiction of state courts to order provisional measures. At the same time, the ECJ declared that the European Commission was required to take all transitional measures necessary 'when the transition to the common organization of the market infringes certain traders' fundamental rights protected by Community law, such as the right to property and the right to pursue a professional or trade activity'. Therefore, the ECJ had to withdraw its first interpretation and admit that the EC regulation could impinge upon fundamental rights, while struggling to maintain exclusive power to issue provisional measures within the supranational domain.

2.2 State acts derogating from free movement

The Treaties lay down a set of grounds, such as public morality, public policy, public security, health, and cultural heritage, under which the states may constrain EU basic freedoms of movement of goods, services, people, and capital.[31] In *ERT*,[32] the ECJ declared that state acts derogating from free movement had to comply with EU fundamental rights to withstand

---

Federal Constitutional Court's 'Banana Decision', 7 EUROPEAN LAW JOURNAL 95 (2001); Ulrich Everling, *Will Europe Slip on Bananas? The Bananas Judgment of the Court of Justice and National Courts*, 33 COMMON MARKET LAW REVIEW 401 (1996).

[28] *Federal Republic of Germany v Council of the European Communities*, C-280/93; *Atlanta Fruchthandelsgesellschaft mbH and others v Bundesamt für Ernährung und Forstwirtschaft*, C-465/93 and 466/93.

[29] German Constitutional Court, 25 January 1995.

[30] *T. Port GmbH & Co. KG v Bundesanstalt für Landwirtschaft und Ernährung*, C-68/95.

[31] Articles 30, 39.3, 46 EC Treaty.

[32] *Elliniki Radiophonia Tileorassi AE v Dimotiki Etairia Pliroforissis and Sotirios Kouvelas*, C-260/89.

scrutiny.[33] Also, besides the express derogation clauses, the ECJ has recognized other grounds (known as 'overriding requirements') that allow member states to constrain the freedoms of movement. These state measures, then, must also comply with EU fundamental rights. Therefore, state acts hindering fee movement, either on the basis of legally established or judicially admitted grounds, are bound by EU and constitutional rights at the same time. Due to the overarching nature of the EU freedoms of movement, almost any state act could be regarded as somewhat constraining free movement. Therefore, there is potential for expanding the scope of application of EU fundamental rights against the states.

For instance, in *Familiapress*,[34] a German weekly magazine offering prizes was banned in Austria under a law containing a general prohibition on offering consumers free gifts linked to the sale of goods or the supply of services. The German publisher claimed that this prohibition restricted free movement of goods within the EU. The Austrian government argued that the goal of this law was to protect press diversity. The ECJ agreed that the interest in maintaining press diversity might constitute an overriding requirement justifying the restriction of the free movement of goods. At the same time, the ECJ declared that overriding requirements had to be examined under the light of EU fundamental rights. Then, the ECJ pointed out that a prohibition on selling publications might detract from the publisher's free speech. Interestingly enough, in this case, there was free speech on both sides: the Austrian law sought to protect free speech (in the form of securing press diversity); and there was also free speech on the side of the publisher whose magazine had been banned. Since the national statute constrained free movement and free speech, the ECJ held that to withstand scrutiny, it had to be proven that this national statute was proportionate to the aim pursued—protecting press diversity—and that there were no less restrictive measures of both intra-EU trade and free speech.

2.3 *Extending the scope of application of EU fundamental rights*

Generally, the ECJ has declared that EU rights are binding on state acts falling within the field of application of EU law. Arguably, this formulation

---

[33] Against the extension of the scope of application of EU fundamental rights to this category of state acts see Francis G. Jacobs, *Human Rights in the European Union: The Role of the Court of Justice*, 26 EUROPEAN LAW REVIEW 331, 336–337 (2001).

[34] *Vereinigte Familiapress Zeitungsverlags- und Vertriebs GmbH v Heinrich Bauer Verlag*, C-368/95.

might include state acts that are not strictly implementing EU law or derogating from EU basic freedoms. Indeed, the scope of application of EU fundamental rights has tended to expand to state acts within the context of EU law, broadly understood. For example, in several cases,[35] the ECJ decided about the compatibility of state affirmative action measures with the EU principle of equal treatment, as enshrined in the Directive 76/207/EEC, 9 February 1976, 'on the implementation of the principle of equal treatment for men and women as regards access to employment, vocational training and promotion, and working conditions'. Yet, these affirmative action measures were not adopted strictly to 'implement' the directive within the state legal order. In *Abrahamsson*,[36] the ECJ examined a Swedish regulation concerning certain professors' and research assistants' posts that established a measure of affirmative action on the basis of sex. The Swedish regulation established that:

[A] candidate belonging to an under-represented sex who possesses sufficient qualifications…must be granted preference over a candidate of the opposite sex who would otherwise have been chosen ('positive discrimination') where it proves necessary to do so in order for a candidate of the under-represented sex to be appointed. Positive discrimination must, however, not be applied where the difference between the candidates' qualifications is so great that such application would give rise to a breach of the requirement of objectivity in the making of appointments.

Ms. Abrahamsson and Mr. Anderson appealed Ms. Fogelqvist's appointment before the Swedish Universities' Appeals Board. This Board referred a question about the interpretation of article 2(1) and (4) of the directive to the ECJ. Article 2(1) of the directive proclaimed the principle of equality and banned discrimination on the basis of sex. Article 2(4) allowed measures 'to promote equal opportunity for men and women, in particular by removing existing inequalities which affect women's opportunities'. The ECJ held that the Swedish method of selection described above was precluded by the directive, since granting automatic preference to candidates belonging to the under-represented sex was considered to be disproportionate to the aim pursued. Hence, as a result of a different understanding of the requirements of the equality principle, member states might be banned from enacting certain kinds of affirmative action measures.

---

[35] *Eckhard Kalanke v Freie Hansestadt Bremen*, C-450/93; *Hellmut Marschall v Land Nordrhein Westfalen*, C-409/95; *Katarina Abrahamsson and Leif Anderson v Elisabet Fogelqvist*, C-407/98.
[36] *Id.*

Remarkably enough, the principle of non-discrimination on grounds of nationality has been applied to monitor state action slightly connected with the field of EU law.[37] In contrast to judicially-made rights, this prinicple is entrenched in article 12 EC Treaty, and it is at the core of the EU system. Arguing that state measures that distinguish between nationals and non-nationals might hinder free movement, the ECJ has extended its power to monitor state action, even if there is no clear connection with the field of EU law. The case of *Bickel and Franz* is very illustrative.[38] Bickel, an Austrian lorry driver, and Franz, a German tourist, were charged with committing two respective crimes while in Italy. Under Italian law, the German-speaking citizens of the Province of Bolzano are entitled to use their own language in relations with the judicial and administrative authorities based in that province. Franz and Bickel requested that the judicial proceedings be conducted in their own language. The state court referred a preliminary question to the ECJ, asking whether the principle of non-discrimination on the basis of nationality (article 12 EC Treaty) and the right of free movement and residence (article 18 EC Treaty) required that the right to have criminal proceedings conducted in German be extended to non-citizens. The ECJ responded that although the rules of criminal procedure were matters under state power, Community law set certain limits to this power: 'Such legislative provisions may not discriminate against persons to whom Community law gives the right to equal treatment or restrict the fundamental freedoms guaranteed by Community law.'[39] Hence, the ECJ concluded that since state provisions concerning the language to be used in criminal proceedings might compromise the right of nationals of other member states to equal treatment in the exercise of their freedom to move and reside in another member state, these state provisions had to comply with the right to non-discrimination on the basis of nationality. To some extent, the argument is circular: free movement is constrained precisely because the state provision only applies to nationals; at the same time, constraining free movement is the basis for enforcing the right to non-discrimination on the basis of nationality within the state.

In any event, it seems that the mere fact of moving from one state to another is considered to be enough connection with EU law to enforce the right to non-discrimination on grounds of nationality to state measures enacted within the field of domestic residual powers. This reasoning might

---

[37] Eeckhout, *supra* n 23, at 959–962.
[38] *Bickel & Franz*, C-274/96.   [39] *Id*. para. 17.

lead to the expansion of the scope of application of other EU fundamental rights: moving EU citizens should enjoy a common set of fundamental
rights, regardless of whether state authorities act within the field of EU law
or not, in order to secure free movement. Along these lines, in *Konstantinidis*,
Advocate General (AG) Jacobs suggested that any European citizen who
develops an economic activity in another member state, should be treated 'in
accordance with a common code of fundamental values, in particular those
laid down in the European Convention on Human Rights. In other words,
any EU citizen should be entitled to invoke that status in order to oppose
any violation of his fundamental rights.'[40] The ECJ, however, did not follow
this line of argument that would have extended the scope of EU fundamental
rights to any moving European citizen vis-à-vis state public authorities. Following Jacobs' lead, AG Poiares Maduro proposed in *Centro Europa* a more
restricted expansion of the scope of the ECJ's powers to review state action
to 'serious and persistent violations which highlight a problem of systemic
nature in the protection of fundamental rights in the Member State.'[41] In the
case at hand, however, the AG advised the ECJ to hold to the conventional
approach. The ECJ decided the case without engaging the question of the
scope of application of EU fundamental rights to the states.

Additionally, the ECJ has extended the application of EU fundamental
rights to the action of EU institutions and state authorities under the third
pillar, which refers to the area of freedom, security, and justice (Title VI EU
Treaty). The application of EU fundamental rights to this area has a great
potential for overlapping with constitutional rights. The third pillar is no
longer about milk quotas and fisheries, but rather immigration and criminal law. Framework decisions under the third pillar, as directives in the first

---

[40] AG Jacobs, *Christos Konstantinidis v Stadt Altensteig- Standesamt und Landratsamt Calw-Ordnungsamt*, C-168/91, para. 46.

[41] AG Poiares Maduro, *Centro Europa 7 Srl. v Ministero delle Comunicazioni e Autorità per le Garanzie nelle Comunicazioni and Direzione Generale Autorizzazioni e Concessioni Ministero delle Comunicazioni*, C-380/05, para. 22: 'My suggestion is not that any violation of fundamental rights within the meaning of Article 6(2) EU constitutes, of itself, an infringement of the rules on free movement. Only serious and persistent violations which highlight a problem of systemic nature in the protection of fundamental rights in the Member State at issue, would, in my view, qualify as violations of the rules on free movement, by virtue of the direct threat they would pose to the transnational dimension of European citizenship and to the integrity of the EU legal order. However, so long as the protection of fundamental rights in a Member State is not gravely inadequate in that sense, I believe the Court should review national measures for their conformity with fundamental rights only when these measures come within the scope of application of the Court's jurisdiction as defined in its case-law to date.'

pillar, require state implementing legislation. In *Advocaten*,[42] the ECJ held that state measures implementing framework decisions were also bound by EU fundamental rights. Hence, these state acts are bound at the same time by EU and constitutional rights. If the constitutional protection is higher, and the state implementing measure is struck down for violating a constitutional right, the efficacy of the framework decision within that member state might be undermined (unless there are other ways of implementing EU law respectful of constitutional rights). In this context, several state constitutional courts ruled that the respective state laws implementing the framework decision regulating the European Arrest Warrant were unconstitutional.[43] This framework decision eliminated the prohibition against extradition of member states' own nationals, and exempted the execution of an arrest warrant from the requirement of double criminality (that the offence be punishable by law in both states) regarding certain crimes. The Polish Constitutional Court, for instance, ruled that the implementing provision of the Polish Criminal Procedural Code was unconstitutional because it clashed with the constitutional prohibition on extraditing Polish nationals.[44] The German Federal Constitutional Court declared the German European Arrest Warrant Act to be unconstitutional and void.[45] The Belgian Arbitration Court (assimilated to a constitutional court), when confronted with this case, submitted a preliminary reference to the ECJ regarding the validity of the framework decision itself. The Belgian Court questioned the framework decision's compatibility with the principles of legality and equality, in connection with the eradication of the requirement of double criminality. The ECJ confirmed its jurisdiction to examine the validity of the framework decision under EU fundamental rights, and thus to monitor the action of EU institutions under the third pillar. At the same time, while admitting that member states had discretion in implementing the framework decision, the ECJ held that state implementing measures had to respect EU fundamental rights.[46] In the particular case, the ECJ ruled that no rights had been violated.

[42] *Advocaten loor de Wereld VZW v Leden van de Ministerraad*, C-303/05.

[43] See Daniel Sarmiento, *European Union: The European Arrest Warrant and the Quest for Constitutional Coherence*, INTERNATIONAL JOURNAL OF CONSTITUTIONAL LAW 1 (2008); Jan Komárek, *European Constitutionalism and the European Arrest Warrant: In Search of the Limits of 'Contrapunctual Principles'*, 44 COMMON MARKET LAW REVIEW 9 (2007).

[44] At the same time, the Polish Constitutional Court limited the effects of its decision temporarily to allow for constitutional amendment and avoid violating EU law, see Komárek, *supra* n 43, at 16–21.

[45] *Id.* at 21–25.

[46] *Advocaten loor de Wereld VZW v Leden van de Ministerraad*, C-303/05, para. 53.

Throughout the Charter's drafting process, defining the scope of application of EU rights was one of the most controversial issues. The wording of article 51.1, regulating the Charter's field of application, received several formulations.[47] The final text reveals a restrictive move when it declares that the Charter provisions are addressed to the Member States 'only when they are implementing Union law'.[48] Yet, the *Explanations* to this article refer back to the ECJ case law.[49] Thus, while aiming at preventing an expansive use of the Charter vis-à-vis member states; this article does not seem to restrict the current scope of application of EU rights, as it has been judicially fashioned.[50] What is more, some commentators clearly favour an expansive interpretation of article 51.1 of the Charter, and the elasticity of the term "implementation" would allow for that.[51] This is a highly relevant debate since the delimitation of EU rights' boundaries has essential implications for state autonomy. The discussion about the scope of EU fundamental rights vis-à-vis state action is ultimately about the ECJ's power to check state action in light of fundamental rights. In this way, by deciding on the scope of EU fundamental rights, the ECJ is deciding on the scope of its own powers, and its capacity to influence upon state policies. In sum, despite the Charter's efforts to constrain the scope of application of EU fundamental rights, the ECJ case law contains the seeds for further enforcing these rights to the states: first, the ECJ has declared that state acts restricting free movement must respect EU fundamental rights (and all of

[47] Gráinne de Búrca, *The Drafting of the European Union Charter of Fundamental Rights*, 26 EUROPEAN LAW REVIEW 126, 136–137 (2001); Eeckhout, *supra* n 23, at 954–958; Ingolf Pernice, *Integrating the Charter of Fundamental Rights into the Constitution of the European Union: Practical and Theoretical Propositions*, 10 COLUMBIA JOURNAL OF EUROPEAN LAW 5, 23–25 (2003–2004).

[48] De Búrca, *supra* n 47, at 137. Favouring a restrictive interpretation, Leonard F. M. Besselink, *The Member States, the National Constitutions and the Scope for the Charter*, 1 MAASTRICHT JOURNAL OF EUROPEAN AND COMPARATIVE LAW 68, 79 (2001); Francis G. Jacobs, *Human Rights in the European Union: The Role of the Court of Justice*, 26 EUROPEAN LAW REVIEW 331, 338–339 (2001).

[49] *Updated Explanations Relating to the Text of the Charter of Fundamental Rights*, CONV 828/1/03 (Brussels, 18 July 2003).

[50] Aida Torres Pérez, *La Dimensión Estructural de la Carta de Derechos Fundamentales de la Unión Europea. Relaciones Verticales y Cláusulas Horizontales*, 67 REVISTA VASCA DE ADMINISTRACIÓN PÚBLICA 253, 281–284 (2003).

[51] Eeckhout, *supra* n 23, at 993: 'if the Charter is to be meaningful, Article 51 should not be interpreted restrictively. The Charter's application to the Member States, when "implementing" EU law, should extend to all cases and contexts where there is a material link wih EU law'; Ricardo Alonso García, *The General Provisions of the Charter of Fundamental Rights of the European Union*, 8 EUROPEAN LAW JOURNAL 492, 495–497 (2002).

them). Secondly, the ECJ has already applied the right to non-discrimination on grounds of nationality to moving citizens arguing that, otherwise, their right to free movement and residence would be hindered. Thus, the current case law is a loaded gun that a binding Charter might contribute to shoot, so that the scope of EU rights would be extended to EU citizens exercising the right to free movement and residence, regardless of the kind of state action under review.[52]

On the whole, when state authorities act 'within the field of application of EU law', blurring as it may be, they operate within the controlling parameters of constitutional and EU rights. As a result of this overlap, state courts face the dilemma of deciding what norm should be applied when the respective interpretations of those rights deviate. On the one hand, from the constitutional law perspective, state courts have the obligation to apply constitutional rights. In most member states, the power of judicial review is centralized in a single constitutional court.[53] If ordinary courts doubt the constitutionality of a piece of legislation applicable to the case, they shall refer a question to the constitutional court.[54] The constitutional court will then decide on the validity of the applicable law. On the other hand, from the EU perspective, state acts falling within the field of application of EU law are also bound by EU fundamental rights. Thus, state courts have the obligation to apply EU fundamental rights when reviewing these state acts. If state courts doubt the interpretation of the applicable EU fundamental right, they might send a preliminary question to the ECJ. To be clear, the ECJ has no powers to strike down state legislation, but the interpretation given to EU fundamental rights will dictate the outcome of state courts' review.[55] Otherwise, if the meaning of the applicable EU right is clear,

---

[52] Once admitted that moving EU citizens should receive the protection of EU rights, irrespective of the kind of state action under review, the next inevitable step would be to consider why only moving EU citizens should fully benefit from these rights, as opposed to the rest. Besides, this situation might give rise to cases of reverse discrimination. See Eeckhout, *supra* n 23, at 969–975.

[53] Ferreres, *supra* n 16, at 461–463.

[54] *Id.* at 465, the possibility to refer a question to the constitutional court exists in most member states with systems of centralized judicial review.

[55] As will be further explained in Chapter 5, the ECJ has used the preliminary reference to decide about the compatibility of EU and state law. For this reason, since in federal systems the power of federal courts to review state provisions is considered to be essential, the preliminary ruling has been regarded as a 'quasi-federal instrument'. See G. Federico Mancini & David T. Keeling, *Democracy and the European Court of Justice*, 57 THE MODERN LAW REVIEW 175, 182–185 (1995); J. Rinze, *The Role of the European Court of Justice as a Federal Constitutional Court*,

state courts are empowered to directly set aside state laws clashing with EU rights.[56] To some extent, state courts are being asked to renounce the constitutional scope of protection in favour of the one defined by the ECJ. The fact that only state acts falling within the field of EU law are bound by EU fundamental rights is not a sufficient reason to replace the constitutional interpretation with that of the ECJ. Besides, as explained above, the scope of application of EU law has been widening steadily, to include state acts only remotely connected with EU law. The ECJ claims authority for interpreting fundamental rights norms that will be applied to review state legislation, sometimes in opposition to the constitutional interpretation of analogous rights. Thus, the key question is not just about the selection of the applicable norm, but rather about the source of the ECJ's legitimacy in adjudicating fundamental rights. For instance, why should national courts follow the ECJ interpretation of the equality principle that bans certain forms of affirmative action in the workplace if those measures are valid under the constitutional interpretation of equality? More generally, what are the bases of the ECJ's legitimacy to mandate that state courts replace the constitutional scope of protection with the EU one? Is the efficacy of EU law a sufficient and satisfactory argument in all cases? Is the argument for the uniformity of fundamental rights convincing, given reasonable disagreements among diverse constitutional polities? What if the ECJ level of protection falls below the one granted by state constitutions? Is this just a question of levels of rights protection? What about the implications for democratic self-government, political identity, and ultimately, for state constitutionalism? In any event, could these conflicts be avoided or managed? Should the ECJ adopt a policy of deference? How should the ECJ interpret

---

Public Law 426, 439 (1993); G. Federico Mancini, *The Making of a Constitution for Europe*, 26 Common Market Law Review 595, 604 (1989).

[56] In *Amministrazione delle Finanze dello Stato v Simmenthal S.p.A*, C-106/77, the ECJ declared that, in virtue of the supremacy principle, state courts were required to set aside state laws clashing with EU law: 'A national court which is called upon, within the limits of its jurisdiction, to apply provisions of community law is under a duty to give full effect to those provisions, if necessary refusing on its own motion to apply any conflicting provision of national legislation, even if adopted subsequently, and it is not necessary for the court to request or await the prior setting aside of such provision by legislative or other constitutional means.' In this vein, one of the effects of the EU supremacy principle has been the 'decentralization' of the system of judicial review of legislation within the states. Note that state courts are forbidden to directly set aside state legislation clashing with the domestic constitution, while they may set aside state legislation clashing with EU law. For an analysis of this transformation see Ferreres, *supra* n 16, at 477–482.

fundamental rights in the face of disagreement among the states? What are the grounds for legitimating its adjudicative function? The following pages expand on some of these questions and offer an answer based on the ideal of dialogue as providing the source for the ECJ's legitimacy in adjudicating fundamental rights norms.

Multilevel Protection of Rights in Europe

Before focusing on the interaction between the ECJ and state courts regarding fundamental rights' adjudication, this chapter will reflect upon the role and impact of yet another court interpreting and protecting rights in Europe: the European Court of Human Rights (ECtHR). The ECtHR was established by the European Convention on Human Rights (ECHR), signed in 1950 within the framework of the Council of Europe. The European Convention was aimed at securing fundamental rights by establishing constraints on states at the international level. The rights enshrined in the Convention are protected and interpreted by the ECtHR, whose judgments are binding on contracting states. Throughout time, the ECtHR has had (and will continue to have) a leading role in defining human rights in Europe. The success of the human rights movement in the international arena, and particularly the success of the ECtHR, has challenged the Westphalian model of international relations, ie, the monopoly of the state over its citizens and, ultimately, the monolithic concept of state sovereignty. Hence, in Europe, there are (minimally) three spheres of human rights protection: national (the states); supranational (the European Union, EU); and international (the ECHR). To be clear about the terminology used throughout the book, first, 'constitutional rights' will refer to fundamental rights laid down by states constitutions, and ultimately interpreted by the respective state constitutional or supreme courts. Secondly, 'EU fundamental rights' are those rights that have been recognized as such by the ECJ as general principles of EU law, and later included in the Charter. Thirdly, 'Convention rights' are those laid down by the European Convention and its Protocols. Although this work does not aim at providing a thorough analysis of the role of the ECtHR and its interplay with state courts and the ECJ, this chapter will consider those elements of all these interactions that are relevant for the model of supranational adjudication of rights that will be advanced for the ECJ.

1 ECtHR vis-à-vis state courts

After the atrocities committed during the Second World War, the main goal of the European Convention was to provide a rights catalogue that all states had to respect and a judicial mechanism for monitoring state action. At present, the jurisdiction of the ECtHR is compulsory, and individuals have standing before this Court against state parties violating Convention rights. Yet, when the Convention was enacted, due to the reluctance of some state governments,[1] individuals were granted a right to petition only before the European Commission of Human Rights and not before the ECtHR. In addition, both this right of individual petition and the jurisdiction of the Court depended on the express acceptance by each state. Protocol 11 (1994) extensively redesigned the judicial protection system.[2] This Protocol eliminated the European Commission of Human Rights and made both the jurisdiction of the ECtHR and individual standing before this Court compulsory.[3] Like any other international treaty, the legal status of the European Convention within the states depends on the national provisions regulating the domestic effect of international law. Thus, whether the Convention is directly enforceable and its hierarchical position within domestic legal orders is determined by state law.[4] At present, all state parties have incorporated the Convention within their domestic systems, although its hierarchical position might vary across countries.[5] Regarding the relationship between the states and this international system of human rights protection, the following procedural and methodological tools have been

[1] See COUNCIL OF EUROPE, II COLLECTED EDITION OF THE TRAVAUX PRÉPARATOIRES 144–200 (1975).

[2] See Andrew Drzemczewski, *The European Human Rights Convention: Protocol No. 11—Entry into Force and First Year of Application*, 21 HUMAN RIGHTS LAW JOURNAL 1 (2000).

[3] Rudolf Bernhardt, *Reform of the Control Machinery under the European Convention on Human Rights: Protocol No. 11*, 89 AMERICAN JOURNAL OF INTERNATIONAL LAW 145, 150–151 (1995).

[4] For studies regarding the reception and effects of the Convention within domestic law, see ROBERT BLACKBURN & JORG POLAKIEWICZ (eds.), FUNDAMENTAL RIGHTS IN EUROPE. THE EUROPEAN CONVENTION ON HUMAN RIGHTS AND ITS MEMBER STATES, 1950–2000 (Oxford University Press 2001); CONOR A. GEARTY (ed.), EUROPEAN CIVIL LIBERTIES AND THE EUROPEAN CONVENTION ON HUMAN RIGHTS. A COMPARATIVE STUDY (Martinus Nijhoff 1997); ALEC STONE SWEET & HELEN KELLER (eds.), A EUROPE OF RIGHTS: THE IMPACT OF THE ECHR ON NATIONAL LEGAL SYSTEMS (Oxford University Press 2008).

[5] For instance, the Convention might be hierarchically superior to the national constitution (the Netherlands); or superior to ordinary legislation, but below the constitution (Spain).

fairly successful in striking a balance between state autonomy and international supervision.

First, the ECtHR is a court of last resort. Thus, before being allowed to bring an action against a state before the ECtHR, individuals must have exhausted all domestic judicial remedies. In addition, as will be further developed in the next chapter, the ECtHR defines a minimum level of protection. National courts are free to interpret constitutional rights as long as the standard of protection does not fall below the standard defined by the ECtHR. This possibility is laid down in article 53 of the Convention: 'Nothing in this Convention shall be construed as limiting or derogating from any of the human rights and fundamental freedoms which may be ensured under the laws of any High Contracting Party or under any other agreement to which it is a Party.'

Moreover, the ECtHR has developed a measure of deference—the so-called 'margin of appreciation' doctrine—to allow for state discretion. The margin of appreciation has to do with the appropriate division of labour between the ECtHR and state courts (and other state authorities) regarding the interpretation of fundamental rights. It has been defined as a methodology by which the ECtHR 'decides upon the scope of its own supervisory powers and, consequently, upon the scope of discretion that will remain vested in the national authorities for the definition, interpretation, and application of the basic human rights guarantees contained in the Treaty.'[6] This judicial doctrine remains highly contested in the literature. Some have voiced concerns about its legitimacy, claiming that it amounts to a denial of justice.[7] Others favoured the legitimacy of judicial self-restraint, offering arguments based upon democracy, cultural diversity, and the subsidiary nature of the ECtHR.[8] There is a widespread concern, however, regarding the uncertainty

---

[6] HOWARD CHARLES YOUROW, THE MARGIN OF APPRECIATION DOCTRINE IN THE DYNAMICS OF EUROPEAN HUMAN RIGHTS JURISPRUDENCE 2 (Martinus Nijhoff Publishers 1996); Thomas A. O'Donnell, *The Margin of Appreciation Doctrine: Standards in the Jurisprudence of the European Court of Human Rights*, 4 HUMAN RIGHTS QUARTERLY 474, 475 (1982).

[7] Lord Lester quoted in Paul Mahoney, *Marvellous Richness of Diversity or Invidious Cultural Relativism?*, 19 HUMAN RIGHTS LAW JOURNAL 1 (1998); Cora S. Feingold, *The Doctrine of Margin of Appreciation and the European Convention on Human Rights*, 53 NOTRE DAME LAWYER 90, 95, 105 (1977), claimed that the margin of appreciation represented an abdication by the Court of its responsibilities.

[8] Mahoney, *supra* n 7, at 2–3; O'Donnell, *supra* n 6, at 476–478; Jeoren Schokkenbroek, *The Basis, Nature and Application of the Margin-of-Appreciation Doctrine in the Case-Law of the European Court of Human Rights*, 19 HUMAN RIGHTS LAW JOURNAL 30, 31 (1998).

surrounding the criteria to decide on the margin of appreciation granted to the states.[9] Some authors have sought to identify these criteria through the analysis of the ECtHR case law.[10] Whether or not there is consensus among the states as to the meaning of a specific right seems to be one of the main criteria used by the Court for determining the scope of the margin of appreciation.[11] If there is consensus among the states parties, the ECtHR will only recognize a narrow margin of appreciation. If consensus is lacking, the margin of appreciation will be wider.[12] Yet, the notion and methodology of consensus itself have been contested.[13]

Generally, these structural arrangements and doctrines have contributed to a relationship of trust and respect between state courts and the ECtHR, which may contain some lessons applicable to the interaction between the ECJ and state courts. This does not mean, however, that the interaction between the ECtHR and state courts is free from controversy. As indicated, the margin of appreciation doctrine still raises strong reactions. In addition, the ECtHR interpretive methods have also generated debate. The weight that the several interpretive methods—textualism, intentionalism, teleological, evolutive—should have is discussed,[14] and the ECtHR laconic reasoning is open to criticism.[15] Besides, enforcement of ECtHR decisions within the states is also a controversial issue. Although ECtHR judgments are binding, there is no coercive mechanism to secure state compliance. The Committee of Ministers is the organ in charge of supervising the execution of judgments, but at the end of the day compliance depends on the willingness of the member states. Although the rate of compliance is high when

---

[9]   Mahoney, *supra* n 7, at 2, 4–5; O'Donnell, *supra* n 6, at 478.

[10]   Yourow, *supra* n 6; Mahoney, *supra* n 7, at 5–6; O'Donnell, *supra* n 6, at 479–490; Schokkenbroek, *supra* n 8, at 34–35.

[11]   Yourow, *supra* n 6, at 193–196; Schokkenbroek, *supra* n 8, at 34. For the justification of this criterion see O'Donnell, *supra* n 6, at 479.

[12]   *Id.*

[13]   Paolo G. Carozza, *Uses and Misuses of Comparative Law in International Human Rights: Some Reflections on the Jurisprudence of the European Court of Human Rights*, 73 NOTRE DAME LAW REVIEW 1217 (1998). Among the critics, some do not necessarily reject a consensus approach to the interpretation of Convention rights, but advocate instead a more rigorous methodology to apply the consensus inquiry, for example, Laurence R. Helfer, *Consensus, Coherence and the European Convention on Human Rights*, 26 CORNELL INTERNATIONAL LAW JOURNAL 133, 135 (1993).

[14]   GEORGE LETSAS, A THEORY OF INTERPRETATION OF THE EUROPEAN CONVENTION ON HUMAN RIGHTS (Oxford University Press 2007).

[15]   Steven Greer, *Constitutionalizing Adjudication under the European Convention on Human Rights*, 23 OXFORD JOURNAL OF LEGAL STUDIES 405, 407 (2003).

states are condemned to pay compensation, they are more reluctant to take positive measures to secure full reparation (*restitutio in integrum*).[16] In this respect, one of the main goals of the new Protocol 14 is reinforcing the role of the Committee of Ministers to monitor state compliance.

In any event, the ECtHR has created a quasi-constitutional order of human rights protection in Europe, and thus this Court is regarded as fulfilling a constitutional role in defining the scope of fundamental rights binding for all state parties.[17] At the same time, the ECtHR case law has become a relevant source for interpreting state constitutional rights. Over time, state courts all over Europe have increasingly referred to the ECHR and its interpretation by the ECtHR to give content to the respective constitutional rights.[18] For instance, the Spanish Constitution expressly mandates that constitutional rights be interpreted according to international treaties on human rights ratified by Spain (article 10.2 Spanish Constitution). In practice, the European Convention is the human rights treaty most commonly cited under this provision, including the ECtHR case law.[19]

2 ECJ vis-à-vis ECtHR

No formal institutional relationship exists between the European Convention and the EU. According to ECJ Opinion 2/94, the EU lacks powers to join the Convention. The ECJ held that accession to the Convention could be brought about only by means of treaty amendment because of its constitutional significance. Since that ruling, both scholars and European institutions have advocated the EU's accession to the European Convention.[20] The

---

[16] Jörg Polakiewicz, *The Execution of Judgments of the European Court of Human Rights*, in FUNDAMENTAL RIGHTS IN EUROPE. THE EUROPEAN CONVENTION ON HUMAN RIGHTS AND ITS MEMBER STATES, 1950–2000 55, 73–76 (Robert Blackburn & Jorg Polakiewicz eds. 2001).

[17] For the constitutional role of the ECtHR, see Greer, *supra* n 15.

[18] See Blackburn & Polakiewicz, *supra* n 4, at 46–53.

[19] For an analysis of this article, see ALEJANDRO SAIZ ARNAIZ, LA APERTURA CONSTITUCIONAL AL DERECHO INTERNACIONAL Y EUROPEO DE LOS DERECHOS HUMANOS. EL ARTÍCULO 10.2 DE LA CONSTITUCIÓN ESPAÑOLA (Consejo General del Poder Judicial 1999).

[20] See, among others, Iris Canor, *Primus Inter Pares. Who is the Ultimate Guardian of Fundamental Rights in Europe?*, 25 EUROPEAN LAW REVIEW 3 (2000); Robert Harmsen, *National Responsibility for European Community Acts Under the European Convention on Human Rights: Recasting the Accession Debate*, 7 EUROPEAN PUBLIC LAW 625 (2001); Hans Christian Krüger & Jörg Polakiewicz, *Proposals for a Coherent Human Rights Protection System in Europe*, 22 HUMAN RIGHTS LAW JOURNAL 1 (2001); Commission of the European Communities, *Memorandum*, Brussels, 4 April

European Constitution included an article stating that 'the Union shall seek accession to the European Convention'. Although the constitutional text failed to complete the ratification process, this article illustrated existing political support for EU membership in the European Convention. The Lisbon Treaty has maintained the clause enabling the EU to join the European Convention.[21]

Despite lacking a formal relationship with the Convention system, the ECJ has drawn inspiration from it. Indeed, the ECJ has repeatedly declared that the European Convention is one of the main sources for interpreting EU fundamental rights.[22] Often, the ECJ refers to articles of the European Convention, and even to ECtHR decisions. For instance, in cases regarding the right to free speech, the ECJ quoted article 10 ECHR;[23] in cases involving the equal protection of transsexuals, the ECJ explicitly referred to decisions of the ECtHR.[24] Nonetheless, the scope of protection delineated by the ECJ and the ECtHR regarding a parallel right might diverge.[25] For example, in *Hoechst*,[26] the ECJ, referring to article 8 ECHR, argued that the right protecting the privacy of the home could not be extended to private

1979; Commission of the European Communities, *Communication on Community Accession to the European Convention for the Protection of Human Rights and Fundamental Freedoms and some of its Protocols*, Brussels, 19 November 1990.

[21] Article 6.2: 'The Union shall accede to the European Convention for the Protection of Human Rights and Fundamental Freedoms.'

[22] *J. Nold, Kohlen- und Baustoffgroßhandlung v Commission of the European Communities*, C-4/73; *Hauer v Land Rheinland-Pfaltz*, C-44/79.

[23] *Elliniki Radiophonia Tileorassi AE and Panellinia Omospondia Syllogon Prossopikou v Dimotiki Etairia Pliroforissis and Sotirios Kouvelas and Nicolaos Avdellas and others*, C-260/89; *Vereinigte Familiapress Zeitungsverlags- und Vertriebs GmbH v Heinrich Bauer Verlag*, C-368/95. Also, regarding the non-retroactivity of criminal law, the ECJ referred to article 7 ECHR: *The Queen v Minister of Agriculture, Fisheries and Food and Secretary of State for Health, ex parte Fedesa and others*, C-331/88; *R v Kent Kirk*, C-63/83.

[24] *P v S and Cornwall County Council*, C-13/94; *K.B. v National Health Service Pensions Agency and Secretary of State for Health*, C-117/01. In the past, the ECJ very rarely cited decisions of the ECtHR. Bruno de Witte, *The Past and Future of the European Court of Justice in the Protection of Human Rights*, in THE EU AND HUMAN RIGHTS 859, n 80 (Philip Alston ed. 1999), pointed out that it was after the ECJ Opinion 2/94 denying the power to join the European Convention, that the ECJ started citing ECtHR decisions, 'as if the Court wanted to console the many commentators that deplore its refusal to recognize an EC competence to accede to the ECHR'.

[25] Harmsen, *supra* n 20, at 627: 'As the Court of Justice interprets fundamental rights through the prism of Community law, it is very likely that it will continue, on occasion, to strike different balances to those struck by the Court of Human Rights'; Dean Spielmann, *Human Rights Case Law in the Strasbourg and Luxembourg Courts: Conflicts, Inconsistencies, and Complementarities*, in THE EU AND HUMAN RIGHTS 757 (Philip Alston ed. 1999).

[26] *Hoechst AG v Commission of the European Communities*, C-46/87 and 227/88.

undertakings; whereas in *Niemietz*,[27] the ECtHR held that this right could afford protection to business premises.[28] In any event, the EU Charter of Fundamental Rights has confirmed the need to interpret EU rights according to the Convention (article 52.3): 'In so far as this Charter contains rights which correspond to rights guaranteed by the Convention for the Protection of Human Rights and Fundamental Freedoms, the meaning and scope of those rights shall be the same as those laid down by the said Convention. This provision shall not prevent Union law providing more extensive protection.' Thus, the Charter also acknowledges the possibility of improving the level of protection granted to EU fundamental rights.

The scope of application of EU and Convention rights might overlap. In principle, the ECtHR has no jurisdiction to check the action of EU institutions.[29] Its jurisdiction over the states might be problematic, however, when state authorities act within the field of application of EU law, since these state measures are also bound by EU fundamental rights. For example, in *Cantoni v France*,[30] the ECtHR emphasized that even though a national provision constituted a transcription of a European directive, almost word for word, that fact did not remove the national provision from the scope of the Convention. In this way, notwithstanding the lack of jurisdiction, the ECtHR might indirectly monitor EU law. In a more recent case—*Bosphorus v Ireland*[31]—however, the ECtHR declared that it would presume that a state had not departed from the Convention when the state did no more than implement legal obligations flowing from its membership to an international organization, as long as fundamental rights within that organization received 'equivalent protection' to that provided by the Convention.[32] In this case, the ECtHR concluded that the protection of fundamental rights within the EU could be considered to be, and to have been at the time of the dispute, equivalent to the protection provided by the Convention system.

---

[27] *Niemietz v Germany*, 16 December 1992.

[28] For other instances of divergence see Spielmann, *supra* n 25, at 766–770.

[29] *Confédération française démocratique du travail v European Communities*, 10 July 1978; *Christiane Dufay v European Communities*, 19 January 1989. In the latter, it was held that complaints brought directly against Community institutions fell outside the ECtHR jurisdiction *ratione personae*.

[30] *Cantoni v France*, 22 October 1996.

[31] *Bosphorus v Ireland*, 30 June 2005.

[32] The doctrine of 'equivalent protection' had already been announced in a decision by the European Commission of Human Rights, *A. M. & Co. v Germany*, 9 February 1990. See Harmsen, *supra* n 20, at 631.

In addition, the ECtHR has asserted jurisdiction over the states in concluding international treaties. In *Matthews v the United Kingdom*,[33] the ECtHR held the United Kingdom liable for violating the right to free elections[34] because Gibraltar citizens had been excluded from the elections to the European Parliament. This exclusion was legally based on a 1976 Council decision, which had treaty status. Hence, the ECtHR might indirectly review international agreements concluded by the states, such as those concerning the EU.[35]

In sum, the ECtHR might indirectly check primary and secondary EU law compliance with the Convention by reviewing state acts concluding treaties or state acts implementing EU law. It is because of this Kafkian situation that most academic literature has advocated the accession of the EU to the European Convention.[36] The accession of the EU to the Convention would make Convention rights binding upon EU institutions and would grant the ECtHR jurisdiction over EU law. Nevertheless, it would not necessarily solve the tensions arising as a consequence of the overlap between constitutional and EU fundamental rights.

3 ECJ vis-à-vis state courts

The structural relationship between the EU and the state legal systems is based upon the principles of supremacy[37] and direct effect[38] of EU law. Direct effect means that EU law confers judicially enforceable rights to individuals. National courts must uphold these rights without the states having to adopt any legislation providing for their application. According to the supremacy principle, EU law always trumps any conflicting domestic provision, be it legislative, executive, or judicial. Consequently, national courts must set aside state provisions that clash with EU law, even if the state provisions have been enacted subsequently. Over time, the supremacy of EU law over

[33] *Matthews v the United Kingdom*, 18 February 1999.
[34] Article 3 of the Additional Protocol to the ECHR (Paris, 20 March 1952).
[35] Note that this would not be a case of overlap between the scope of application of EU and Convention rights. Indeed, EU Treaties and other norms at the Treaty level are not subject to EU fundamental rights and therefore cannot be reviewed by the ECJ.
[36] Canor, *supra* n 20, at 21.   [37] *Flaminio Costa v ENEL*, C-6/64.
[38] *NV Algemene Transport- en Expeditie Onderneming van Gend & Loos v Netherlands Inland Revenue Administration*, C-26/62.

ordinary domestic law has been generally accepted. The legitimacy of this principle has been contested, however, with regard to the supremacy of EU law over state constitutions.[39]

The ECJ took the initiative in recognizing fundamental rights as a part of the EU legal system.[40] The 'general principles of law' were employed as the legal means for the introduction of fundamental rights in the EU legal order.[41] The declared sources of interpretation to give content to these general principles were the constitutional traditions common to the member states and the European Convention on Human Rights. As explained, not only did the ECJ enforce EU fundamental rights against EU institutions, but the ECJ applied them to state authorities as well. The incorporation of EU rights to the states, however, had a 'limited' scope,[42] in that not all state measures were declared to be bound by EU fundamental rights, but only those enacted 'within the field of application of EU law'. It should be pointed out that the model delineated by the ECJ case law is somewhat different from the one that evolved in the US.[43] The original US federal Bill of Rights was binding only upon the federal government. After the Civil War, as a result of the enactment of the Reconstruction Amendments and the Supreme Court's interpretation of the Due Process Clause, most rights became binding upon any and all state action. Throughout the so-called process of 'incorporation', the main debate questioned which rights from the federal Bill would become binding upon the states.[44] In the EU, the debated question is not so much which rights are incorporated, but rather

[39] Regarding the reception of the supremacy principle by national courts see ANNE-MARIE SLAUGHTER, ALEC STONE SWEET & JOSEPH H. H. WEILER (eds.), THE EUROPEAN COURT AND NATIONAL COURTS, DOCTRINE AND JURISPRUDENCE: LEGAL CHANGE IN ITS SOCIAL CONTEXT (Hart Publishing 2000).

[40] *Stauder v City of Ulm*, C-29/69; *Internationale Handelsgesellschaft mbh v Einhfuhr-und Vorratsstelle für Getreide und Futtermittel*, C-11/70; *J. Nold, Kohlen- und Baustoffgroßhandlung v Commission of the European Communities*, C-4/73; *Hauer v Land Rheinland-Pfaltz*, C-44/79.

[41] In the words of TREVOR C. HARTLEY, THE FOUNDATIONS OF EUROPEAN COMMUNITY LAW 130 (Oxford University Press 1998), the ECJ 'has utilized general principles of law to cloak the nakedness of judicial law-making'.

[42] Aida Torres Pérez, *La Dimensión Estructural de la Carta de Derechos Fundamentales de la Unión Europea. Relaciones Verticales y Cláusulas Horizontales*, 67 REVISTA VASCA DE ADMINISTRACIÓN PÚBLICA 253, 276–281 (2003).

[43] Koen Leanerts, *Fundamental Rights to be Included in a Community Catalogue*, 16 EUROPEAN LAW REVIEW 367, 368–372 (1991); Torres, *supra* n 42, at 255–265, 275–281.

[44] The competing theories of Justice Frankfurter, who rejected the theory of incorporation, Justice Brennan, who defended a 'selective incorporation', and Justice Black, who affirmed a 'total incorporation', dominated the debate. See AKHIL R. AMAR, THE BILL OF RIGHTS 221 (Yale University Press 1998).

what kind of state action is constrained by them. As discussed in the previous chapter, the scope of application of EU rights upon the states has been defined case by case in an expanding way. At this point, it should be clear that certain state acts are bound concurrently by constitutional and EU fundamental rights. Conflicts might arise when the respective national and supranational standards of protection deviate. The standard of protection established by the ECJ is not a minimum, as it is the one defined by the ECtHR. Instead, EU rights claim to be both a floor and a ceiling that states are required to respect.

The interplay between state courts and the ECJ, and more particularly the adjudication of fundamental rights by the ECJ within the EU *sui generis* institutional structure are at the core of this inquiry. A complete picture of rights protection in Europe requires that the role of the ECtHR be taken into account. The relationship between the ECtHR and state courts, however, responds to different parameters. The ECtHR was created by an international treaty whose main goal was protecting human rights. Individuals have been granted a direct action against the states before the ECtHR. Yet, the intervention of the ECtHR is subsidiary, and individuals must exhaust all domestic judicial remedies before filing a complaint before the ECtHR. Additionally, Convention rights only set a floor of protection that states may improve. In contrast, the ECJ was created to secure compliance with EU law and the realization of common market goals within a broader supranational organization, whose institutions enact binding law. EU fundamental rights were judicially crafted by the ECJ, which also decided to extend their scope of application to the states. Individuals have not been granted a direct action against the states before the ECJ. In practice, the preliminary reference has been the mechanism through which the ECJ has decided about the compatibility between state action and EU fundamental rights. The intervention of the ECJ through the preliminary reference, though, is not subsidiary. Finally, according to the supremacy principle, EU fundamental rights do not only set a floor of protection, but claim to prevail over national law, including constitutional law, in all circumstances. Hence, the terms in which the ECJ and the ECtHR interact with state courts structurally and methodologically differ.

In any event, should the EU accede to the European Convention, the ECtHR would acquire jurisdiction over EU institutions contributing to clarify the current situation. The Convention, interpreted by the ECtHR, would provide a common set of binding rights for the states and the EU. Accession to the European Convention, however, would not necessarily address potential conflicts between the EU and state legal systems. Accession would extend the jurisdiction of the ECtHR over EU institutions, and the EU could be condemned for violating the Convention. The Convention, however, only establishes a floor of protection. Even if EU institutions respected the Convention, and EU rights were not interpreted below this floor, the potential conflicts between EU and constitutional rights would not necesarily disappear. Member states may still grant a higher level of protection than the ECtHR and the ECJ. This is admitted by the Convention system, but clashes with the EU supremacy principle. Thus, even if the EU acceded to the ECHR, the normative inquiry regarding the ECJ's adjudication of fundamental rights within the EU institutional structure would deserve specific analysis. On the whole, the function of protecting human rights in Europe is being 'disaggregated',[45] in that this function is now shared by different institutions from different, possibly overlapping spheres. Traditional constitutional theory, built upon the assumption of state boundaries, falls short of giving an account of this new reality.

---

[45] Christian Walter, *Constitutionalizing (Inter)national Governance—Possibilities for and Limits to the Development of an International Constitutional Law*, 44 GERMAN YEARBOOK OF INTERNATIONAL LAW 171, 196–201 (2001).

PART II

EU Rights within a Pluralist Framework

From Hierarchy to Pluralism

The debate regarding fundamental rights conflicts in the European Union (EU) has engaged both courts and scholars. Much of the debate, including work by Theodor Schilling[1] or Ingolf Pernice,[2] has focused on whether state constitutions or EU law should be regarded as supreme. Conflicts between norms are commonly solved on the basis of a pre-established hierarchical relationship between them. Generally, if two norms are applicable to the same case and they command different results, the superior norm prevails. According to this view, the question to be answered in the EU would be the following: which norm is at the top of the hierarchy, state constitutions or EU law? The discussion that follows will briefly present the positions and main arguments for the respective supremacy of state constitutions and EU law. Each of these arguments will be critically assessed, with both approaches ultimately rejected. On the other hand, several scholars have opposed hierarchy as the ordering principle between national and supranational fundamental rights norms within the EU. Alternative non-hierarchical accounts to address these conflicts have been proposed. These alternative proposals will also be critically analysed. Ultimately, in spite of dismissing these specific proposals, a pluralist framework for institutional and norm interaction will be advanced.

[1] Theodor Schilling, *The Autonomy of the Community Legal Order—An Analysis of Possible Foundations*, 37 HARVARD INTERNATIONAL LAW JOURNAL 389 (1996).

[2] Ingolf Pernice, *Multilevel Constitutionalism and the Treaty of Amsterdam: European Constitution-Making Revisited?*, 36 COMMON MARKET LAW REVIEW 703 (1999).

1 Hierarchical models

1.1 *State constitutional supremacy*

First, the thesis supporting the supremacy of state constitutions asserts that since the constitution, by definition, is the supreme law of the land, all state acts must comply with it, even if they are enacted within the field of application of EU law. European integration may not impair constitutional rights' protection. Secondly, according to constitutional theory, the ultimate source of legitimacy for a legal system resides with the people. The legal authority of the EU system, however, does not emanate from an act of original, constituent power expressing the will of the people, but from the consent of the member states, according to their own constitutions. Since the validity of the EU legal system is based, ultimately, upon state constitutions, EU law cannot override state constitutional law. Consistent with this, several constitutional courts have affirmed their power to determine whether state acts, despite being enacted within the field of application of EU law, comply with state constitutional rights.[3]

1.1.1 *State constitutions as comprehensively regulating and limiting power*

The first argument in favour of the supremacy of state constitutions is ontological in nature. It derives from the concept that the constitution, by definition, is the supreme norm of a national legal system and is comprehensive in scope.[4] Accordingly, all public power exercised in a given state is regulated and limited by the constitution as the ultimate source of legitimacy. To be more specific, the constitution establishes the structure of government and the constraints upon public authority, such as fundamental rights. From the perspective of modern constitutionalism, no legal act applied within the state territory can escape constitutional scrutiny. Hence,

---

[3] For example, the German Constitutional Court in *Solange I* (1974) and *Solange II* (1986), and the Spanish Constitutional Court in STC 64/1991, 22 March 1991. These courts were not necessarily challenging the validity of EU legislation, but rather reviewing state acts falling within the field of application of EU law. Still, such judicial review might well challenge the efficacy of EU law.

[4] Dieter Grimm, *The Constitution in the Process of Denationalisation*, in DIE ZUKUNFT DER VERFASSUNG, 1, 13 (Suhrkamp 2002), defines the function of a constitution as 'the comprehensive legal regulation of public power'; this author clarifies that the constitution is comprehensive 'in that constitutional legitimation is necessary to the exercise of power and no sovereign act that does not meet the requirements of the constitution can claim legal validity'.

it is argued, the application of EU law within the state cannot trump the national constitution, in particular constitutional rights.

Moreover, the transfer of powers to the EU has been performed according to specific constitutional provisions allowing for this transfer.[5] This 'constitutionally permitted' transfer cannot tolerate the violation of fundamental rights enshrined in the state constitution. Thus, the creation of a supranational regime cannot justify the circumvention of constitutional rights. For example, in *Solange I* (1974), the German Constitutional Court held that the constitutional clause allowing for the transfer of powers did not allow legislation enacted by supranational institutions to change the basic structure of the German Constitution. Fundamental rights were deemed part of this basic structure.[6] In 1992, this constitutional clause was amended to expressly acknowledge German fundamental rights as limits to European integration.[7] On the whole, the recognition and enforcement of EU law within the states stems from domestic constitutional law. The transfer of powers to this supranational organization was only possible because state constitutions enabled it. Thus, state constitutions are still supreme. Furthermore, as argued, this transfer involves only the 'exercise' of powers. States are still the 'holders' of the powers transferred, and therefore these powers could be recovered by the states at any time.[8]

1.1.2 *State constitutions as the expression of popular sovereignty*

The claim for the supremacy of state constitutions is commonly grounded in 'popular sovereignty', as the ultimate source of legitimacy of the state legal

---

[5] For example, article 11 of the 1948 Italian Constitution, article 24(1) of the 1949 German Constitution, (now article 23 after the 1992 amendment), article 93 of the 1978 Spanish Constitution. See Bruno de Witte, *Sovereignty and European Integration: The Weight of Legal Tradition*, in THE EUROPEAN COURT AND NATIONAL COURTS, DOCTRINE AND JURISPRUDENCE. LEGAL CHANGE IN ITS SOCIAL CONTEXT 277 (Anne-Marie Slaughter, Alec Stone Sweet & Joseph H. H. Weiler eds. 1998).

[6] Juliane Kokott, *Report on Germany*, in THE EUROPEAN COURT AND NATIONAL COURTS, DOCTRINE AND JURISPRUDENCE. LEGAL CHANGE IN ITS SOCIAL CONTEXT 77, 92 (Anne-Marie Slaughter, Alec Stone Sweet & Joseph H. H. Weiler, eds. 1998).

[7] De Witte, *supra* n 5, at 296–297.

[8] For example, the House of Lords (1991) argued that the limitation upon parliamentary sovereignty as a consequence of entering the EU was legitimate because it had been voluntarily consented by the enactment of the European Communities Act 1972, and it may be revoked at any time by derogating this law and withdrawing from the EU. See Paul Craig, *Report on the United Kingdom*, in THE EUROPEAN COURT AND NATIONAL COURTS, DOCTRINE AND JURISPRUDENCE. LEGAL CHANGE IN ITS SOCIAL CONTEXT 195, 202 (Anne-Marie Slaughter, Alec Stone Sweet & Joseph H. H. Weiler eds. 1998).

order. The state constitution realizes the ideal of self-government by the 'people' subject to that constitution. This argument holds that European integration has not changed the location of popular sovereignty, which still resides in the state. Hence, state constitutions are still supreme within the respective territories.

Clearly, the concept of sovereignty has evolved over time. Sovereignty was traditionally understood as the limitless power to rule without being bound by any rules. This power was originally attibuted to the monarch. Over the sixteenth and seventeenth centuries, the centralization of power in the monarch contributed to the emergence of the modern sovereign states, which were conceived as monopolizing the legitimate use of force over their territory.[9] Jean Bodin articulated the concept of sovereignty, and Thomas Hobbes provided its justification from the standpoint of political philosophy.[10] By the end of the eighteenth century, with the liberal French and American revolutions, sovereignty was transferred from the monarch to the people, and then 'popular sovereignty' became the relevant concept.[11] In constitutional democracies, sovereignty—the ultimate and supreme power—resides with the people. Some scholars note that when sovereignty was transferred from the monarch to the people, the nature of this concept changed. It was no longer adequate to describe the exercise of power within the state,[12] as it had become a legitimating mechanism according to which 'all political and legal power ought to rest on the will and consent of those among or over whom power is exercised.'[13] Popular sovereignty is mainly expressed in the act of giving birth to the constitution, which regulates the institutions that will actually exercise public power. In other words, the people, acting as the 'constituent power',[14] create and legitimite the new legal order by establishing a constitution.

---

[9] Concerning the origins of the concept of sovereignty and the modern state, see Dieter Grimm, *The Modern State: Continental Traditions*, in GUIDANCE, CONTROL AND EVALUATION IN THE PUBLIC SECTOR 89, 91–94 (Franz-Xaver Kaufmann et al. eds. 1986).

[10] De Witte, *supra* n 5, at 277–279; NEIL MACCORMICK, QUESTIONING SOVEREIGNTY. LAW, STATE AND NATION IN THE EUROPEAN COMMONWEALTH 123–124 (Oxford University Press 1999), LUIS MARÍA DÍEZ PICAZO, CONSTITUCIONALISMO DE LA UNIÓN EUROPEA 121–123 (Civitas 2002).

[11] De Witte, *supra* n 5, at 279–280; Grimm, *supra* n 9, at 96–97.

[12] De Witte, *supra* n 5, at 280, argues that popular sovereignty is 'utterly empty. It seems to offer little or no value for explaining the effective functioning of today's constitutional systems. In the countries of continental Europe, the "people" may well formally hold the ultimate authority in the state, but it is barred from the immediate exercise of state power.'

[13] MacCormick, *supra* n 10, at 130.

[14] As Sieyès famously put it, this is the 'pouvoir constituant'. He differentiated between the 'pouvoir constituant' and the 'pouvoir constitué'. Grimm, *supra* n 4, at 10: 'The *pouvoir constituant*

Hence, EU law cannot claim supremacy over state constitutions because the EU founding Treaties were not established by the will of the people but by the consent of the member states. In signing and ratifying these Treaties, state governments and parliaments were not exercising a constitution-making (or constituent) power.[15] In general, the procedures for the ratification of these Treaties required less qualified majorities than those needed for constitutional amendment. They were negotiated through the usual diplomatic channels employed to conclude international agreements, with member states' citizens excluded from negotiations and ratification processes. Not only did the Treaties lack a popular foundation, but there was no single 'European people' (or *demos*) capable of acting at the supranational level. To put it differently, member states' citizens did not share a belief in a European collective identity and still do not.[16] The locus of political identity has largely remained within the states. The Treaties have always referred to the 'peoples' of Europe in the plural. Also, those concluding the Treaties are identified as the 'high contracting parties' (article 1 EC Treaty). Even the text of the failed EU Constitution kept the plural form 'peoples' in the preamble. Despite the ambiguous double reference in article I-1 to the 'will of the citizens and the States of Europe' as the origin of the Constitution, the consent of only the states (and all the states) was required for its approval and future amendments. Although some states decided to convoke referenda before ratifying the constitutional text, this was not compulsory according to the EU legal system. Furthermore, there was no provision for a European-wide referendum in which all the peoples of Europe would speak as a single body. Therefore, even the proposed EU Constitution could not have been attributed to the will of a single European people. In conclusion, the supremacy of the EU Treaties over state constitutions cannot be sustained because the legitimacy of the EU legal order does not directly derive from the European people, but from the member states acting according to their

spawns the *pouvoir constitué* and in this birthing process it is itself not legally bound. But it does not go beyond creating and regulating legitimate power. It is for the *pouvoir constitué* to actually exercise the power. However, it can only act on the basis and within the limits of the constitution. In the constitutional state, there can be no extra-constitutional or supra-constitutional powers beyond the *pouvoir constituant*.' This distinction fairly corresponds with the distinction between higher and normal law-making tracks in Ackerman's terminology. BRUCE ACKERMAN, WE THE PEOPLE: FOUNDATIONS (Harvard University Press 1993).

[15] Schilling, *supra* n 1, at 390–395.

[16] Dieter Grimm, *Does Europe Need a Constitution?*, 1 EUROPEAN LAW JOURNAL 282, 291–297 (1995).

constitutions. Hence, popular sovereignty, the ultimate source for the legitimacy of public power, still resides with state constitutions.

1.1.3 *State constitutionalism in light of European integration*

The foregoing arguments underpinning state constitutional supremacy fail to acknowledge the transformations that have occurred as a result of the European integration process; instead, they faithfully follow from modern state constitutionalism, which posits the constitution as comprehensively regulating and limiting power within the state territory, legitimated by an act of the people as the ultimate source of authority. Traditional concepts of state sovereignty and constitutionalism, however, are less and less capable of accounting for and regulating the new EU reality.

Although the transfer of sovereign powers to a supranational organization was constitutionally permitted, such constitutional provisions opened up state constitutions to supranational modes of governance. Admittedly, the transfer of powers to the EU modified state constitutions since, by virtue of that very act, state constitutions no longer regulate all public power exercised within the state. In this vein, the transfer of powers did not modify the text, but the scope of the constitution. The transfer of powers was performed through procedures (usually legislative statutes ratifying the Treaties) not necessarily the same as those required for constitutional amendment. Yet, this alteration of the constitution through procedures that differed from constitutional amendment was not unconstitutional because the same constitution had enabled this. Still, the concept of constitutionalism was compromised. After transferring sovereign powers to a supranational regime, whose laws have direct effect within state territories, state constitutions cannot fulfil their claim of comprehensiveness because all public powers exercised within the state are no longer regulated by that state's constitution as the ultimate source of legitimacy. Public powers exercised within the states are now defined and limited in several 'constitutional' documents.[17] To put it differently, member states' constitutions need to be supplemented with the EU Treaties to obtain a comprehensive picture of the structure of public authority. In this context, constitutions are better seen as 'partial constitutions',[18] since they no longer regulate public authority exercised within the state on a comprehensive level. Although it might be formally argued that since each state consented to the transfer of powers according to

---

[17] Christian Walter, *Constitutionalizing (Inter)national Governance—Possibilities for and Limits to the Development of an International Constitutional Law* 44 GERMAN YEARBOOK OF INTERNATIONAL LAW 171(2001), at 194.

[18] *Id.* at 193–196.

its constitution, that constitution is still governing, in reality, those powers are regulated in the text of the EU Treaties and exercised by EU institutions. Moreover, member states are bound to enforce legislation enacted by those supranational institutions. Law-making within the EU does not require unanimity of the member states on an increasing number of issues. In addition, recovery of the powers transferred is not contemplated in the Treaties. Even though, for the first time, the text of the failed EU Constitution regulated the possibility of withdrawal from the Union (article I-60), and this possibility has been kept in the Lisbon Treaty (article 50), the political and economic costs for a state acting unilaterally would make such a withdrawal quite unfeasible.[19]

With regard to the second argument stemming from popular sovereignty, admittedly the source of the EU Treaties is not a single 'European people'. The people, however, are not necessarily an existing prior entity.[20] As discussed above, popular sovereignty is a legitimating mechanism to justify the exercise of public power upon individuals. Constitutional theory tends to presuppose the existence of a people as the constituent power, but this legal presupposition often does not correspond with political and social realities.[21] The founding patterns of sovereign states around the world vary. Bruce Ackerman distinguishes between two scenarios: 'new beginnings', in which the 'constitution emerges as a symbolic marker of a great transition in the political life of the nation',[22] and 'federalism', in which a treaty among a group of states evolves into a constitution.[23] The former would correspond to the traditional view of the emergence of a new legal order in a 'constitutional moment', at which point, the people establish the principles that henceforth will govern them. But this pattern is not the sole means for creating a legal order that might claim popular sovereignty. For example, nobody today would question that the legitimacy of the US Constitution derives from 'We the People'. However, at the moment of enactment, its 'constitutional' nature

[19] Neil MacCormick, *The Maastricht-Urteil: Sovereignty Now*, 1 EUROPEAN LAW JOURNAL 259, 265 (1995).

[20] MacCormick, *supra* n 10, at 131.

[21] Joseph H. H. Weiler, *Federalism Without Constitutionalism: Europe's Sonderweg*, in THE FEDERAL VISION 54, 56 (Kalypso Nicolaidis & Robert Howse eds. 2003): 'In many instances, constitutional doctrine presupposes the existence of that which it creates: the *demos* which is called upon to accept the constitution is constituted, legally, by that very constitution, and often that act of acceptance is along the first steps towards a thicker social and political notion of constitutional *demos*.'

[22] Bruce Ackerman, *The Rise of World Constitutionalism*, 83 VIRGINIA LAW REVIEW 771, 778 (1997).

[23] *Id.* at 775–776.

was much more ambiguous and the concept of a unitary 'people' much more questionable, all of which was not resolved until the Civil War and the enactment of the Reconstruction amendments. Despite this difficult and traumatic historical evolution, popular American constitutional beliefs accept as an inviolable truth that the US Constitution, from its outset to this day, is legitimated through the unwavering support of 'We the People'. Ackerman conceives both the US, from the 1780s through the 1860s, and the European Union, from its birth in the 1950s to the present, as 'combined scenarios'. Regarding the EU, he writes, 'The Treaty of Rome, like the Articles of Confederation, was negotiated and approved by sovereign states without any of the plebiscites and constitutional convention that characteristically accompany a "new beginning".'[24] He proceeds to describe the process through which the 'treaty' has been converted into a more 'constitution-like' document. Hence, in theory, a notion of 'We the People of Europe' may evolve in the future to be the ultimate source of legitimacy for the EU legal order. Another question is how this notion should be understood. The notion of people does not require a pre-existent ethno-cultural community. Indeed, some would argue that a European people should not be defined in ethno-cultural terms.[25] 'The people' is a concept of the political imagination. It is argued that a notion of people might emerge as the belief in a collective identity evolves among a defined group of individuals on the basis of civic and political commitments. Among the prerequisites for the emergence of a European people, some indicate the need of a public sphere for transnational debate about issues of common interest and the development of links of solidarity among the members of a European civil society.[26] Beyond the debates about 'the people' as the ultimate source of authority, the legitimacy of the EU legal order from the perspective of its links with the people at the 'higher lawmaking' track has slowly improved. Regarding the ratification process, some states modified the majorities needed to pass legislation ratifying the EU Treaties in order to have the same majorities as needed for constitutional amendment.[27] In addition, several member states held referenda for their

---

[24] *Id.* at 793.

[25] See Jürgen Habermas, *Comment on the Paper by Dieter Grimm: Does Europe need a Constitution?*, 1 EUROPEAN LAW JOURNAL 303, 305 (1995); JOSEPH H. H. WEILER, THE CONSTITUTION OF EUROPE 344 (Cambridge University Press 1999).

[26] Habermas, *supra* n 25, at 305–307; DEIRDRE M. CURTIN, POSTNATIONAL DEMOCRACY. THE EUROPEAN UNION IN SEARCH OF A POLITICAL PHILOSOPHY, 43, 56–61 (Kluwer 1997).

[27] For instance, in 1992, the German Constitution was amended and now article 23 requires a two-thirds majority of the legislature for approving EU Treaty amendments. This is the same

accession to the EU and the ratification of the successive Treaty amendments.[28] Many had planned to convoke referenda regarding the ratification of the proposed EU Constitution.[29] The talk about a European Constitution increased the awareness of the population in general, generating more interest and public debate across Europe. In addition, regarding the drafting process, a convention was set up to elaborate the constitutional text.[30] National and European, executive and legislative institutions were represented at this convention.[31] In total, more than two-thirds of the members were parliamentarians, who directly represent their constituencies. In addition, participation of organizations from the civil society was promoted throughout the debate. The drafting process was public and transparent, offering citizens access to documents through the internet, such as the successive drafts and proposed amendments. As opposed to the Intergovernmental Conference model, the convention furthered diverse participation, deliberation, and transparency.[32] The Lisbon Treaty, which was concluded by means of the traditional Intergovernmental Conference, regulates the possibility to convene a convention for future Treaty amendments, composed of representatives of the national parliaments, the heads of state or government of the member states, and representatives of the European Parliament and of the Commission (article 48 EU Treaty). For all these reasons, although the

majority required for amending the constitution, instead of the simple majority required by previous article 24. See Kokott, *supra* n 6, at 92.

[28] In Ireland and Denmark referenda were compulsory for acceding to the EU (1973). In Ireland, referendum is compulsory for ratifying Treaty amendments as well. Austria, Finland, and Sweden held referenda to approve their accession, becoming members in 1995. It was only compulsory in Austria. See SIMON HUG, VOICES OF EUROPE. CITIZENS, REFERENDUMS, AND EUROPEAN INTEGRATION (Rowman & Littlefield Publishers 2002); BRUNO KAUFMANN & M. DANE WATERS (eds.), DIRECT DEMOCRACY IN EUROPE. A COMPREHENSIVE REFERENCE GUIDE TO THE INITIATIVE AND REFERENDUM PROCESS IN EUROPE (Carolina Academic Press 2004).

[29] Among others, the Czech Republic, Denmark, France, Ireland, Luxembourg, the Netherlands, Poland, Portugal, Spain, and the United Kingdom announced that referenda would be held.

[30] The 'convention' model had been used before only once, for drafting the EU Charter of fundamental rights. The convention does not substitute the Intergovernmental Conference. It produces the text that will be discussed by the representatives of the member states in the Intergovernmental Conference.

[31] This convention was composed of 15 representatives of the heads of state or government (one per state); 30 members of national parliaments (two per state), 16 members of the European Parliament and two representatives of the Commission. European Council, *Laeken Declaration—The future of the European Union* (2001).

[32] Lars Hoffmann, *The Convention on the Future of Europe— Thoughts on the Convention-Model*, Jean Monnet Working Paper 11/02, 11 (New York School of Law 2002).

EU legal order cannot be attributed to the popular consent of 'the European people', its legitimacy has been slightly promoted.

To conclude, in the EU, modern nation-states have undergone a profound transformation as a consequence of their participation in this supranational form of governance. In the words of MacCormick, 'No state in Western Europe any longer is a sovereign state. None is in a position such that all the power exercised internally in it, whether politically or legally, derives from purely internal sources.'[33] State functions are being disaggregated and allocated at different levels of governance.[34] Hence, there is a plurality of legal systems regulating public power within the state. We should stop trying to determine which is the ultimate sovereign authority in Europe and acknowledge the reality of a new form of a supranational community embracing a plurality of polities interpreting fundamental rights. In short, claims based upon sheer state constitutional supremacy or ultimate popular sovereignty fail to acknowledge these transformations. The values brought by constitutionalism should be preserved, within a context of blurring state boundaries. In a globalized world, the challenge to reconcile state sovereignty with the proliferation of sources of law requires the development of forms of governance and adjudication capable of dealing with supranational pluralism.

1.2 *EU law supremacy*

An alternative hierarchical model posits the supremacy of EU law, which has been advanced by the European Court of Justice (ECJ) itself. This Court defined the supremacy of EU law in absolute terms: all EU law (including both primary and secondary law)[35] is always supreme over both state constitutions and state law. In *Internationale Handelsgesellschaft*, the ECJ formulated the principle of supremacy and stated its consequences as follows:

The law stemming from the Treaty, an independent source of law, cannot, because of its very nature, be overridden by rules of national law, however framed, without being deprived of its character as EC law and without the legal basis of the EC itself being called into question. Therefore the validity of a EC measure or its

---

[33] Neil MacCormick, *Beyond the Sovereign State*, 56 THE MODERN LAW REVIEW 1, 16 (1993).

[34] Anne-Marie Slaughter, *The Real New World Order*, 76 FOREIGN AFFAIRS 183, 184 (1997): 'The state is not disappearing, it is disaggregating into its separate, functionally distinct parts.'

[35] 'Primary law' includes the Treaties and other documents at the Treaty level; 'secondary law' includes all binding legal acts emanating from EU institutions.

effect within a Member State cannot be affected by allegations that it runs counter to either fundamental rights as formulated by the constitution of that State or the principles of a national constitutional structure.[36]

The reference to national law 'however framed' indicates the supremacy of EU law over any kind of national norms, including constitutional and ordinary law. Particularly, according to the ECJ, state courts cannot rely on state constitutional rights to review the validity of EU law or impair its effect within the member states. Several arguments have been advanced to support the unlimited supremacy of EU law.

1.2.1 *The autonomy of the EU legal order*

In *Costa v ENEL*,[37] the 1964 case in which the supremacy principle was first advanced, the ECJ justified the supremacy of EU law on the basis of the creation of an autonomous legal order. The ECJ put forward a view of the EU legal order as separate from both international law and state legal orders. The autonomy of the EU was premised in the kind of organization created, to which the member states had transferred sovereign powers, self-limiting their own sovereignty for an unlimited period of time.[38] Despite the fact that the EU had its origin in an international treaty, the ECJ argued that it had become 'an independent source of law'.[39] Thus, EU law was not subject to any higher law. The ECJ attributed a constitutional nature to the Treaty,[40] expressly calling it a 'constitutional charter' and proclaiming its supremacy over any form of state law:

The EEC-Treaty, albeit concluded in the form of an international agreement, none the less constitutes the constitutional charter of a Community based on the rule of law.... The essential characteristics of the Community legal order ... are in

[36] *Internationale Handelsgesellschaft mbh v Einhfuhr- und Vorratsstelle für Getreide und Futtermittel*, C-11/70.
[37] *Flaminio Costa v ENEL*, C-6/64.
[38] Jan Wouters, *National Constitutions and the European Union*, 1 LEGAL ISSUES OF ECONOMIC INTEGRATION 25, 64–66 (2000); Eric Stein, *Lawyers, Judges, and the Making of a Transnational Constitution*, 75 AMERICAN JOURNAL OF INTERNATIONAL LAW 1, 11–14 (1981).
[39] *Internationale Handelsgesellschaft mbh v Einhfuhr- und Vorratsstelle für Getreide und Futtermittel*, C-11/70.
[40] About the role of the ECJ in the 'constitutionalization' of the Treaties see, among others, Stein, *supra* n 38; J. Rinze, *The Role of the European Court of Justice as a Federal Constitutional Court*, PUBLIC LAW 426 (1993); G. Federico Mancini, *The Making of a Constitution for Europe*, 26 COMMON MARKET LAW REVIEW 595 (1989); ALEC STONE SWEET, GOVERNING WITH JUDGES. CONSTITUTIONAL POLITICS IN EUROPE (Oxford University Press 2000).

particular its primacy over the law of the Member States and the direct effect of a whole series of provisions.[41]

All EU legislation can be traced back to a single norm as the ultimate source of validity, namely, the Treaties. Hence, if it is admitted that the Treaties are an independent source of law, state law cannot determine the validity of EU law. As such, the EU legal order would have its own Grundnorm.

1.2.2 *Member states' consent*

Although the original Treaties did not include a supremacy clause, some authors claim that the supremacy of EU law was implicitly accepted through the ratification of the Treaties.[42] Since the EU was created to achieve an efficient structure for political action at the supranational level, this argument maintains, the ratifying states necessarily consented to the supremacy of EU law. Also, it has been held that, even if the states did not consent to the supremacy principle through the Treaties' ratification, this was consented to over time as state courts accepted the supremacy of EU law.[43]

Some have claimed that had the EU Constitution been ratified, the supremacy of EU law over state constitutions would definitely have been established and validated by the states. The draft EU Constitution incorporated the principle of supremacy in article I-6: 'The Constitution and law adopted by the Union's Institutions in exercising competences conferred on it shall have primacy over the law of the Member States.' It is held that this article would have consecrated the ECJ case law, which clearly asserts the supremacy of EU law over constitutional and ordinary state law.

1.2.3 *Uniformity and efficacy of EU law*

There is a more pragmatic argument in favour of the supremacy of EU law: if state courts applied the respective constitution to control the enforcement

---

[41] ECJ Opinion 1/91. Also, in *Parti écologiste 'Les Verts' v European Parliament*, C-294/83, the ECJ called the Treaty 'basic constitutional charter'. The ECJ held that all measures adopted by the member states or the EU institutions had to comply with it.

[42] Supporting this thesis, Wouters, *supra* n 38, at 68: 'It is submitted that the essential legal basis of the precedence of Community law over national law—with the inclusion of constitutional norms—is found in the voluntary decision by the Member States to establish the European Communities and the European Union or to accede to these afterwards, after ratification of the relevant Treaties "in accordance with their respective constitutional requirements".'

[43] Exploring and rejecting this possibility see Schilling, *supra* n 1, at 395–398.

of EU law within the state, the uniformity and efficacy of law would be jeopardized.[44] In *Internationale Handelsgesellschaft*, the ECJ declared that neither the 'validity' of an EU measure nor its 'effect' within a member state should be altered by allegations that 'it runs counter to either fundamental rights as formulated by the constitution of that state or the principles of its constitutional structure'.[45] In *Hauer*, the ECJ articulated the reasons why as follows:

[T]he introduction of special criteria for assessment stemming from the legislation or constitutional law of a particular Member State would, by damaging the substantive unity and efficacy of Community law, lead inevitably to the destruction of the unity of the Common Market and the jeopardizing of the cohesion of the Community.[46]

The ECJ claimed its sole power for reviewing the validity of EU legislation in light of EU fundamental rights.[47] If domestic courts suspect that an applicable EU provision might violate fundamental rights, they should refer a preliminary question about the validity of that EU provision to the ECJ. Domestic courts cannot set aside EU law on their own motion.

The efficacy of EU law might also be challenged if courts from several states set aside state measures enacted within the field of application of EU law for violating constitutional rights. For example, the invalidation of domestic measures enforcing the European regulation regarding the banana market on the grounds that these state measures clash with constitutional rights might endanger the uniform application and efficacy of this regulation. Generally, to avoid this result, the ECJ requires that domestic courts follow the supranational understanding of the fundamental right at stake (instead of following the constitutional interpretation). If in doubt as to the supranational interpretation, state courts may always refer a preliminary question to the ECJ to clarify how that fundamental right should be interpreted.[48]

---

[44] Wouters, *supra* n 38, at 64–65.
[45] *Internationale Handelsgesellschaft mbh v Einhfuhr- und Vorratsstelle für Getreide und Futter-mittel*, C-11/70.
[46] *Hauer v Land Rheinland-Pfaltz*, C-44/79.
[47] *Foto-Frost v Hauptzollamt Lübeck-Ost*, C-314/85.
[48] The ECJ, however, is surreptitiously deciding about the compatibility of state acts with EU fundamental rights through the preliminary reference.

1.2.4 *EU law supremacy in light of state constitutionalism*

The arguments supporting the supremacy of EU law over state constitutions are not conclusive. They do not provide sufficient grounds to sustain the unlimited supremacy of EU law over state constitutions. First, recognizing a certain degree of autonomy to the EU legal order does not necessarily imply the supremacy of EU law over state constitutions. All would concur that the EU initially emerged from an agreement among states acting under international law and according to their respective constitutions. Hence, the EU legal order was not the outcome of 'higher lawmaking'. Even the so-called EU Constitution was still an international treaty. The unanimity of the states has always been required for ratifying and amending the Treaties; it still is. As a result, the EU is not auto-determined, but hetero-determined by the member states. Thus, the EU legal order cannot have 'original autonomy'. This kind of autonomy belongs to a 'legal order that is not derived from any other legal order. It is ultimately created by its own original constituent power.'[49] At the same time, even if a legal order derives from another, once created, it might be independent from the contents of the other, ie, 'derivative autonomy'. The Treaties might then derive their validity from the member states' consent acting according to their constitutions under international law; yet, the validity of secondary EU law might solely depend on the Treaties, as interpreted by the ECJ.[50] Even admitting this kind of derivative autonomy, however, the claim that EU Treaties are the sole source of validity of secondary EU law does not validate the conclusion that EU Treaties have supremacy over state constitutions when their respective applications overlap. In these overlapping areas, domestic courts face a conflict between two obligations: the obligation to apply constitutional rights (and give effect to their state constitutions) and the obligation to apply EU fundamental rights (and give effect to EU law). On the one hand, if domestic courts applied state constitutional rights and set aside state implementing acts under review, the efficacy of EU law in the territory might be endangered. On the other hand, if domestic courts applied EU fundamental rights when they have been interpreted by the ECJ in a less protective or different manner, the constitutional protection would no longer be effective. Thus, even if the derivative autonomy of EU law were admitted, this would not justify the supremacy of EU rights over constitutional rights in reviewing state

---

[49]   Schilling, *supra* n 1, at 389.

[50]   For the difference among original, derivative, and interpretive autonomy, see *id.* at 389–390.

legislation. State authorities cannot escape being subject to their respective state constitutions just because they act within the field of EU law.

In addition, the argument for the supremacy of EU law based upon consent, in its several forms, cannot be sustained. Admittedly, through the ratification of the Treaties, the states consented to the exercise of sovereign powers by supranational institutions. The states, however, did not consent to the supremacy of EU law over state constitutions, and they certainly did not consent to the subordination of the rights enshrined in these constitutions as a result of European integration. As Rasmussen put it, 'The absence of a Treaty-provision on supremacy strongly inspires one to believe that the negotiators could not agree on it.'[51] A clause of such importance would not just have been 'forgotten'. Neither did member states consent to the supremacy of EU law vis-à-vis state constitutions over time.[52] Although state courts later consented to the supremacy of EU law over ordinary state law, some have explicitly and recurrently opposed EU supremacy over state constitutions.[53] Furthermore, when state courts acquiesced to the supremacy of EU law, it was not on the basis of the autonomy of the EU legal order, but rather on the basis of the respective state constitutional provisions, with the corresponding limitations.[54] Along these lines, several constitutional courts affirmed their powers to check that constitutional rights were not impaired as a consequence of state participation in the EU, usually through the control of state measures enforcing or generally falling within the field of EU law. For example, the Spanish Constitutional Court admitted that it had no powers to review the validity of EU acts. This Court, however, confirmed its power to review state acts in light of constitutional fundamental rights, even if they fell within the field of EU law.[55] In *Solange II* (1986), the

---

[51] Hjalte Rasmussen, On Law and Policy in the European Court of Justice 392 (Martinus Nijhoff Publishers 1986).

[52] Schilling, *supra* n 1, at 396–398.

[53] See the national reports in Anne Marie Slaughter, Alec Stone Sweet & Joseph H. H. Weiler (eds.), The European Court and National Courts, Doctrine and Jurisprudence: Legal Change in its Social Context (Hart Publishing 2000).

[54] Another question would be why national courts accepted the supremacy of EU law over state law. Some have argued that state courts accepted supremacy in order to increase their own powers within the state (as they would acquire the power to review state legislation), or on the basis of diverse judicial interests in enhancing their independence, influence, and authority. See Karen Alter, Establishing the Supremacy of European Law. The Making of an International Rule of Law in Europe (Oxford University Press 2001).

[55] The Spanish Constitutional Court (STC 64/1991, 22 March 1991) held that transferring powers to supranational organizations did not imply that state authorities were no longer bound by the domestic legal order when acting according to obligations derived from their

German Federal Constitutional Court declared that it would not exercise its power of review as long as the ECJ 'ensures an effective protection of the basic rights against acts of the Communities, which basically corresponds to the protection of basic rights compelled by the [German] Basic Law'.[56] Hence, the German Constitutional Court conditioned the exercise of its review power, but without giving it up. In *Fragd* (1989), the Italian Constitutional Court even claimed that it would 'test the consistency of individual rules of Community law with the fundamental principles for the protection of human rights that are contained in the Italian constitution'.[57] Lastly, the proposed EU Constitution did not clearly establish the supremacy of EU law over 'state constitutions'. The wording of article I-6 did not explicitly declare such supremacy,[58] as did the US Constitution in 1787, for example. Article VI of the US Constitution explicitly established the supremacy of the federal constitution and federal law over both state constitutions and state law. Arguably, the reference to 'the law of member states' in article I-6 might be thought to include state constitutions. Nonetheless, since the supremacy of EU law over state constitutions has been the source of profound debate and state constitutional courts have not generally accepted it, the failure to address the status of state constitutions means the issue had not been resolved. It cannot be thought that the drafters 'forgot' to mention state constitutions.[59] Remarkably, the Lisbon Treaty has omitted

---

participation in those organizations. The Constitutional Court argued that, even in these cases, state public authorities were still subject to the Constitution and the rest of the Spanish legal order. See Diego J. Liñán Nogueras & Javier Roldán Barbero, *The Judicial Application of Community Law in Spain*, 30 COMMON MARKET LAW REVIEW 1135, 1142–1143 (1993).

[56] Kokott, *supra* n 6.

[57] Marta Cartabia, *The Italian Constitutional Court and the Relationship Between the Italian Legal System and the European Union*, in THE EUROPEAN COURT AND NATIONAL COURTS, DOCTRINE AND JURISPRUDENCE. LEGAL CHANGE IN ITS SOCIAL CONTEXT 133 (Anne-Marie Slaughter, Alec Stone Sweet & Joseph H. H. Weiler, eds. 1998).

[58] Article I-6 of the European Constitution: 'The Constitution and law adopted by the Union's Institutions in exercising competences conferred on it shall have primacy over the law of the Member States.'

[59] In this sense, Víctor Ferreres & Alejandro Saiz Arnaiz, *Realmente Hay que Reformar la Constitución Española para Adecuarla a la Cláusula de Primacía de la Constitución Europea?*, 645 ACTUALIDAD JURIDICA ARANZADI 1 (2004): 'The lack of an explicit reference to the national constitutions in article I-6 is not due to a simple "oversight". If there is no explicit reference, it is because the members of the convention did not dare to take this step, given the constitutional and political problems that this would bring about' [author's translation]. Also, Miguel Azpitarte Sánchez, *Las Relaciones entre el Derecho de la Unión y el Derecho del Estado a la Luz de la Constitución Europea*, 1 REVISTA ESPAÑOLA DE DERECHO CONSTITUCIONAL EUROPEO 75, 94–95 (2004), emphasized the difficulties within the drafting convention to include this provision.

any supremacy clause. In sum, the supremacy principle has been admitted in the relationship between EU law and state ordinary law, but it has not been definitely established in the relationship between EU law and state constitutional law.

Finally, the unlimited supremacy of EU law cannot be grounded in the interest in securing the uniformity and efficacy of EU law. The success of the integration process is undoubtedly an interest all member states share. In certain circumstances, however, reviewing state measures within the field of application of EU law under constitutional rights would not necessarily render EU law wholly ineffective, even if that review affected the uniform application of a specific EU measure. This is not to deny force to the argument based upon the need to guarantee the uniform application of EU law, but this argument is formulated in overly broad terms. The formula 'within the field of application of EU law' spans state acts directly implementing EU law as well as others remotely connected to the sphere of EU law. For instance, diverse interpretations regarding the admissibility of affirmative action measures on the basis of sex in the marketplace do not necessarily or significantly undermine the efficacy of EU law or lead to the 'destruction of the unity of the Common Market and the jeopardizing of the cohesion of the Community'. In this vein, in *Abrahamsson*,[60] the case concerning the Swedish affirmative action measure, the ECJ could have deferred the decision about the validity of such a measure to state courts without having to renounce the EU integration goals. Indeed, the imposition of supranational standards when there is disagreement among the states might mislead undermine the cohesion of the EU. Thus, recognizing a certain degree of diversity in the interpretation of rights does not necessarily challenge the efficacy of a particular regulation or endanger general integration goals. The impact upon the EU legal order will depend on the kind of state act under review.

To sum up, the quest for the ultimate source of validity to evaluate the supremacy claim will not provide a definitive answer to fundamental rights conflicts. Recognizing a measure of autonomy to the EU legal order does not imply unlimited supremacy of EU law over state constitutions. At the same time, such supremacy was neither consented to at the foundational moment nor accepted by state courts over time. The proposed EU Constitution would not have definitely established it.[61] Although the argument for

---

[60] *Katarina Abrahamsson and Leif Anderson v Elisabet Fogelqvist*, C-407/98.

[61] Even if supremacy were to be generally declared in a future constitutional document, this would not mean that EU rights should prevail in any case. For instance, in the US, the fact that

supremacy relying on the uniformity and efficacy of EU law has merit and needs to be addressed, it is not conclusive and does not support the whole-sale subordination of constitutional rights to EU law. Hence, the supremacy principle is not the most proper way to approach the conflict between fundamental rights norms in the EU.

2 Beyond hierarchy

Some scholars have formulated alternative proposals to address fundamental rights conflicts that do no rely on hierarchy as the structuring principle between national and supranational systems. Basically, these alternatives consist of (i) adopting a conflict rule according to which EU fundamental rights set a floor of protection or (ii) establishing a supra-adjudicative institution in charge of deciding what interpretation should prevail in case of conflict.

2.1 *EU fundamental rights as a floor of protection*

The interaction between overlapping catalogues of rights might be config-ured in a manner that establishes one of the catalogues setting a floor of protection. According to this rule, EU fundamental rights would constitute a floor of protection that member states must respect. At the same time, state courts would be free to enforce constitutional rights in case of conflict as long as constitutional rights provided a better level of protection than par-allel EU rights.

This solution is quite common concerning international treaties for the protection of human rights: human rights treaties set a floor of protec-tion that states must respect. In the case of diverging interpretations, state courts may follow the constitutional interpretation should it be more pro-tective than the international one. This model secures the best protection for individuals in all cases. This conflict rule is explicitly incorporated in the text of several human rights treaties. For instance, article 53 of the

the supremacy clause is expressly established in the Constitution does not mean that the federal interpretation of the Bill of Rights always trumps state interpretations of parallel state constitu-tional rights. State courts are free to interpret state constitutional rights in reviewing state acts, as long as the state level of protection does not fall below the federal standard established by the US Supreme Court.

European Convention on Human Rights (ECHR) declares the following: 'Nothing in this Convention shall be construed as limiting or derogating from any of the human rights and fundamental freedoms which may be ensured under the laws of any High Contracting Party or under any other agreement to which it is a party.' Similar provisions are found in article 5(2) of the International Covenant on Economic, Social and Cultural Rights; article 5(2) of the International Covenant on Civil and Political Rights; article 42 of the Convention for the Rights of the Child; and article 23 of the Convention for the Elimination of All Forms of Discrimination against Women.

Even in a federal state like the US, in which the supremacy of the federal constitution and federal law over state constitutions is explicitly articulated in the Constitution, federal rights are regarded as setting a floor of protection. State courts may surpass this floor when interpreting the rights enshrined in the state constitutions.[62] Thus, when reviewing state laws, state courts are free to interpret state constitutional rights, as long as they do not fall below the federal constitutional floor of protection. It should be remarked that, originally, the US federal Bill of Rights was not binding upon the states. Federal rights were only binding upon federal authorities, and state rights were only binding upon state authorities.[63] Thus, the supremacy clause did not speak to the conflicts between federal and state constitutional rights because there was no overlap in their scope of application. After the Civil War and the enactment of the Fourteenth Amendment, federal rights were progressively incorporated against the states by the Supreme Court.[64] In the words of Justice Brennan, the incorporation 'transformed the basic structure of constitutional safeguards for individual political and civil liberties in the nation and profoundly altered the character

---

[62] William J. Brennan, Jr., *The Bill of Rights and the States: The Revival of State Constitutions as Guardians of Individual Rights*, 61 NEW YORK UNIVERSITY LAW REVIEW 536 (1986); William J. Brennan, Jr., *State Constitutions and the Protection of Individual Rights*, 90 HARVARD LAW REVIEW 489 (1977).

[63] *Barron v Mayor and City of Baltimore* 32 US 243 (1833): '[The question] is of great importance, but not of much difficulty. The constitution was ordained and established by the people of the United States for themselves, for their own government, and not for the government of the individual states.... [The amendments] are limitations of power, granted in the instrument itself, not of distinct governments, framed by different persons and for different purposes. [If] these propositions be correct, the Fifth Amendment must be understood as restraining the power of the general government, not as applicable to the [states]. These amendments contain no expression indicating an intention to apply them to the state governments. This Court cannot apply them.'

[64] See AKHIL R. AMAR, THE BILL OF RIGHTS (Yale University Press 1998).

of our federalism'.[65] State courts were then confronted with the dilemma of applying state constitutional rights or the federal ones when reviewing state measures. What standard of protection should be enforced when the respective interpretations differ? An absolute interpretation of the supremacy clause would answer that federal constitutional rights should always prevail. Following Justice Brennan, however, it is admitted that should the state interpretation be more protective, state courts would be free to enforce state constitutional rights.[66] Therefore, diversity is possible over and above the federal floor of protection.[67] Supremacy means that federal constitutional rights cannot be violated, rather than federal constitutional rights must be applied, no matter what.

One might think that article 53 of the European Charter of Fundamental Rights should be interpreted as incorporating this conflict rule. This article reads as follows: 'Nothing in this Charter shall be interpreted as restricting or adversely affecting human rights and fundamental freedoms as recognized, in their respective fields of application ... by the Member States' constitutions.' If it were interpreted that the Charter sets a floor of protection, above which state courts would be free to enforce their respective constitutional rights, the Charter would not restrict or adversely affect constitutional rights. This interpretation is based upon the analogous relationship of this provision to the clauses codified in international treaties for the protection of human rights, such as the ones mentioned above.[68]

2.2 The inadequacy of the floor of protection rule in the EU

Given the particular dynamics of the EU supranational order, adopting this conflict rule without further restrictions might generate tensions and threaten to undermine the uniformity and efficacy of EU law.[69] It should be

---

[65] Brennan, *The Bill of Rights and the States, supra* n 62, at 543.

[66] Also, following Brennan's lead, among others, Stewart G. Pollock, *State Constitutions as Separate Sources of Fundamental Rights*, 35 RUTGERS LAW REVIEW 707, 709 (1983): 'A state may add to those rights [federal Bill of Rights], but may not substract from them. That is, the Bill of Rights in the United States Constitution establishes a floor for basic human liberty'; Hans E. Linde, *E Pluribus. Constitutional Theory and State Courts*, 18 GEORGIA LAW REVIEW 165, 179 (1984).

[67] Brennan, *The Bill of Rights and the States, supra* n 62, at 549–550.

[68] Ricardo Alonso García, *The General Provisions of the Charter of Fundamental Rights of the European Union*, 8 EUROPEAN LAW JOURNAL 492, 507–508 (2002).

[69] Rejecting the interpretation of article 53 as a minimum floor of protection or in any way limiting the supremacy of EU law, see Jonas Bering Liisberg, *Does the EU Charter of Fundamental Rights Threaten the Supremacy of Community Law? Article 53 of the Charter: A Fountain of*

pointed out that in the EU legal order the enforcement of EU law within the states is left, to a great extent, to state authorities. Therefore, if state courts were absolutely free under a more protective constitutional standard to review and set aside state acts implementing EU law, the uniformity and efficacy of EU law within the territory of each member state might be undermined. For example, if state courts simply set aside state legislation implementing the framework decision regulating the European Arrest Warrant to ensure constitutional rights protection, the efficacy of that EU framework decision could be jeopardized. As argued before, even though the efficacy argument does not justify the absolute supremacy of EU law, it needs to be addressed.

The same problem does not arise either in the US or within the framework of international treaties due to the different institutional structures of these three types of political organizations. In the US, the federal government generally enforces federal law and the states enforce state law. Moreover, according to the 'anticommandeering principle', the federal government cannot require state legislative or executive branches to enforce federal law.[70] Consequently, if state laws are reviewed and set aside under a more protective interpretation of state constitutional rights, the uniform application of federal law is not necessarily impaired. On the other hand, within the framework of international human treaties, state courts' review of state measures, eventually striking them down under more protective state constitutional rights, does not impair the efficacy of those treaties because the international floor of protection is secured. The purpose of human rights treaties is to guarantee respect for a minimum level of human rights protection by national authorities, rather than ensuring the success of a system of supranational regulation.

On the whole, according to this conflict rule, state courts would be free to make a more protective constitutional right prevail over a parallel EU right in reviewing state acts within EU law's field of application, irrespective of the consequences for the efficacy of EU law. Understood in this way, this conflict rule would be self-defeating, since it would not account for the

---

Law or Just an Inkblot?, Jean Monnet Working Paper 4/01; Francisco Rubio Llorente, *Mostrar los Derechos sin Destruir la Unión (Consideraciones sobre la Carta de Derechos Fundamentales de la Unión Europea)*, 64 REVISTA ESPAÑOLA DE DERECHO CONSTITUCIONAL 13, 43–44 (2002).

[70] In contrast, as Ernest A. Young, *Protecting Member State Autonomy in the European Union: Some Cautionary Tales from American Federalism*, 77 NEW YORK UNIVERSITY LAW REVIEW 1612, 1705–1709 (2002), put it, the system in the EU might be regarded as one of 'exclusive commandeering'.

interest in the uniform application and efficacy of EU law.[71] This is not to say, however, that a uniform interpretation of EU rights must be imposed on the states no matter what. Accommodating a degree of diversity in the interpretation of rights does not always significantly undermine the efficacy of EU law, let alone the success of the entire integration project. Thus, the questions to be answered are how, and by whom, diversity should be accommodated. This is different from maintaining that state courts are free to make a more protective standard prevail in any case. Additionally, a further difficulty in applying the floor of protection rule would be that often, and particularly when there are several rights in conflict, it is difficult to determine which legal system provides better protection. Some scholars conclude that article 53 of the EU Charter is just an empty clause.[72] It was politically useful to calm the anxieties of some member states and to reassure them that the potential enactment of the Charter would not undermine constitutional protection.[73] Chapter 6 will offer an alternative interpretation that accounts for judicial deference to domestic courts in specific circumstances.

2.3 *A supra-adjudicative institution for conflict resolution*

Within state borders, disagreements about the meaning of rights tend to be resolved by setting up a judicial authority with the last word. In Europe, the competing legal orders, those of the states and the EU, have their own courts with ultimate authority to interpret their respective rights norms. Among the authors who reject a hierarchical model to regulate the interaction between the EU and national legal orders, there are some who propose the establishment of a supra-adjudicative institution for the resolution of conflicts. Neil MacCormick is one of the leading scholars advancing a pluralistic approach to the interaction between legal systems in the EU. Constitutional pluralism is defined as a situation in which there is a plurality of institutional normative orders, each with a functioning constitution, which are not hierarchically ordered. They mutually recognize each other's validity, but with different grounds for that recognition.[74] MacCormick supports a

[71] Rubio Llorente, *supra* n 69, at 44.
[72] Liisberg, *supra* n 70; Rubio Llorente, *supra* n 69.
[73] Liisberg, *supra* n 70, regarding article 53: 'It is a politically useful inkblot meant to serve as an assurance to Member States, and eventually the electorate, that the Charter does not replace national constitutions and that it does not, by itself, threaten other, better or different, human rights.'
[74] MacCormick, *supra* n 10, at 102–104, 118: 'The legal systems of member states and their common legal system of EC law are distinct but interacting systems of law, and hierarchical

model of 'pluralism under international law'.[75] This model conceives the EU and the member states as self-referential legal systems, not constitutionally dependent on each other, whose non-hierarchical, interactive relationship is nonetheless subject to norms of international law.[76] Therefore, when conflicts cannot be avoided, international arbitration or adjudication would be an open avenue to find a solution.[77]

MacCormick did not fully develop this international law avenue for the resolution of conflicts, but building upon his insights on legal pluralism and institutional theory, Christoph Schmid further elaborated this proposal.[78] Schmid also opposes a hierarchical relationship between legal orders, and argues that public international law is applicable to EU constitutional conflicts, compelling the establishment of a conciliation body above the ECJ and domestic courts.[79] His argument runs as follows: principles of public international law should be applied to fill the gap in the Treaties as to the resolution of constitutional conflicts. In particular, he regards the 'theory of relevance' (codified in article 46 of the Vienna Convention on the Law of the Treaties) as customary law. According to the theory of relevance, manifest violations of essential internal law regarding the powers to conclude treaties entitle the state to a neutral conciliation procedure. Schmid interprets the reference to 'essential internal law regarding the powers to conclude treaties' as to embrace 'all domestic provisions limiting the powers of state organs to conclude treaties, including in particular substantive constitutional provisions like fundamental rights'.[80] Therefore, a breach of essential internal law, particularly constitutional law, as a consequence of the ratification of the EU

---

relationships of validity within criteria of validity proper to distinct systems do not add up to any sort of all-purpose superiority of one system over another.'

[75] *Id.* at 117–121.

[76] *Id.* at 118: 'The obligations of international law set conditions upon the validity of state and of Community constitutions and interpretations thereof, and hence impose a framework on the interactive but not hierarchical relations between systems.'

[77] *Id.* at 121.

[78] Christoph U. Schmid, *From Pont d'Avignon to Ponte Vecchio. The Resolution of Constitutional Conflicts Between the European Union and the Member States through Principles of Public International Law*, European University Institute Working Paper No. 98/7 (1998).

[79] *Id.* at 31: 'Even without any action by the European legislator, such a conciliation procedure is already obligatory under standing law: Public International Law, whose significance for EC law is sometimes underestimated, contains principles on the relevance of violations of internal law by an international treaty and on an obligatory conciliation mechanism which may be resorted to for the sake of conflict resolution.'

[80] Christoph U. Schmid, *All Bark and No Bite: Notes on the Federal Constitutional Court's 'Banana Decision'*, 7 EUROPEAN LAW JOURNAL 95, 111 (2001).

Treaties or the enactment of EU secondary law, would entitle member states to a neutral conciliation procedure. Public international law commands a conciliation solution, but it does not indicate the form, procedure, or composition of the conciliation body. According to Schmid, given the special nature of the EU, the conciliation body should be, out of necessity, different from a conciliation commission in international law. 'An organ deciding as the ultimate umpire over the recognition of a national constitutional standard in human rights...must be democratically legitimated.'[81] He argued that this body should be set up preferably by Treaty amendment; its members should be judges from the constitutional or highest state courts and from the ECJ; and its decisions should be generally binding.[82]

Without relying on international law, Joseph H. H. Weiler proposed the creation of a Constitutional Council, modelled after the French one, to resolve the conflicts about competences (*Kompetenz-Kompetenz*). This Council would be composed of judges from the state constitutional courts and the ECJ. It would review EU legislation only *ex ante*, before coming into force, to check whether EU institutions had exceeded the powers conferred upon them by the Treaties.[83] According to this proposal, the Constitutional Council would have jurisdiction only over conflicts regarding competences, but one might consider the possibility to extend its jurisdiction to the resolution of fundamental rights conflicts.

2.4 *Further complicating the EU judicial architecture*

The establishment of a third neutral body as the ultimate umpire is not the most satisfactory solution for the resolution of fundamental rights conflicts in the EU. First, for reasons of institutional economy, it would be advisable to seek a solution within the existing institutional framework. Adding a third body to the EU judicial architecture would be procedurally complex, and it would lengthen procedures that are already taking too long. Secondly, according to the proposals examined, this adjudicative or conciliatory body would have the capacity to issue binding decisions. However, it is not clear why, from the national perspective, a decision by an international body would be more authoritative than a decision taken by the ECJ when constitutional rights are at stake. It is also not clear what sources would guide its activity in deciding which interpretation should

---

[81] Schmid, *supra* n 78, at 46.   [82] *Id*. at 47.
[83] Weiler, *supra* n 25, at 322–323, 353–354; Joseph H. H. Weiler, *The European Union Belongs to its Citizens: Three Immodest Proposals*, 33 EUROPEAN LAW REVIEW 150, 155–156 (1997).

prevail. The legitimacy problem concerning the authority of the ECJ to impose a particular interpretation upon the states would be transferred to this adjudicative institution. To ground its legitimacy, Schmid proposed that the members of this body should be judges from the highest or constitutional courts of the member states and the ECJ. Should this be the key to the legitimacy problem, instead of creating a third institution, it would be easier to modify the composition of the ECJ. With regard to the extension of Weiler's Constitutional Council to the resolution of constitutional rights conflicts, it is contended that *ex ante* review is not adequate to secure compliance with fundamental rights. Often, a violation is difficult to detect until a legislative act has been applied to concrete cases. In any event, this institutional solution would not address the dilemma that national courts face in reviewing state acts within the field of application of EU law.

Finally, given the special nature of the relationship between the EU and its member states, using international law to regulate their interaction does not seem to be effective. The EU Treaties were created under international law, and international law might have some subsidiary application to certain issues. Regarding fundamental rights conflicts, however, international law does not get us very far. According to MacCormick, not only does international law indicate an institutional solution, but it also has interpretive consequences. EU and state legal systems in the interpretation of their respective constitutional norms 'ought both to have regard to the international obligations which still subsist.... Such an approach would help to diminish the risk of normative collisions.'[84] This author does not add much about what these obligations entail or how they would help to avoid or solve constitutional conflicts. At a very general level, he refers to the normative significance of *pacta sunt servanda*, which means that the parties must comply with their agreements. But this is precisely the point under discussion: from the national perspective, the agreement to give effectiveness to EU law, derived from the Treaties' ratification, did not entail compromising constitutional rights. Additionally, there is no need for recourse to international law to assert these mutual obligations. They already exist under the EU Treaties. On the one hand, article 10 EC Treaty establishes the obligation to comply and give effectiveness to EU law: 'Member States shall take all the appropriate measures, whether general or particular, to ensure fulfilment of the obligations arising out of this Treaty or resulting from action taken by the institutions of the Community. They shall facilitate the achievement of

---

[84] MacCormick, *supra* n 10, at 121.

the Community's tasks.' On the other hand, the EU has the obligation to exercise its powers 'under the conditions and for the purposes provided for' in the Treaties (article 5 EU Treaty) and 'respect the national identities of its Member States' (article 6.3 EU Treaty). Therefore, international law does not add much to the mutual obligations already existing under the Treaties. Hence, it is difficult to see how international law would contribute substantively to resolve the constitutional conflicts under analysis.

To conclude, setting up a third adjudicative body is not the most advisable solution to fundamental rights conflicts in the EU. Without denying some applicability to international law, it cannot impose the obligation of creating a conciliation body, and it does not seem to offer any interpretive guidance either. Some might think that, instead of creating yet another international adjudicative institution, the European Court of Human Rights (ECtHR) could resolve these conflicts once the EU joined the European Convention. Notwithstanding the benefits emerging from regulating the interaction between the ECJ and the ECtHR, the accession of the EU to the European Convention would not necessarily address the potential conflicts between EU and state legal systems. As argued in the previous chapter, this accession would extend the jurisdiction of the ECtHR over EU legislation. Hence, the ECtHR would have the power to hold the EU liable for violating Convention rights. The Convention, however, only establishes a floor of protection, whereas EU fundamental rights not only claim to be a floor but also a ceiling. Even if EU authorities respected the Convention, and EU fundamental rights were not interpreted below this floor, the potential conflicts between EU and constitutional rights would not necessarily disappear because the member states might still grant a higher level of protection.

3 Constitutional pluralism in the European Union

Although discourses based upon supremacy, either national or supranational, are common in the judicial and political arena, hierarchical models are not responsive to the European reality. Neither do they offer the best framework for structuring interaction between the EU and state systems in the fundamental rights sphere. The traditional notion of a supreme and comprehensive constitution governing over a sovereign nation-state does not fairly account for the transformations that member states have undergone as a consequence of the integration process. At the same time, an ultimate sovereign authority has not been reconstructed at the supranational level. As MacCormick put it, 'The Community is a non-sovereign polity... comprising no-longer-fully-sovereign states, and the relationships of the various parts will depend in the long run on a still-to-be-elaborated principle of subsidiarity, rather than on a zero-sum game of competition for sovereignty.'[85] Thus, the EU unprecedented political structure—neither a state itself, premised upon a vibrant *demos*, nor a mere constellation of sovereign nation-states—does not fit the traditional, conceptual framework for the organization of public power.

One could possibly acknowledge the descriptive claim about the transformations stemming from EU integration and at the same time struggle for either the return of the nation-state or the reconstitution of an ultimate sovereign authority at the supranational level. The difficulties inherent in articulating a clear-cut alternative to the modern nation-state might lead many to try explaining and reconstructing this new reality through the lenses of statist categories of sovereignty. Nonetheless, a constitutional pluralist framework—understood as a community constituted by partly separate but interdependent legal orders, whose foundational norms are not hierarchically ordered—not only provides a better account of the new reality but should be normatively embraced as well. Along these lines, Neil Walker holds that the normative claim for pluralism 'acknowledges the account given by explanatory pluralism and welcomes its implications, contending that the only acceptable ethic of political responsibility for the new Europe is one that is premised upon mutual recognition and respect between national and supranational authorities'.[86]

Hence, constitutional pluralism should be welcomed as valuable and not regarded as a temporary stage in the integration process that needs to be overcome. A constitutional pluralist framework offers the possibility to overcome the dangers of exacerbated national sovereignty through a mutual system of checks and balances between national and supranational orders within an overarching community. The emergence of the modern sovereign

---

[85] MacCormick, *supra* n 10, at 95.

[86] Neil Walker, *The Idea of Constitutional Pluralism*, 65 The Modern Law Review 317, 337 (2002). Nico Krisch, *The Open Architecture of Human Rights Law*, 71, The Modern Law Review 183, 215–216 (2008) also favours pluralism and indicates: 'By leaving questions of fundamental norms and ultimate authority undecided, pluralism migh give postnational law the flexibility it needs in order to deal with principled contestation—contestation might be easier to circumnavigate than in a constitutional order built on the ideal that these questions are settled in one way or another.'

state predated constitutionalism. After the liberal revolutions at the end of the eighteenth century, constitutionalism provided a theory upon which to establish the limits of state power. Basically, public power would be limited by fragmenting it among different institutions checking each other and by protecting individual rights against encroachment by state action. Also, according to the republican strand of constitutionalism, the ultimate source of legitimacy of public authority would be located in the 'people'. Modern constitutionalism, however, did not explicitly address the limitation of state power in its relationship to other nation-states. Even more, as has been claimed, 'A regime of nation-states was a regime at war or anticipating the possibility of war.'[87] The limitation of state power regarding other states and peoples was the main task of international law. Nonetheless, international law, time and again, has proven not to be so successful in constraining state violence against 'others'. The goal of the European integration project was to limit the potential excesses of sovereign (even constitutional) nation-states through the creation of a broader supranational community.[88] This supranational entity would not be a state itself, resting on a single nation.[89] It would be composed of states that had partly given up their sovereignty. Thus, the power of the state would be fragmented, and state functions allocated at the supranational level. The project of integration would bring about transformations not only for the states in their interaction with the supranational order but also for the member states in their interaction among each other. Consistent with this, one finds at the core of the EU the principles of free movement of people, goods, services, and capital across national territories. Free movement is buttressed by a bedrock principle: no discrimination on the basis of nationality is tolerated.[90] Hence, member states are compelled to treat 'others' as they treat their own citizens. Consequently, state borders and the monolithic concept of the nation tend to blur. In sum, constitutional pluralism should be welcomed as an opportunity to establish mutual

[87] Paul Kahn, *The Question of Sovereignty*, 40 STANFORD JOURNAL OF INTERNATIONAL LAW 259, 264 (2004).
[88] Weiler, *supra* n 25, at 341: 'A central plank of the project of European integration may be seen, then, as an attempt to control the excesses of the modern nation-state in Europe, especially, but not only, its propensity to violent conflict and the inability of the international system to constrain that propensity. The European Community was to be an antidote to the negative features of the state and statal intercourse.'
[89] *Id.* at 341: 'It would be more than ironic if a polity set up as a means to counter the excesses of statism ended up coming round full circle and transforming itself in a (super) state.'
[90] *Id.* at 342–343.

checks and balances between the national and supranational spheres.[91] The supranational order might serve a corrective role for the excesses of state constitutionalism. In turn, state constitutionalism might counteract the concentration of power at the supranational level. In short, 'constitutional pluralism' might be an important mechanism for the limitation of public power in the context of a supranational community.

In this work, the notion of constitutional pluralism is meant to indicate the absence of a hierarchy between the foundational-constitutional documents of the interacting national and supranational legal orders. Although a constitutional pluralist framework might look too precarious to be sustainable, the national and the supranational are so closely intertwined that the interdependence of goals and functions[92] will secure the continuity of this community. For example, the EU Treaties rely on the states for the composition of EU institutions.[93] Moreover, in many instances, authorities from both legal systems share functions in the same policy areas. As indicated, sovereign powers of the state have been transferred to the EU legal order. As such, instability might come precisely from insisting in imposing an ultimate supreme authority. Indeed, Nico Krisch has argued that in the context of European human rights law the pluralist structure has contributed to the stability of the regime: 'by leaving issues of principle open, the pluralist structure has limited the antagonism between the different institutions involved and has helped them move to a stage where they could mutually benefit from a cooperative relationship'.[94] Admittedly, within this pluralist framework there is a potential for conflict as a consequence of the overlap between national and supranational norms protecting rights. Therefore, any conceptual model of interaction should determine how to manage these conflicts, while securing enough stability to prevent the system from collapsing.

---

[91] Miguel Poiares Maduro, *Las Formas del Poder Constitucional de la Unión Europea*, 119 REVISTA DE ESTUDIOS POLÍTICOS 11, 36–37 (2003), argued that the lack of an ultimate authority in the EU might be linked to values of constitutionalism consisting of the limitation of power and mutual checks and balances.

[92] For this interdependence, as revealed in the text of the Treaties, see Wouters, *supra* n 38, at 28–36.

[93] For instance the Council shall consist of 'a representative of each Member State at ministerial level, authorized to commit the government of that Member State' (article 203 EC Treaty); member states propose the members of the Commission (article 214 EC Treaty); the justices that compose the ECJ are also proposed by the member states' governments (article 223 EC Treaty).

[94] Krisch, *supra* n 86, at 214–215.

4

The Tension between Uniformity and Diversity

Although hierarchical models provide straightforward solutions, they are not the best framework to address the challenges posed by potential rights' conflicts in the process of European integration. A pluralist framework for the European Union (EU) acknowledges the claims of authority coming from different sites and aims at co-ordinating them in a coherent manner. It is important to avoid forced homogenization and excessive fragmentation since both might endanger stability of the entire system. Writing for the US, Robert M. Cover and Alexander Aleinikoff remarked that, under both, the 'hierarchical imposition of federally determined values' or 'a model of fragmentation justifying value choices by the states... one system has exclusive or preeminent voice as to the value to be chosen or imposed. Such political model suffers from the lawyer's disease of sovereignty'.[1] The main purpose will be to examine the tensions between the normative ideals of supranational uniformity and national diversity regarding the European Court of Justice's (ECJ) adjudicative function in interpreting fundamental rights. The ECJ, given its position at the top of the overall system composed of the EU and the state legal orders, is destined to play a prominent role in managing fundamental rights conflicts. In shaping a normative model for ECJ adjudication, one must answer the following question: should rights be interpreted uniformly or should a certain degree of diversity be accommodated?

The tension between uniformity and diversity is endemic to any divided-power system.[2] In a broad sense, the interaction between legal

---

[1] Robert M. Cover & T. Alexander Aleinikoff, *Dialectical Federalism: Habeas Corpus and the Court*, 86 THE YALE LAW JOURNAL 1035, 1047–1048 (1977).

[2] Eric Stein, *Uniformity and Diversity in a Divided-Power System: The United States' Experience*, 61 WASHINGTON LAW REVIEW 1081 (1986).

systems in the EU can be understood through the lense of federalism. The EU is not a federal *state*, and the failed EU Constitution would not have created one. Nevertheless, one can regard the relationship between the national and supranational systems under a *federal* perspective, as a community in which public power is allocated among different levels of governance. In this sense, Daniel Elazar pointed out that the federal principle should not be confused with its manifestation in the federal state.[3] As Pierre Pescatore put it,

The methods of federalism are not only a means of organizing states. Federalism is a political and legal philosophy which adapts itself to all political contexts on both the municipal and the international level, wherever and whenever two basic prerequisites are fulfilled: the search for unity, combined with genuine respect for the autonomy and the legitimate interests of the participant entities.[4]

The model of rights protection in federal compounds is always debated, as the US experience demonstrates. The US literature converging on federalism and rights might provide valuable insights for this inquiry.[5] The core of the chapter will be devoted to discussing the arguments underpinning national diversity and supranational uniformity. In many cases, the arguments for state diversity do not go beyond state sovereignty, which is no longer adequate given the EU political structure. At the same time, the virtues of supranational uniformity tend to be assumed without questioning the reasons underpinning this claim. Reaching to the conclusion, it will be claimed that the ECJ should not impose uniformity for its own sake. Although there are good reasons to argue for uniform fundamental rights, the creation of a supranational community to establish a form of collective action regarding certain subject matters does not in and of itself justify

[3] Daniel J. Elazar, *Options Problems and Possibilities in Light of the Current Situation*, in SELF RULE-SHARED RULE 3–4 (Daniel J. Elazar ed. 1979).

[4] Pierre Pescatore, *Preface*, in COURTS AND FREE MARKETS ix–x (Terrance Sandalow & Eric Stein eds. 1982). In the EU context, as Kalypso Nicolaidis & Robert Howse, *Introduction: The Federal Vision, Levels of Governance and Legitimacy*, in THE FEDERAL VISION 1, 5–6 (Kalypso Nicolaidis & Robert Howse eds. 2003), noted: the '"new Europe" has already begun the experiment of emancipating the federal idea from statist categories of sovereignty and constitutional supremacy'.

[5] ELLIS KATZ & G. ALAN TARR (eds.), FEDERALISM AND RIGHTS ix (Rowman & Littlefield Publishers 1984), began their introduction to this volume with the following question: 'Does federalism promote or undermine rights?'; Stein, *supra* n 2, at 1081: 'The concern for diversity has remained a part of the public discourse in America even though the forces of the industrial, post-industrial, and "post-material" revolution have worked mightily against diversity and for uniformity and a uniform rule.'

homogenizing fundamental rights. The values underlying state autonomy require that certain degree of diversity be accommodated and justify a measure of deference to state courts.

1 Federalism and rights

The model of rights protection in the forms of government with a politically decentralized structure tends to be contested. This is especially true in the EU, given the elusive character of this supranational form of government. In pluralist/federal compounds, the model of rights protection is inextricably linked to structural elements. As a consequence of this structural dimension of rights' catalogues, several institutional questions need to be addressed: are the constituent states bound by the federal/supranational rights? How are the powers to regulate and enforce fundamental rights to be allocated between the states and the central government? How are interpretive conflicts between levels of governance to be resolved? Indeed, the so-called 'horizontal provisions' included in the EU Charter of fundamental rights are aimed at answering them.[6] Underlying all these questions there is an under-theorized theme regarding the normative ideal about how to strike the balance between state diversity and supranational uniformity. These same questions have been faced in the US throughout the process of building the federation. At present, the incorporation of the federal Bill of Rights vis-à-vis the states is generally accepted, but this was a highly debated issue for a long time.[7] Empowering the federal Congress to enforce the Bill of Rights against the states, under section 5 of the Fourteenth Amendment, still gives rise to controversy.[8] Moreover, scholars have shown increasing interest in state constitutionalism and the diverging interpretations of parallel federal

---

[6] See Title VII: 'General Provisions Governing the Interpretation and Application of the Charter', particularly articles 51, 52, and 53.

[7] See AKHIL R. AMAR, THE BILL OF RIGHTS 137–294 (Yale University Press 1998); R.C. CORTNER, THE SUPREME COURT AND THE SECOND BILL OF RIGHTS. THE FOURTEENTH AMENDMENT AND THE NATIONALIZATION OF CIVIL LIBERTIES (University of Wisconsin Press 1981); Arthur E. Wilmarth, Jr., *The Original Purpose of the Bill of Rights: James Madison and the Founders' Search for a Workable Balance between Federal and State Power*, 26 AMERICAN CRIMINAL LAW REVIEW 1261 (1989).

[8] *Katzenbach v Morgan* 384 US 641 (1966), *City of Boerne v Flores* 521 US 507 (1997), *United States v Morrison* 529 US 598 (2000). Michael W. McConnell, *Institutions and Interpretations: A Critique of City of Boerne v Flores*, 111 HARVARD LAW REVIEW 153 (1997); Evan H. Caminker, *'Appropriate' Means-Ends Constraints on Section 5 Powers*, 53 STANFORD LAW REVIEW 1127 (2001).

and state rights.[9] Over time, the structural dimension of the Bill of Rights has brought about considerable case law and a vast literature converging on the topic of federalism and rights. Thus, US federalism may well provide illuminating insights for EU dilemmas. It is not, however, suggested that the EU model should necessarily reproduce US answers. The historical and political circumstances greatly differ. Yet, from a conceptual standpoint, the questions that the EU faces are very similar to those that emerged in America.

The arguments for states' rights (or federalism) formulated in the US might be particularly suited to the EU.[10] The main proponent of states' rights in the domain of constitutional interpretation, above the federal floor of protection, has been Justice William J. Brennan,[11] whose lead has been followed by other judges and scholars.[12] The Supreme Court in *Gregory v Ashcroft* summarized the arguments for states' rights as follows:[13]

This federalist structure of joint sovereigns preserves to the people numerous advantages. It assures a decentralized government that will be more sensitive to the diverse needs of a heterogeneous society; it increases opportunity for citizen involvement in democratic processes; it allows for more innovation and experimentation in government; and it makes government more responsive by putting the

[9] Among others, Akhil R. Amar, *Of Sovereignty and Federalism*, 96 YALE LAW JOURNAL 1425 (1987); Akhil R. Amar, *Foreword: Lord Camden Meets Federalism—Using State Constitutions to Counter Federal Abuses*, 27 RUTGERS LAW JOURNAL 845 (1996); William J. Brennan, Jr. *The Bill of Rights and the States: The Revival of Sate Constitutions as Guardians of Individual Rights*, 61 NEW YORK UNIVERSITY LAW REVIEW 536 (1986); Lawrence Friedman, *The Constitutional Value of Dialogue and the New Judicial Federalism*, 28 HASTINGS CONSTITUTIONAL LAW QUARTERLY 93 (2000); Paul W. Kahn, *Interpretation and Authority in State Constitutionalism*, 106 HARVARD LAW REVIEW 1147 (1993).

[10] It should be kept in mind that, in the current US debate, to favour 'federalism' means to support states' rights or state autonomy, whereas, in the EU debate, 'federalism' refers to the empowerment of central authorities. To avoid confusions, the arguments for federalism in the US will be referred to as arguments for states' rights or state autonomy, meaning to favour a measure of state diversity as opposed to complete centralization.

[11] Brennan, *supra* n 9; William J. Brennan, Jr., *State Constitutions and the Protection of Individual Rights*, 90 HARVARD LAW REVIEW 489 (1977).

[12] Among others, Stewart G. Pollock, *State Constitutions as Separate Sources of Fundamental Rights*, 35 RUTGERS LAW REVIEW 707, 709 (1983); Hans E. Linde, *E Pluribus. Constitutional Theory and State Courts*, 18 GEORGIA LAW REVIEW 165, 179 (1984); Donald E. Wilkes Jr., *First Things Last: Amendomania and State Bills of Rights*, 54 MISSISSIPPI LAW JOURNAL 223 (1984); Robert F. Williams, *In the Supreme Court's Shadow: Legitimacy of State Rejection of Supreme Court Reasoning and Result*, 35 SUPREME COURT LAW REVIEW 353 (1984); Friedman, *supra* n 9, advocates the possibility of a state independent interpretation of state constitutional provisions protecting individual rights and liberties.

[13] *Gregory v Ashcroft* 501 US 452 (1991).

States in competition for a mobile citizenry....Perhaps the principal benefit of the federalist system is a check on abuses of government power....Just as the separation and independence of the coordinate Branches of the Federal Government serves to prevent the accumulation of excessive power in any one Branch, a healthy balance of power between the States and the Federal Government will reduce the risk of tyranny and abuse from either front....'If their rights are invaded by either, they can make use of the other as the instrument of redress.' The Federalist No. 28, pp. 180–181 (C. Rossiter ed. 1961).

Without entering fully into the American debate, the benefits of states' rights in the US are actually quite controversial. Indeed, the arguments underpinning state autonomy in the US do not seem to be as compelling as they may be in the EU. The political structure of the EU—not a state itself, while embracing a plurality of constitutional democracies—reinforces the arguments for state autonomy, given the lower degree of integration and homogeneity among EU member states. Also, in the US, the particular history of racial discrimination sheds a dark light over arguments for states' rights.[14]

Regardless of the contested nature of the federation at its foundational moment and until the Civil War, it is undisputed today that the US is a federal state legitimated by the will of 'We the People'. Several scholars emphasize the impact of the Reconstruction amendments upon the US federal structure and the system of rights protection. To be precise, Reconstruction sought to empower the central government against the states for the protection of civil rights. Consequently, several American authors strongly oppose state diversity in rights interpretation. For example, Michael W. McConnell holds that uniformity of rights protection is required by the Fourteenth Amendment.[15] Others emphasize that

---

[14] Ernest A. Young, *Protecting Member State Autonomy in the European Union: Some Cautionary Tales from American Federalism*, 77 NEW YORK UNIVERSITY LAW REVIEW 1612, 1731 (2002): 'Our debates are a prisoner of our history; the categories tend to be frozen in terms defined by Reconstruction, the New Deal, and the civil rights struggles of the 1960s....It is hard, for example, to make an argument for "states' rights" without being accused of harboring racist sympathies.'

[15] McConnell, *supra* n 8, at 193–194 (1997): 'By its very text, however, the Fourteenth Amendment rejects the idea that the rights of citizens should vary from state to state and group to group. Prior to the adoption of the Fourteenth Amendment, the source and protection of the basic rights of citizens was grounded in state law....As antebellum history had shown, the states were unreliable guardians of the rights of the people....The Fourteenth Amendment enshrined fundamental rights (including those listed in the Bill of Rights) in the federal Constitution as "privileges or immunities of citizens of the United States" and empowered Congress to enforce those

there are no normative reasons supporting states' rights since the states are not distinct sovereigns any more[16] and a relevant degree of homogeneity has been reached.[17] Edward L. Rubin and Malcolm Feeley argue that the states only serve a function of administrative decentralization since they are not heterogeneous political communities with particular identities.[18]

In addition, the states' rights discourse in the US is seen under the light of the particular US history linked to slavery and segregation. It has been stated that 'federalism has an image problem'.[19] In this sense, Jean Yarbrough explains how the problem of racism and securing rights for blacks has operated to undermine states' rights in the present time.[20] When the Reconstruction amendments were enacted, there was great distrust concerning the states.[21] In this context, state autonomy was regarded as impairing civil rights; whereas the Supreme Court was regarded as their main protector. As some scholars point out, however, the situation is no longer the same.[22] In some cases, states have improved the federal standards of protection. Justice Brennan observed that between 1970 and 1984, state courts published around 250 opinions holding that the constitutional

rights against recalcitrant states. The Framers of the Fourteenth Amendment thus rejected the idea that rights such as the free exercise of religion should vary from state to state....Nothing was more central to the Fourteenth Amendment than the idea that all citizens should be equal in their enjoyment of civil rights.' Caminker, *supra* n 8, at 1194–1195.

[16] For instance, Kahn, *supra* n 9, at 1148, argued: 'The diversity of state courts is best understood as a diversity of interpretive bodies, not as a multiplicity of representatives of distinct sovereigns'; Andrzej Rapaczynski, *From Sovereignty to Process: The Jurisprudence of Federalism after Garcia*, SUPREME COURT REVIEW 341 (1985); Edward L. Rubin & Malcolm Feeley, *Federalism: Some Notes on a National Neurosis*, 41 UCLA LAW REVIEW 903 (1994).

[17] Edward L. Rubin, *Puppy Federalism and the Blessings of America*, 574 ANNALS AM. ACAD. POL. & SOC. SCI. 37, 45–46 (2001); James A. Gardner, *The Failed Discourse of State Constitutionalism*, 90 MICHIGAN LAW REVIEW 761, 823, 827–830 (1992).

[18] Rubin & Feeley, *supra* n 16, at 944, 946: 'There are no regions in our nation with a separate history or culture....Most of our states, the alleged political communities that federalism would preserve, are mere administrative units....Although some of the original thirteen states had unique political communities resulting from their separate origins, their uniqueness has long since given way to the national culture....American federalism is nothing more than decentralization because the normative claim of political community is not available to it.'

[19] Lynn A. Baker & Ernest A. Young, *Federalism and the Double Standard of Judicial Review*, 51 DUKE LAW JOURNAL 75, 162, 143–149 (2001), claim that one of the reasons for which states' rights are seen as normatively unattractive is due to the historical linkage with slavery and segregation.

[20] Jean Yarbrough, *Federalism and Rights in the American Founding*, in FEDERALISM AND RIGHTS 57, 70 (Ellis Katz & G. Alan Tarr eds. 1984).

[21] McConnell, *supra* n 8, at 193–194.   [22] Young, *supra* n 14.

minimums defined by the Supreme Court 'were insufficient to satisfy the more stringent requirements of state constitutional law'.[23]

By contrast, in the EU, a federal state does not yet exist (and the failed EU Constitution would not have created one). The member states are constitutional democracies with strong identities, based on distinct cultures, histories, and languages.[24] The degree of integration and homogeneity among EU member states is lower than in the US. Hence, state autonomy cannot be disregarded since it relates to the principle of self-government of democratic polities, while the democratic legitimacy of the EU is still controversial. By ratifying the Treaties, the member states surrendered their sovereign powers over certain subject matters conferred upon the EU. Nonetheless, they preserved their powers to interpret rights constraining state action. Even when fundamental rights have been recognized at the supranational level, this does not mean that member states have lost their powers of interpretation or that constitutional rights are no longer effective. There is a plurality of bills of rights, all of them supreme within their respective systems. There are also several courts with the ultimate power to interpret and enforce these rights. Even if the Lisbon Treaty is eventually ratified, and the EU Charter acquires legally binding force, constitutional catalogues of rights would still stand. The EU Charter reiterates that EU rights were only incorporated to state acts implementing EU law (article 51); that the Charter would not create new powers for the EU (article 52); and that constitutional rights would not be restrictively affected (article 53).[25] Additionally, in contrast to the US history of state discrimination, the incorporation of EU fundamental rights to the states was not guided by a perceived lack of protection within the states, but rather by the need to secure the efficacy and uniformity of EU law.[26] Indeed, some fear that the levels of protection of certain rights

[23] William J. Brennan Jr., *The Bill of Rights and the States: The Revival of State Constitutions as Guardians of Individual Rights*, in THE BILL OF RIGHTS AND THE STATES 81, 94 (Paul L. Murphy ed. 1990). For several examples of fields in which the states have been more protective, see Baker & Young, *supra* n 19, at 154.

[24] George A. Bermann, *Taking Subsidiarity Seriously: Federalism in the European Community and the United States*, 94 COLUMBIA LAW REVIEW 331, 450 (1994): 'In Europe, geography still brings along with it differences in culture, language, and social and political values that are far more pronounced than the generally prevailing differences in the United States.'

[25] The precise interpretation of these clauses, as discussed in other parts of this work, is very much disputed.

[26] Joseph H. H. Weiler, *Eurocracy and Distrust: Some Questions Concerning the Role of the European Court of Justice in the Protection of Fundamental Rights within the Legal Order on the European Communities*, 61 WASHINGTON LAW REVIEW 1103, 1119 (1986).

might diminish as a consequence of the integration process. While the arguments for states' rights have for long been discussed within the US judicial and academic debate, they have not been thoroughly examined in the EU context. Hence, this chapter will first examine the reasons for uniform fundamental rights to demonstrate that they do not necessarily support full homogeneity in the EU. Secondly, the reasons for state autonomy and the benefits of a system that accommodates diversity will be explored.

2 Supranational uniformity

Arguably, in the EU, uniformity of fundamental rights might (i) foster unity and supranational identity; (ii) secure the efficacy and uniform application of EU law within the member states; (iii) guarantee equality across the union; and (iv) enhance the legitimacy of the whole system. The values underpinning uniformity of rights must be acknowledged; on occasion, however, they are misconceived or they are not necessarily achieved by invariably imposing a common supranational interpretation.

2.1 *Unity and supranational identity*

The integrative force of a common bill of rights is a classic idea. Common values expressed in a single document might contribute to forge a common allegiance.[27] In the EU, sharing the same basic rights might further the belief among the citizens of the several member states that, despite their differences, they are part of a broader political community.[28] Thus, the commitment to a common bill of rights might contribute to the project of identity building at the supranational level and buttress the notion of European citizenship.[29] Along these lines, some scholars point out the political use made of the US and Canadian bills of rights as tools to strengthen national

---

[27] Jochen Abr. Frowein, Stephen Schulhofer & Martin Shapiro, *Fundamental Human Rights as a Vehicle of Integration in Europe*, in INTEGRATION THROUGH LAW. EUROPE AND THE AMERICAN FEDERAL EXPERIENCE 231 (MAURO CAPPELLETTI, MONICA SECCOMBE & JOSEPH H. H. WEILER eds. 1986).

[28] ANDREW CLAPHAM, I HUMAN RIGHTS AND THE EUROPEAN COMMUNITY: A CRITICAL OVERVIEW 14 (Nomos Verlagsgesellschaft 1991): 'Talking about human rights may sometimes bestow identity on Community citizens.'

[29] Koen Leanerts, *Fundamental Rights in the European Union*, 25 EUROPEAN LAW REVIEW 575, 593 (2000): 'Citizenship of the Union acquires its full meaning only when it includes an assurance that all the Member States respect the fundamental rights guaranteed by the Community legal order.'

unity and hold together citizens with diverse backgrounds and cultures.[30] Similarly, it is thought the enactment of a written catalogue of rights for the EU might have a symbolic effect as the document that enshrines the rights common to all European citizens.[31] Indeed, one of the main goals underlying the drafting of an EU catalogue of rights was to render these rights (most of them already protected by the ECJ case law) more visible. This would increase the citizens' awareness of sharing a common set of rights.[32] Hence, the purpose of the EU Charter was not limited to legal protection. Rather, it had a larger political purpose: enhancing integration and strengthening the common identity of all European citizens.

Nonetheless, it should be realized that fundamental rights have a divisive potential as well.[33] The imposition of uniformity by a supranational authority when there is diversity among the states might well provoke tensions, especially when moral issues and essential social and political values are at stake, such as abortion or the right of homosexuals to marry or adopt children.[34] Particularly, enforcing EU rights to the states might give rise to resistance when the standard of protection given by the ECJ is lower or clashes with entrenched constitutional values. In spite of its aspirations, the EU Charter does not seem to offer sufficient grounds upon which to build a common identity at the supranational level. Given the fact that fundamental

---

[30] MAURO CAPPELLETTI (ed.), THE JUDICIAL PROCESS IN COMPARATIVE PERSPECTIVE 395 (Clarendon Press 1989): 'There is hardly anything that has greater potential to foster integration than a common bill of rights, as the constitutional history of the United States has proved'; ALAN CAIRNS, CHARTER VERSUS FEDERALISM: THE DILEMMAS OF CONSTITUTIONAL REFORM 49 (McGill-Queens University Press 1992): 'The Charter was always more than an instrument to protect the rights of Canadians against their governments. The larger political purpose...was to strengthen national unity by providing constitutional support to a new definition of Canadians as a rights-bearing citizenry regardless of location.'

[31] Annie Gruber, *La Charte des Droits Fondamentaux de l'Union Européenne: Un Message Clair Hautement Symbolique*, 15 PETITES AFFICHES. LA LOI 4, 16 (2001), emphasized the highly symbolic value of the Charter.

[32] European Council, *European Council Decision on the Drawing up of a Charter of Fundamental Rights of the European Union. Presidency Conclusions* (annex X), Cologne, June 1999: 'There appears to be a need, at the present stage of the Union's development, to establish a Charter of fundamental rights in order to make their overriding importance and relevance more visible to the Union's citizens.'

[33] Gráinne de Búrca, *The Language of Rights and European Integration*, in NEW LEGAL DYNAMICS OF EUROPEAN INTEGRATION 29, 46–49 (Jo Shaw & Gillian More eds. 1995).

[34] Clapham, *supra* n 28, at 15, argued that rights have an important role in the process of European integration, but that 'they may well operate as a double edged sword. Not only are they a cohesive force but they may well be divisive. Should the Community move to tackle questions such as divorce, contraception, abortion, blasphemy, surrogacy, etc., rights might no longer be handy tools for integration but vehicles of division and disintegration.'

rights are already enshrined in state constitutions and that the European Convention on Human Rights (ECHR) already provides a common set of rights, yet another rights' catalogue is not likely to have an integrative impact. The strength of the diverse national identities is based upon myriad elements that go well beyond legal texts, such as a common culture, history, and language. In addition, the failure to include the Charter in the Treaty of Nice (December 2000) demonstrated the inability of the member states to agree on the binding force to this common bill of rights. As Jospeh H. H. Weiler argued, the failure to agree upon the binding force of the Charter could have exactly the opposite effect to that sought by its drafting, which was furthering integration and identity.[35] Later on, the inclusion of the Charter in the failed European Constitution, and the recognition of its legal value by the Lisbon Treaty illustrate existing political agreement on its binding force. Nonetheless, some scepticism persists among those who regard the Charter as an instrument to enlarge EU powers and intrude on areas of state autonomy. The so-called 'horizontal provisions' governing its interpretation and application reflect the attempt to reassure that the Charter will not impair constitutional rights or extend EU powers.

2.2 *Efficacy of EU law*

Arguably, the uniform interpretation of fundamental rights would secure the uniform application and efficacy of EU law. Otherwise, if fundamental rights were interpreted differently and state acts implementing EU law were set aside by state courts, the uniform application and efficacy of EU law within the state territories might be undermined. In this line of argument, followed by the ECJ, safeguarding uniformity seems to be only instrumentally about fundamental rights. To be clear, when claiming the need to preserve the uniformity of EU law, the ECJ does not seem so concerned about uniform fundamental rights as it is about the uniform application of the EU piece of legislation at stake. In this way, in order to ensure the uniform application of EU legislation in all member states, fundamental rights need to be interpreted uniformly across the states. Thus, the ECJ interest is not so much to secure a common interpretation of fundamental rights, as to prevent state courts from reviewing state acts implementing EU law under the respective constitutional rights.

[35] Joseph H. H. Weiler, *Editorial: Does the European Union Truly Need a Charter of Rights?*, 6 EUROPEAN LAW JOURNAL 95, 95–96 (2000), claimed that, instead, it could become a 'symbol of European incompetence and refusal to take rights seriously'.

The efficacy of EU law within the states, however, does not require uniformity in the interpretation of fundamental rights in each and every case. This argument was developed in the previous chapter: the interest in the uniformity and efficacy of EU law does not justify the unlimited suprem- acy of EU law over constitutional rights. Hence, the recognition of a certain degree of diversity in the interpretation of rights does not necessarily render EU legislation ineffective nor threaten the success of the integration project. For example, it is difficult to see why the existence of diverse state affirma- tive action measures favouring women's access to public posts would signifi- cantly jeopardize the efficacy and goals of the EU system. On the contrary, the imposition of uniformity for its own sake might increase the scepticism of some states.

2.3 *Equal protection*

The drive towards uniformity is not only about efficacy, but also about equal- ity of protection. Thus, a powerful argument for uniformity is grounded on equality. Arguably, all European citizens should be granted the same level of fundamental rights protection. In the US, this was a strong argument to support the application of federal rights to all American citizens irrespective of the state where they lived against the action of federal and state authorities indistinctively.[36] At the same time, one needs to acknowledge the political structure of the EU. In the EU, there is a plurality of polities interpret- ing fundamental rights enshrined in their respective constitutions, based on their own sources. As a consequence of the process of European integra- tion, a supranational legal order has emerged, in which rights are protected and interpreted by a supranational court. The interpretation of fundamen- tal rights, owing to their open texture and essentially contested content, is highly controversial. Additionally, they may conflict with public interests or other fundamental rights. The balance between them may be legitimately resolved differently in diverse legal systems. Since it is uncertain whether there is only one 'correct' interpretation, and even if there is, there is no agreement on how to reach it, diverse political communities might 'reason- ably disagree' about the meaning of fundamental rights.[37]

The creation of a supranational community to establish a form of col- lective action regarding certain subject matters does not itself justify

---

[36] McConnell, *supra* n 8, at 194: 'Nothing was more central to the Fourteenth Amendment than the idea that all citizens should be equal in their enjoyment of civil rights.'

[37] JEREMY WALDRON, LAW AND DISAGREEMENT (Oxford University Press 1999).

homogenizing fundamental rights. Undeniably, citizens from all member states should receive the same protection from the EU legal order against the action of EU institutions. At the same time, standards of protection given to parallel constitutional rights might reasonably diverge from one state to the other. In the face of reasonable disagreement, other values, such as democratic self-government or political identity, might justify co-existing, differing interpretations. EU member states constitute democratic constitutional polities for the self-government of a group of people with a collective identity living under the same constitution. Thus, some degree of autonomy to interpret constitutional rights should be respected, even within the field of application of EU law. In short, equality does not require that state diversity be immediately rejected in favour of supranational uniformity.

2.4 *Legitimating the EU legal order*

The legitimacy of any legal order directly imposing obligations upon individuals, as the EU legal order does, requires guaranteeing the protection of fundamental rights against encroachment by public authorities. This constitutes one of the main tenets of liberal constitutionalism: securing individual rights against state action, usually by providing judicial remedies. As explained, no fundamental rights were recognized in the text of the foundational Treaties. In addition, the ECJ declared that state constitutional rights were not binding upon EU institutions.[38] Particularly after the proclamation of EU law's supremacy, it became evident that the action of EU institutions was not at all constrained by fundamental rights. Consequently, there were reasons to cast doubt on the legitimacy of the EU legal order from the perspective of fundamental rights protection.[39] Some argued that since EU powers were steadily expanding and reaching fields well beyond the

---

[38] *Friedrich Stork & Cie v High Authority of the European Coal and Steel Community*, C-1/58; *Präsident Ruhrkolen-Verkaufsgesellschaft mbH, Geitling Ruhrkohlen-Verkaufsgesellschaft mbH, Mausegatt Ruhrkohlen-Verkaufsgesellschaft mbH and I. Nold KG v High Authority of the European Coal and Steel Community*, C-36, 37, 38, and 40/59. In these early cases, individuals challenged EU measures on the basis of state constitutional rights. The ECJ argued that it was not its task to interpret domestic law, and that the validity of EU law was not determined by domestic law, let alone constitutional law. The ECJ avoided answering the question whether the EU legal system included fundamental rights with which EU institutions had to comply.

[39] Weiler, *supra* n 26, at 1119, argued that the ECJ case law inaugurating the protection of fundamental rights as general principles of EU law was an 'attempt to protect the concept of supremacy which was threatened because of the inadequate protection of fundamental rights in the original Treaty system'.

economic realm, coupled with the decision-making democratic deficit, the legitimacy of the EU legal system required the guarantee of fundamental rights' protection.[40] Furthermore, the explicit recognition of fundamental rights could enhance the legitimacy of the EU in the international sphere: 'the concept of human and fundamental rights may be seen as capable of providing a moral grounding to a legal order which on its face was established principally to support the pursuit of economic goals'.[41] With regard to the EU Charter, some argued that a written rights' catalogue would enhance the legitimacy of the EU system as a whole,[42] by making the commitment with fundamental rights more visible. Also, the Charter would contribute to the legitimacy of the ECJ's case law, by replacing sheer judicial activism with the outcome of a wide political consensus.[43]

All these arguments may very well support the need to protect fundamental rights vis-à-vis EU institutions to secure the legitimacy of the EU legal order, but they do not necessarily justify imposing a uniform interpretation to the states. In the US, the incorporation of federal rights to the states was justified by the enactment of the Reconstruction amendments and the need to secure the protection of fundamental rights against state action. In the EU, the ECJ did not rely upon any Treaty provision to incorporate EU rights against the states. Moreover, the justification for this expansion could not be traced to a lack of protection at the state level, since the states protected the rights enshrined in their constitutions and were all parties to the European Convention on Human Rights. Some argued that by incorporating EU fundamental rights to the states, the ECJ made an 'offensive' use of those rights to foster EU integration and 'extend its jurisdiction into areas previously reserved to member states' courts and to expand the influence of the Community over the activities of the member states'.[44] In any event, beyond the debate about incorporation, the underlying point is that

---

[40] Antonio Vitorino, *La Charte des Droits Fondamentaux de l'Union Européenne*, 3 Revue du Droit de l'Union Européenne 499, 501 (2000); Natividad Fernández Sola, *À Quelle Nécessité Juridique Répond la Négociation d'une Charte des Droits Fondamentaux de l'Union Européenne?*, 442 Revue du Marché Commun et de l'Union Européenne 595, 596 (2000).

[41] De Búrca, *supra* n 33, at 43.

[42] Fernández Sola, *supra* n 40, at 596.

[43] Montserrat Pi Llorens, Los Derechos Fundamentales en el Ordenamiento Comunitario 129 (Ariel 1999).

[44] Jason Coppel & Aidan O'Neill, *The European Court of Justice: Taking Rights Seriously?*, 29 Common Market Law Review 669, 669–670 (1992); opposing this view, Joseph H. H. Weiler & Nicolas Lockhart, *'Taking Rights Seriously' Seriously: The European Court and its Fundamental Rights Jurisprudence*, 32 Common Market Law Review 51 (1995).

the legitimacy of the EU legal order from the perspective of the commitment to fundamental rights cannot justify imposing uniformity to the states. Indeed, ignoring state constitutional rights might undermine the legitimacy of the ECJ's claim to authority.

3 State diversity

The argument for states' rights (or state autonomy) in the interpretation of fundamental rights is an argument for a measure of diversity, as opposed to complete uniformity. State autonomy in interpreting fundamental rights is valued to the extent that it promotes individual freedom in both a republican (freedom as self-government) and a liberal (freedom as rights protection) sense. State autonomy also furthers experimentation, which might promote legal innovation. Accordingly, the arguments for state autonomy are grouped in three main categories: (i) democratic self-government of political communities; (ii) protection of individual liberty; and (iii) experimentation leading to innovation.

3.1 *Democratic self-government of political communities*

Because the EU suffers from a democratic deficit, there are reasons that justify respecting state interpretations of constitutional rights. The EU falls short of fulfilling the conditions for being a full democratic political community from the perspective of both, law-making procedures and the dubious existence of a European *demos*.

3.1.1 *Democratic self-government*

A common argument for states' rights in the US is that the proper functioning of democracy is promoted when decisions are taken closer to the people: citizens have more opportunities to participate in the decision-making procedures so that civic democratic participation is fostered;[45] the accountability of public authorities is enhanced;[46] and decision-makers are better

---

[45] As the Supreme Court stated in *Gregory v Ashcroft* 501 US 452 (1991), a federalist structure 'increases opportunity for citizen involvement in democratic processes'.

[46] DAVID L. SHAPIRO, FEDERALISM. A DIALOGUE 91–92 (Northwestern University Press 1995); Deborah Jones Merritt, *The Guarantee Clause and State Autonomy: Federalism for a Third Century*, 88 COLUMBIA LAW REVIEW 1, 7–8 (1988).

able to accommodate the needs of their constituencies.[47] This argument is easily applicable to support state autonomy in the EU. All member states are democratic polities, which, by definition, offer mechanisms for the representation and participation of citizens in law-making processes. Thus, if decisions are taken by state authorities, closer to the people than EU institutions, citizens have more possibilities to participate and engage in public debate. Also, decision-makers at the state level are more accountable and can better accommodate the sensibilities and interests of their constituencies. By contrast, EU institutions invariably fail to promote civic democratic participation. They are too remote from the European citizenry. The EU Parliament, which is the only institution directly elected by the people, does not play a main role in the law-making process. Furthermore, the pervasive low turnout in European parliamentary elections demonstrates the inability of the EU Parliament to foster democratic participation, although this might be explained by its perceived secondary role. In addition, there are no European political parties. Generally speaking, the development of a robust transnational debate about matters of public interest is still wishful thinking. Although enhancing democracy and transparency of decision-making procedures was one of the main reasons to draft a constitution for the EU,[48] the final text did not manage to improve significantly the democratic nature of law-making procedures.[49]

3.1.2 *Political community and identity*

A further argument in favour of state autonomy is that EU member states are the locus of political communities with a collective identity. A political community is defined as a group of people committed to a project of democratic self-government who also share a sense of belonging together (collective identity). The commitment to a project of self-government is usually expressed in a constitution. 'The constitution is a document that

[47] Baker & Young, *supra* n 19, at 150–151: 'In the absence of consensus, imposition of a uniform national solution almost always will satisfy fewer people, and therefore may result in decreased aggregate social welfare, than would allowing for state-by-state diversity.' The Supreme Court, in *Gregory v Ashcroft*, 501 US 452 (1991), argued that federalism 'assures a decentralized government that will be more sensitive to the diverse needs of a heterogeneous society'.

[48] As declared by the European Council, *Laeken Declaration—The Future of the European Union*, 15 December 2001.

[49] Gráinne de Búrca, *The Drafting of a Constitution for the European Union: Europe's Madisonian Moment or a Moment of Madness?*, 61 WASHINGTON & LEE LAW REVIEW 555, 557 (2004), examined the changes introduced by the proposed EU Constitution to the internal structure concluding that 'they do not in any significant way address the problems of democratic legitimacy which seemed to motivate the impetus for a constitutional debate at its outset'.

self-consciously defines a communal identity…meant to identify a political community and to set out some of the most fundamental principles according to which the members of the community wish to live their lives.'[50] Collective identity might be based upon several factors, such as a common history, culture, and language. According to some scholars, if not the main source in current multicultural societies, the commitment to live under the same constitution contributes to build a collective identity.[51] Self-identity as well as mutual recognition among the members of the 'we' is partly constituted through participation in this self-governing enterprise within state boundaries.[52] Hence, living together under the same constitution provides shared meanings and the possibility of a meaningful discussion about public issues, including the substantive content of fundamental rights. Constitutional fundamental rights tend to encapsulate essential values of a specific political community.

EU member states are the locus of political communities self-governing themselves under the respective constitution. Hence, there is a normative argument for state autonomy and thus for accommodating a certain degree of diversity. Generally, the citizens of each member state share a collective identity.[53] Beyond the discussion about the origin of current national groups,[54] membership in these communities is still relevant today for the understanding of the self as a part of a larger group, whose individuals mutually recognize each other.[55] Thus, in spite of the transformations incurred as a consequence of the integration process, the member states can still be regarded as true political communities with their own respective identities.

---

[50] Gardner, *supra* n 17, at 769–770.

[51] JÜRGEN HABERMAS, THE INCLUSION OF THE OTHER (MIT Press 1998), argued that 'constitutional patriotism can take the place originally occupied by nationalism'.

[52] Rubin & Feeley, *supra* n 16, at 939: 'Members of a group may function as a community because they engage in a collective decision-making process regarding major questions of self-governance.'

[53] Admittedly, some member states embrace more than one national group within their borders.

[54] It is not suggested that nations naturally emerged. As is widely admitted by the literature about nationalism, in many cases, nations were the result of deliberate policies of nation-building aimed at promoting a common identity among the inhabitants of a concrete territory so as to legitimate state power. See NEUS TORBISCO CASALS, GROUPS RIGHTS AS HUMAN RIGHTS (Springer 2006); WILL KYMLICKA, LIBERALISM, COMMUNITY AND CULTURE (Clarendon Press 1989); YAEL TAMIR, LIBERAL NATIONALISM (Princeton University Press 1993).

[55] As BENEDICT ANDERSON, IMAGINED COMMUNITIES: REFLECTIONS ON THE ORIGIN AND SPREAD OF NATIONALISM (Verso 1983), put it, nations are 'imagined communities'. What is relevant is what people believe, beyond the objective elements defining a nation or the circumstances of the nation-building process.

At the same time, a European *demos*, in other words, a 'European people' with a sense of collective identity is still lacking. Although some scholars believe that a common European identity could evolve in the future, most agree it does not yet exist.[56] For some it is not even desirable if this means replicating national identity.[57] All member states are constitutional democracies, and almost all are governed by written constitutions embodying a catalogue of fundamental rights. Political and social diversity among these communities might influence the way essential public values and constitutional rights in particular are conceived in each state. For instance, Scandinavian countries have proved to be quite progressive, adopting measures to advance equality on the basis of sex and sexual orientation. In short, diverse constitutional polities might bring about distinct interpretations of analogous fundamental rights. These political communities and corresponding constitutional understandings deserve a measure of respect as well as the possibility to develop further within a broader EU pluralist structure.

To conclude, the arguments based upon self-government and political identity justify accommodating some degree of diversity. This is not to say, however, that democratic self-government and identity are essentially linked to state boundaries. While, at this moment, they seem to be better realized at the state level, other *infra-* or *supra*-national possibilities should not be excluded.[58] In addition, constitutional-political identity is not the only possible source of identity and mutual recognition. For instance, there are groups with the potential for building transnational identities on the basis of gender or other common traits.

3.2 *Protection of individual liberty*

3.2.1 *Liberty as dual protection*

An important argument for federalism in the US is that it furthers liberty by diffusing power and establishing checks between the federal and the state governments. As the classic Madison no. 51 (Federalist Papers) reads:

---

[56] Dieter Grimm, *Does Europe Need a Constitution?*, 1 EUROPEAN LAW JOURNAL 282, 297 (1995); Joseph H. H. Weiler, *Does Europe Need a Constitution? Reflections on Demos, Telos and the German Maastricht Decision*, 1 EUROPEAN LAW JOURNAL 219 (1995).

[57] JOSEPH H. H. WEILER, THE CONSTITUTION OF EUROPE 341 (Cambridge University Press 1999): 'It would be ... ironic if the ethos which rejected the boundary abuse of the nation-state gave birth to a polity with the same potential for abuse.'

[58] Specifically, one of the main purposes of the EU project was to overcome the exclusionary trends of a national ethos among the members of this supranational community. See Weiler, *supra* n 57, 340–343.

Whilst all authority in it will be derived from and dependent on the society, the society itself will be broken into so many parts, interests and classes of citizens, that the rights of individuals, or of the minority, will be in little danger from interested combinations of the majority.... In the compound republic of America, the power surrendered by the people is first divided between two distinct governments, and then the portion allotted to each subdivided among distinct and separate departments. Hence a double security arises to the rights of the people. The different governments will control each other, at the same time that each will be controlled itself.[59]

Madison emphasized the vertical separation of powers between the central government and the states as a mechanism to secure individual rights against abuses of power.[60] The US Supreme Court in *Gregory* stated: 'Perhaps the principal benefit of the federalist system is a check on abuses of government power.'[61] Regarding rights protection in particular, state judiciaries provide an interpretive counterpoint to the US Supreme Court, and vice-versa. Justice Brennan argued that the strength of the US federal system was that it provided 'a double source of protection' for the citizens' rights.[62] He encouraged state courts to interpret state constitutional rights as giving a broader scope of protection than the parallel federal provisions. As he said, 'As tempting as it may be to harmonize results under state and national constitutions, our federalism permits state courts to provide greater protection to individual civil rights and liberties.'[63] Hence, diversity should be allowed above the federal floor of protection. For example, some states have gone further than the federation in protecting minority rights or free speech.[64]

In the EU, the power to interpret rights is allocated among different institutions from different systems, checking each other. This pluralist structure creates benefits emerging from a dual source of protection. National and supranational participation in this interpretive activity contributes to limit the excesses and detect the shortcomings of each other, eventually furthering individual protection.[65] Hence, the potential dangers

---

[59] ALEXANDER HAMILTON, JAMES MADISON & JOHN JAY, THE FEDERALIST PAPERS 321–323 (Clinton Rossiter ed. 1999).

[60] Merritt, *supra* n 46, at 4–7.

[61] *Gregory v Ashcroft* 501 US 452 (1991).

[62] Brennan, *supra* n 11, at 490.   [63] Brennan, *supra* n 9 at 551.

[64] See the examples quoted by Brennan, *supra* n 23, at 94; Shapiro, *supra* n 46, at 99.

[65] Miguel Poiares Maduro, *Las Formas del Poder Constitucional de la Unión Europea*, 119 REVISTA DE ESTUDIOS POLÍTICOS 11 (2003).

of restricting the scope of rights' protection for the sake of efficacy at the supranational level can be counteracted by state constitutionalism. In this vein, state courts might push for further protection in the common market. For example, in *Wachauf*,[66] the intervention of state courts fostered the ECJ's recognition of the right to compensation for measures equivalent to expropriation. This case involved a German farmer who had developed a thriving dairy business on leased land over a period of around twenty-five years. After the renewal of the lease was denied, he claimed for monetary compensation provided by a 1985 EC regulation to dairy farmers who decided to reduce or abandon their milk production. The German Government, responsible for enforcing this regulation, refused to grant compensation because the regulation required the consent of the landowner, who had refused to give it. The case was brought before a German court, which submitted a question to the ECJ, suggesting that the EC regulation had the effect of an 'unconstitutional expropriation without compensation'. The ECJ, in line with the German interpretation, proceeded to hold that, despite the regulation's language, this should be construed to grant compensation in such a case to secure compliance with EU fundamental rights. Hence, constitutional rights protected by state courts might boost better individual protection at the supranational level.

At the same time, exclusionary trends existing at the national level can be counteracted at the supranational one. The availability of a supranational forum might further the protection of certain groups. For example, the ECJ's interpretation of the right to sex equality in *Dekker*[67] and *Webb*[68] favoured the situation of pregnant women in the workplace. *Dekker* involved a woman, three months' pregnant at the time, who had been denied a teaching position in a formative centre for young adults because the employment insurance did not cover sick leave for illnesses that would occur during the first six months of employment and could be anticipated at the time of hiring. Consequently, the employer could not recover the daily benefits due during maternity leave. After the district court and the regional court of appeal dismissed her lawsuit, Ms. Dekker appealed to the Dutch Supreme Court, which referred a question to the ECJ. The ECJ declared that the decision not to hire her amounted to sex discrimination. This Court asserted that

---

[66]   *Hubert Wachauf v Bundesamt für Ernährung und Forstwirtschaft*, C-5/88.

[67]   *Elisabeth Johanna Pacifica Dekker v Stichting Vormingscentrum voor Jong Volwassenen Plus*, C-177/88.

[68]   *Carole Louise Webb v EMO Air Cargo (UK) Ltd.*, C-32/93.

employers violate the equal protection clause if they refuse to enter into a contract with a pregnant female candidate considered to be suitable for the job, regardless of national rules on unfitness for work assimilating pregnancy and illness. In *Webb*, a woman was hired by an air cargo company in the UK to replace another female employee during the latter's maternity leave. During the training period, she discovered she was pregnant and was subsequently dismissed by the company. She lost the successive appeals before ordinary courts because the 1975 British Sex Discrimination Act would not afford her protection. Eventually, the House of Lords referred a question to the ECJ. The ECJ held that dismissal of a female worker on account of her pregnancy constituted direct discrimination on grounds of sex.[69]

In both these cases, female workers were able to get protection from the ECJ, after having been turned down by state courts. Therefore, such a dual source might improve the scope of individual protection. Interpreting rights in Europe is a co-operative enterprise that incorporates diverse viewpoints from different levels of governance. In the end, this system may well be more inclusive and protective. Indeed, this argument runs in two directions: it recognizes the benefits of state constitutionalism as a counterpoint to supranational adjudication, while also recognizing the benefits of supranational adjudication in developing common understandings. Ultimately, the argument for dual protection is grounded on the benefits of securing checks and balances between institutions from different levels of governance, preventing the concentration of power in one single interpretive authority.

3.2.2 Liberty through exit

As has been argued in the US, state autonomy enhances individual liberty by providing freedom to choose among diverse legal regimes, according to one's own preferences.[70] Different states offer diverse packages of taxes and services, including state constitutional rights and laws. As David L. Shapiro

---

[69] Following *Dekker*, the ECJ held: 'The situation of a woman who finds herself incapable, by reason of pregnancy discovered very shortly after the conclusion of her employment contract, of performing the task for which she was recruited could not be compared with that of a man similarly incapable for medical or other reasons, since pregnancy is not in any way comparable with a pathological condition, and even less so with unavailability for work on non-medical grounds' (*Carole Louise Webb v EMO Air Cargo (UK) Ltd.*, C-32/93).

[70] Baker & Young, *supra* n 19, at 139, argued that 'federalism provides an additional level of freedom to individuals, beyond that provided by specific guarantees of individual rights, by conferring the freedom to choose from among various diverse regulatory regimes the one that best suits the individual's preferences'.

put it, 'The existence of separate polities ... when coupled with a reasonable degree of mobility, may significantly enhance individual freedom whenever a state acts against personal preferences.'[71] In this context, the precondition for benefiting from state diversity is the 'right to exit',[72] in other words, the possibility to move and settle in another territory under a different set of laws. This is guaranteed in the EU on the basis of the principle of free movement. Specifically, the EU contains as one of its core principles the right of every citizen of the Union 'to move and reside freely within the territory of the member states' (article 18 EC Treaty). Also, the right to non-discrimination on the basis of nationality is secured (article 12 EC Treaty). Therefore, citizens have the right to move to states that better accommodate their preferences regarding fundamental rights and social policies in general.

3.3 *Experimentation leading to innovation*

An argument formulated by some scholars and judges in the US claims that federalism fosters state experimentation, and thus innovation. This argument is known under the metaphor of 'states as laboratories'.[73] The notion is that states might experiment with new social policies before these policies might be implemented at the federal level.[74] In this way, experimentation enhances innovation, without risk for the system as a whole. For instance, as Justice O'Connor claimed in her dissent in *Federal Energy Regulatory Commission v Mississippi*:

The 50 States serve as laboratories for the development of new social, economic and political ideas. This state innovation is no judicial myth. When Wyoming became a State in 1890, it was the only State permitting women to vote. That novel idea

---

[71] Shapiro, *supra* n 46, at 95–96; Seth Kreimer, *Federalism and Freedom*, 574 ANNALS AM. ACAD. POL. & SOC. SCI 66, 72 (2001), refers to various examples.

[72] Richard A. Epstein, *Exit Rights Under Federalism*, 55 LAW AND CONTEMPORARY PROBLEMS 147, 149 (1992): 'The individuals who are subject to state regulation need not be content with a "voice" in the political process but can protect their interests through the right of "exit", that is, through the ability to avoid the difficulties of further association by picking up stock and going elsewhere.'

[73] Introduced by Justice Brandeis in his dissent in *New State Ice Co. v Liebman* 285 US 262 (1932), see Akhil R. Amar, *Five Views of Federalism: 'Converse-1983' in Context*, 47 VANDERBILT LAW REVIEW 1229, 1233–1235 (1995).

[74] See examples cited by Merritt, *supra* n 46, at 9; Shapiro, *supra* n 46, at 87–88: 'Sometimes, an idea born and bred in a particular state serves as a basis for developments in other states or throughout the Nation.'

did not bear national fruit for another 30 years, Wisconsin pioneered unemployment insurance, while Massachusetts initiated minimum wage laws for women and minors.[75]

Shapiro indicates several areas in which the states in the US have introduced new and innovative regulations, such as workers' compensation programmes, welfare reform, health care, penology, and environmental protection.[76] Moreover, innovation is furthered by inter-state competition. And inter-state competition is fostered by the recognition of the right to exit.[77] As Akhil R. Amar remarked, 'The counterpart of citizen choice and self-selection is state competition for the allegiance of citizens.'[78] In this situation, states have incentives to adopt new policies and regulations that might better accommodate the needs and ideals of individuals. According to McConnell, 'There is a powerful incentive for decentralized governments to make things better for most people.'[79] In the domain of rights protection, the states might compete by offering better standards of protection to individuals, for example regarding equal protection or workers' rights.

Also in the EU, state autonomy allows for experimenting with social policies and rights in the several member states. Experimentation contributes to create new solutions to new problems. The possibility for the states to experiment by enacting diverse regulatory frameworks or interpreting their respective constitutional rights to include new situations would allow the EU to test different solutions and examine their consequences before adopting certain interpretation at the supranational level.[80] Eventually, experimentation could lead to raising the standards of protection through a bottom up process. After states had agreed on extending the scope of protection of a specific right, this interpretation could be adopted at the supranational level. For instance, in the 1970s, several member states proceeded

[75] Quoted in Amar, *supra* n 73, at 1233.

[76] Shapiro, *supra* n 46, at 87–88. A few scholars have questioned the view of states as innovators, for example, Susan Rose-Ackerman, *Risk Taking and Reelection: Does Federalism Promote Innovation?*, 9 JOURNAL OF LEGAL STUDIES 593, 603–605 (1980).

[77] Charles Fried, *Federalism—Why Should We Care?*, 6 HARVARD JOURNAL OF LAW AND PUBLIC POLICY 1, 2–3 (1982).

[78] Amar, *Supra* n 73, at 1238.

[79] Michael McConnell, *Federalism: Evaluating the Founder's Design*, 54 UNIVERSITY OF CHICAGO LAW REVIEW 1484, 1498–1499 (1987).

[80] Klaus Gretschmann, *The Subsidiarity Principle: Who Is to Do What in an Integrated Europe?*, in SUBSIDIARITY: THE CHALLENGE OF CHANGE 45, 50–51 (Proceedings of Colloquium organized by the European Institute of Public Administration, 21–22 March 1991), asserts that European diversity 'represents a playground for experiments'.

to give a legal response to transsexuality by passing legislation authorizing transsexuals to amend their birth certificates to include reference to their new sexual identities.[81] As a result, following the respective state legislation, transsexuals may enjoy the right to marry, adopt children, and enjoy pension rights according to their acquired sexual identity. Over time, other states followed suit, either in the form of laws, regulations, or judicial decisions.[82] Eventually, the ECJ took into account these state legal developments to interpret the EU ban on sex discrimination to include transsexuals. In *P v S and Cornwall County Council*, the ECJ held that the equal protection clause precluded the dismissal of a transsexual for reasons related to gender reassignment.[83]

4 Accommodating diversity within a pluralist framework

This chapter started with a question: given the EU pluralist framework, should fundamental rights be interpreted uniformly or should a certain degree of diversity be respected? Our answer is that the values underpinning state autonomy require that a certain degree of diversity be accommodated. Accordingly, in certain circumstances, the ECJ should defer to state courts for interpreting fundamental rights.[84] At the same time, this is not to argue against uniform supranational fundamental rights. The development of common supranational understandings should not be attempted, however, through the hierarchical imposition of ECJ standards. The commitment to the European integration process does not in itself justify homogenizing fundamental rights. Then, the question is how these rights should be constructed for the authority claim of the ECJ to be justified. As will be argued, rights should be interpreted through an ongoing dialogue between national and supranational courts. Dialogue offers a way of articulating diversity in a non-hierarchical manner, reaching

---

[81] For example, Sweden in 1972, Denmark in 1976, Greece in 1977, Germany in 1980. See the Opinion of Advocate General Tesauro, C-13/94, and the Opinion of Advocate General Ruiz-Jarabo Colomer, C-117/01.

[82] For example, Italy in 1982, Finland in 1988, Austria in 1996, Belgium in 1999.

[83] *P v S and Cornwall County Council*, C-13/94; *K.B. v National Health Service Pensions Agency and Secretary of State for Health*, C-117/01.

[84] As will be further developed in Chapter 6.

convergence over time. Thus, state diversity should be acknowledged in the process of norm construction, by taking into consideration state constitutional understandings in giving meaning to supranational rights. Also, state diversity should be acknowledged in the exercise of judicial authority, by deferring to state courts in certain circumstances. The EU constitutional structure, manifested throughout the Treaties, confirms that any model addressing fundamental rights adjudicative conflicts has to comply with a double aim: developing common understandings at the supranational level while respecting state constitutionalism (article 6 EU Treaty). Along these lines, the preamble of the Charter reads: 'The Union contributes to the preservation and to the development of these *common values* [human dignity, freedom, equality and solidarity] while *respecting the diversity* of cultures and traditions of the peoples of Europe as well as the national identities of the Member States' [emphasis added]. In short, the goal of any conceptual model to guide ECJ adjudication in its interaction with national courts should be building common understandings without neglecting to accommodate diversity.

PART III

Judicial Dialogue

5

Judicial Dialogue as the Source of Legitimacy of Supranational Adjudication

National legal orders generally provide rules for resolving conflicts between norms within the respective states. The European Union (EU), however, is not a unified system under a single constitution but a pluralist structure, constituted by distinct, yet interdependent, national and supranational legal orders. In cases of potential conflict, one should no longer insist on selecting the applicable norm, either constitutional or EU fundamental rights. Rather, the main inquiry should focus on the legitimacy of the European Court of Justice's (ECJ) claim of authority in adjudicating EU fundamental rights. The fact that the ECJ is a supranational court interpreting supranational rights that need to be followed by state courts, even if they clash with constitutional rights, poses particular problems for the ECJ's claim of authority. To be clear, the purpose here is not to undermine the authority of the ECJ as a judicial institution, but to explore the grounds for its legitimacy and the limits imposed on it when the ECJ adjudicates the meaning of fundamental rights. Given the EU pluralist structure, the regulative ideal of judicial dialogue might provide a conceptual model for the ECJ's legitimacy in adjudicating fundamental rights.

1 Legitimacy and authority

Legitimacy, an elusive concept, has been used and defined in a myriad of ways.[1] In this work, legitimacy refers to the justification of

[1] Daniel Bodansky, *The Legitimacy of International Governance: A Coming Challenge for International Environmental Law?*, 93 AMERICAN JOURNAL OF INTERNATIONAL LAW 596, 600–601, n 29 (1999).

authority: 'legitimate authority' means 'justified authority'.[2] In this vein, 'theories of legitimacy attempt to specify what factors might serve as justifications'[3] for the claim of authoritativeness. Legitimacy might refer to the authority of the law in general as well as to the authority of a specific legal text, such as the constitution. Also, legitimacy might refer to an institution, such as the legislature or the courts, as well as to decisions coming from those institutions. In this work, the inquiry focuses neither on the legitimacy of the EU legal system in general nor on the legitimacy of the ECJ as a judicial institution. Rather, it questions the legitimacy of the ECJ's decisions on fundamental rights.

The notion of legitimacy might be used in a normative or a descriptive sense.[4] For example, there is a difference between saying that ECJ interpretations are legitimate and saying that they are perceived as legitimate. In a normative sense, legitimacy refers to the conditions or reasons that justify the claim of authoritativeness. Normative legitimacy aims to determine why the law or a particular institution should be obeyed. What are the grounds that justify this claim to obedience? An institution or legal system is legitimate if it fulfils the specified conditions for legitimacy. On the other hand, in a descriptive sense, legitimacy implies that a legal system or institution is perceived as legitimately binding by those under its jurisdiction, thus making a justified claim to obedience. This notion was coined by Max Weber, who held that a social order was legitimate when it enjoyed 'the prestige of being considered binding'.[5] The belief in legitimate authority might be based on factors such as tradition, myth, demagoguery, or established democratic procedures. 'Legitimacy as an empirical fact only reports an attitude held by individuals or groups toward domination.'[6] Since it looks into the motives for obedience, this notion is empirical-psychological. Hence, obedience is not, in and of itself, a measure of (normative or descriptive) legitimacy. For example, I might obey a dictator's rules to avoid being executed.[7] According to the Weberian notion of legitimacy, a social order is

---

[2] *Id.* at 601.   [3] *Id.*

[4] For this distinction see Jens Steffek, *The Legitimation of International Governance: A Discourse Approach*, 9 EUROPEAN JOURNAL OF INTERNATIONAL RELATIONS 249, 253–254 (2003); Bodansky, *supra* n 1, at 601–603.

[5] Weber quoted in Steffek, *supra* n 4, at 253.   [6] *Id.*

[7] H. L. A. HART, THE CONCEPT OF LAW 82–88 (Oxford University Press 1997) remarking on the distinction between 'being obliged' to obey and 'having an obligation' to obey. One might 'be obliged' to obey without 'having an obligation' to do so.

only legitimate when it is obeyed for reasons based on the belief of its rightful binding force.[8]

As for the relationship between the normative and descriptive notions of legitimacy, an institution might be legitimate in a descriptive sense because it is obeyed on the basis of a perception of legitimacy, but it might not fulfil the conditions for normative legitimacy. For instance, this is the case when the perception of legitimacy is based on myth or demagoguery. In turn, if an institution fulfils the conditions for normative legitimacy, the perception of legitimacy might be enhanced. In other words, an institution might be perceived as legitimate (and obeyed) for the same reasons that make it normatively legitimate. For example, if a system is democratic (normative legitimacy), this fact may well give rise to a perception of legitimacy and foster obedience on the basis of that reason (descriptive legitimacy). The more a system or institution is perceived as legitimate, the more effective it is likely to be.[9] As such, legitimacy is certainly relevant for the effectiveness of an institution and the stability of a legal system. There is a widespread agreement among social and legal theorists that it would not be possible to secure the stability of a legal system solely on the basis of fear.[10]

We can also distinguish between a normative and a descriptive notion of authority. Authority is a relational notion in which one has a claim of obedience upon another.[11] From a normative perspective, an institution is authoritative when it ought to be obeyed, regardless of whether it is actually obeyed or not. Accordingly, the question to be answered is whether or not there are legitimate reasons that justify the claim of authoritativeness. From a descriptive perspective, an institution has authority when the rules or decisions emanating from it are actually obeyed by those to whom the rules or decisions are addressed. From this standpoint, whether an institution has authority or not is a factual question. Thus, it can be answered through the

[8] Steffek, *supra* n 4, at 254.
[9] MAX WEBER, I ECONOMY AND SOCIETY 31 (Bedminster Press 1968).
[10] TOM R. TYLER, WHY PEOPLE OBEY THE LAW 22 (Yale University Press 1990): 'It has been widely suggested that in democratic societies, the legal system cannot function if it can influence people only by manipulating rewards and costs'; Weber, *supra* n 9, at 31: 'An order which is adhered to from motives of pure expediency is generally much less stable than one upheld on a purely customary basis through the fact that the corresponding behavior has become habitual....But even this type of order is in turn much less stable than an order which enjoys the prestige of being considered binding, or, as it may be expressed, of "legitimacy".'
[11] Michael J. Perry, *The Authority of Text, Tradition, and Reason: A Theory of Constitutional 'Interpretation'*, 58 SOUTHERN CALIFORNIA LAW REVIEW 551, 553 (1985).

observation of facts in the world. What needs to be investigated is whether the conduct of those to whom the rules or decisions are addressed conforms to the commands contained in those rules or decisions. As for the relationship between normative and descriptive notions of authority, if an institution that has normative authority is not actually obeyed by the majority of those to whom it is addressed, the assertion that it has authority might be regarded as empty.[12] On the other hand, an institution that is obeyed, without being legitimate, such as a dictatorship, will be authoritarian, but not authoritative.

With reference to the notions of legitimacy and authority combined, normative legitimacy specifies the conditions for normative authority. An institution should be obeyed if it complies with the conditions that justify its power. On the other hand, descriptive legitimacy does not necessarily correspond with descriptive authority. An institution might be obeyed for reasons different from the belief in its rightful binding force, such as a fear of punishment or a cost-benefit rational calculation.[13] Therefore, an institution might have descriptive authority (if it is obeyed) but not descriptive legitimacy (if it is obeyed for reasons different from the belief in its legitimacy). Legitimacy describes only one specific class of reasons for rules' compliance.[14]

This work does not investigate whether the ECJ is actually obeyed by state courts,[15] nor the actual reasons for which state courts comply (or not) with ECJ rulings.[16] Instead, a normative perspective toward legitimacy and

---

[12] Hart, *supra* n 7.

[13] Tyler, *supra* n 10, at 3, distinguishing between an instrumental and a normative perspective on why people obey the law.

[14] For the distinction between compliance and legitimacy, see Steffek, *supra* n 4, at 254–255.

[15] The descriptive inquiry about state courts' compliance with ECJ rulings is pending. As some authors have noted, there is no comprehensive and systematic study about the reception of ECJ references by state courts. See Claire Kilpatrick, *Community or Communities of Courts in European Integration? Sex Equality Dialogues between UK Courts and the ECJ*, 4 EUROPEAN LAW JOURNAL 121 (1998).

[16] Political scientists have attempted to explain state courts' acceptance (or resistance) to specific ECJ doctrines, such as EU supremacy over state law. The most common explanations refer to rational calculations or judicial self-interest. See Walter Mattli & Anne-Marie Slaughter, *The Role of National Courts in the Process of European Integration: Accounting for Judicial Preference and Constraints*, in THE EUROPEAN COURT AND NATIONAL COURTS, DOCTRINE AND JURISPRUDENCE. LEGAL CHANGE IN ITS SOCIAL CONTEXT 253 (Anne-Marie Slaughter, Alec Stone Sweet & Joseph H. H. Weiler eds. 1998); KAREN ALTER, ESTABLISHING THE SUPREMACY OF EUROPEAN LAW. THE MAKING OF AN INTERNATIONAL RULE OF LAW IN EUROPE (Oxford University Press 2001).

authority is adopted. Hence, the purpose is to develop an account for the legitimacy of the ECJ's claim to authority regarding fundamental rights' adjudication. Given the weakness of traditional sources of judicial authority as applied to the ECJ, it is an important normative task to provide such an account.[17] At the outset, it should be kept in mind that the ECJ lacks enforcement powers to compel compliance with its decisions within the territory of the member states. In particular, ECJ decisions in preliminary rulings are binding upon state courts (article 234 EC Treaty). These are not just advisory opinions.[18] The ECJ, however, cannot make recourse to the legitimate use of force to secure compliance. Therefore, the ECJ needs the collaboration of state courts for its decisions to be effective.[19] Judicial authority might be justified on the basis of institutional virtues that judicial decisions might help realize. The particular mode of judicial decision-making might foster certain interests, such as the continuity of traditional social values or the stability of the political system, by securing the final settlement of questions about public values.[20] The institutional virtue of the ECJ's adjudication of fundamental rights, however, is not evident. The interest in securing the continuity of European values is problematic since in the EU there is a plurality of democratic societies each with their own values. Indeed, critics have raised a democratic concern regarding the ECJ's interpretive activity of fundamental rights because a lawful interpretation of rights within a democratic polity could be overridden by a supranational court's interpretation. With regard to the interest in stability, the ECJ's authority could be

[17] Lawrence R. Helfer & Anne-Marie Slaughter, *Toward a Theory of Effective Supranational Adjudication*, 107 YALE LAW JOURNAL 273, 285 (1997), arguing that international courts, given the lack of coercive powers, need to rely on factors such as 'their own legitimacy and the legitimacy of any particular judgment reached'; Jed Rubenfeld, *Legitimacy and Interpretation*, in CONSTITUTIONALISM. PHILOSOPHICAL FOUNDATIONS 194, 210 (Larry Alexander ed. 1998): 'Legitimacy is obviously not the only desideratum of law. Let us say that it is a necessary condition of law's acceptability.'

[18] The preliminary reference or preliminary ruling is the procedural mechanism through which national courts may send a question to the ECJ about the validity or interpretation of EU law. The ECJ has firmly reiterated the binding character of these decisions, such as in *Benedetti v Munari*, C-52/76: 'A preliminary ruling...is binding on the national court.' L. NEVILLE BROWN & FRANCIS G. JACOBS, THE COURT OF JUSTICE OF THE EUROPEAN COMMUNITIES 233 (Sweet & Maxwell 1983).

[19] MAURO CAPPELLETTI, THE JUDICIAL PROCESS IN COMPARATIVE PERSPECTIVE (Clarendon Press 1989): 'In practice...the Community system of review requires the co-operation and goodwill of the courts of the member states'; Joseph H. H. Weiler, *A Quiet Revolution. The European Court of Justice and its Interlocutors*, 26 COMPARATIVE POLITICAL STUDIES 510, 523 (1994): 'Without the cooperation of the national judiciary, the ECJ's power was illusory.'

[20] OWEN FISS, THE LAW AS IT COULD BE 165 (New York University Press 2003).

justified on the basis of securing the efficacy of EU law and ultimately the success of the integration process. Admittedly, this could be a good reason to assert the normative authority of the ECJ in general. However, the claim for normative authority based on stability has limits and needs to be refined. Otherwise, it could be used to justify a dictator's authority. In the context of ECJ rights adjudication, the value of stability is not enough to account for the legitimacy of interpretive decisions about fundamental rights. Indeed, instead of securing stability, the judicial imposition of supranational uniform standards might give rise to some degree of resistance and discontent among the states. At the same time, the normative authority of the ECJ cannot be based on the claim of having correctly applied a body of established legal rules that emanate from the ultimate sovereign (formal rationality). This claim cannot be sustained because the supremacy of EU law as an autonomous legal order trumping constitutional rights has not been definitively established in the Treaties or accepted by domestic courts. Moreover, since the meaning of fundamental rights is essentially contested, claiming to merely 'correctly apply' the law is not convincing. The adjudication of fundamental rights entails interpretation, which should not be viewed as a mechanical, non-creative activity.[21]

In sum, this inquiry focuses on the reasons that justify the ECJ's claim to authority in adjudicating fundamental rights from a normative standpoint. In this context, the ECJ cannot fully rely on sources of normative authority such as institutional virtue or formal rationality. The contention is that the legitimacy of ECJ fundamental rights' adjudication might be grounded in the ideal of dialogue. Some might agree on the legitimating potential of dialogue in the abstract, but it is still necessary to demonstrate how the ideal of dialogue might support the ECJ's claim to normative authority when adjudicating fundamental rights. This is not to deny other elements related to the same process of judicial decision-making that might bolster judicial legitimacy, such as impartiality or reasoned decision-making.[22] These elements that contribute to the legitimacy of judicial decisions in general are acknowledged, and they may actually be reinforced in a model of judicial dialogue. The implications of the dialectical ideal for judicial reasoning and the interpretive method will be explored in the next chapter.

---

[21] Owen Fiss, *Conventionalism*, 58 SOUTHERN CALIFORNIA LAW REVIEW 177, 178–182 (1985): 'It seems important... to recover the concept of interpretation and to avoid the mechanistic view of that activity. It seems important to understand that interpretation permits the judge or reader a creative role.'

[22] Helfer & Slaughter, *supra* n 17, at 284.

2 The turn to dialogue as a source of legitimacy

In the last decades, constitutional and democratic theories have increasingly embraced a dialogic ideal, which emerged in the realm of moral and
political philosophy. The communitarian and postmodern critiques of
liberalism and modernity have presided over this turn to dialogue. The
postmodernist critique, as Stephen A. Gardbaum put it, consists of the
'rejection of the enlightenment faith in foundationalist and universalistic
modes of normative argument in favor of discourse ethics, hermeneutic
understanding and contextualism'.[23] Generally speaking, postmodernism involves a move from universal and ultimate truths to particular and
evolving truths. Moreover, it emphasizes dialogue as a means of reaching
knowledge. In turn, the communitarian critique encompasses a variety
of claims,[24] some of which seek to rethink main tenets of liberalism, such
as the concept of the individual, the source of values, and the neutrality
principle, without necessarily rejecting the liberal paradigm. In particular, communitarianism insists that values are constituted at the level of
community. In this vein, the context of particular historical communities
becomes crucial for the validity of normative claims. Normative orders are
neither derived from universal and timeless truths nor totally subjective.
Instead, values are intersubjectively constituted within specific communities. This approach does not imply abandoning rationality. Rationality
adopts the form of 'communicative rationality' as a dialogue or discourse
oriented toward understanding.[25] The concept of community as the locus
for bounded rational discourse and the epistemological and legitimating
value of dialogue have reached a central position in political philosophy
as well as constitutional and democratic theory. According to Drucilla
Cornell, 'dialogic reciprocity' might constitute the regulative ideal at the
basis of the normative authority of law.[26] Bruce Ackerman emphasizes
the value of dialogue as the means to justify the principles of the liberal

---

[23] Stephen A. Gardbaum, *Law, Politics and the Claims of Community*, 90 MICHIGAN LAW REVIEW
685, 689 (1992).

[24] *Id.* for a detailed analysis of the several communitarian claims.

[25] JÜRGEN HABERMAS, THE THEORY OF COMMUNICATIVE ACTION 285–288 (Beacon Press 1984);
JOHN S. DRYZEK, DELIBERATIVE DEMOCRACY AND BEYOND. LIBERALS, CRITICS, CONTESTATIONS
21–22 (Oxford University Press 2000).

[26] Drucilla Cornell, *Two Lectures on the Normative Dimensions of Community in the Law*, 54
TENNESSEE LAW REVIEW 327 (1997).

state[27] and conceives (neutral) dialogue as the first obligation of citizens.[28] Constitutional theory has stressed the importance of dialogue in providing the grounds for the legitimacy of law's normative claim to obedience. Basically, dialogue occupies a central role in the thinking of the so-called new republicans. The institutional location of dialogue varies from the people's representatives in Cass R. Sunstein's account,[29] to the Supreme Court justices in Frank I. Michelman's,[30] or to the people acting in constitutional moments, as interpreted by the Supreme Court, in Ackerman's.[31]

Dialogue is at the core of the deliberative turn in democratic theory. Jürgen Habermas shaped a new paradigm of deliberative democracy grounded on the theory of discourse, which he developed in previous writings.[32] This scholar advocated the 'discourse principle' for the impartial justification of norms. This discourse principle establishes that 'just those action norms are valid to which all possibly affected persons could agree as participants in rational discourses'.[33] According to Habermas, consensus is only a measure

---

[27] BRUCE ACKERMAN, SOCIAL JUSTICE IN THE LIBERAL STATE 361 (Yale University Press 1980): 'Liberalism's ultimate justification is to be found in its strategic location in a web of talk that converges upon it from every direction.'

[28] Bruce Ackerman, *Why Dialogue?*, 86 THE JOURNAL OF PHILOSOPHY 5 (1989).

[29] Cass R. Sunstein, *Beyond the Republican Revival*, 97 YALE LAW JOURNAL 1539, 1589 (1988); Cass R. Sunstein, *Interest Groups in American Public Law*, 38 STANFORD LAW REVIEW 29, 41 (1985): 'The representatives of the people would be free to engage in a process of discussion and debate from which the common good would emerge.'

[30] Frank I. Michelman, *Traces of Self-Government*, 100 HARVARD LAW REVIEW 4, 74–76 (1986), arguing for the need of dialogue in providing legitimacy: 'Every norm, every time, requires explanation and justification in context. As we have seen, the task calls for practical reason, and practical reason involves dialogue.... The courts and especially the Supreme Court, seem to take on as one of their adscribed functions the modeling of active self-government that citizens find practically beyond reach. Unable as a nation to practice our own self-government (in the full, positive sense), we—or at any rate we of "the reasoning class"—can at least identify with the judiciary's as we idealistically construct it.'

[31] BRUCE ACKERMAN, WE THE PEOPLE: FOUNDATIONS (Harvard University Press 1993). For a critique of all these accounts relying on the concept of a discursive community, see Paul W. Kahn, *Community in Contemporary Constitutional Theory*, 99 YALE LAW JOURNAL 1 (1990).

[32] JÜRGEN HABERMAS, BETWEEN FACTS AND NORMS (MIT Press 1998).

[33] *Id.* at 107–110. Action norms include both moral and legal norms. The discourse principle, which 'is only intended to explain the point of view from which norms of action can be *impartially justified*', branches into the moral and the democratic principle. In this book, Habermas wants to distinguish between both of them: 'The moral principle first results when one specifies the general discourse principle for those norms that can be justified if and *only* if equal consideration is given to the interests of all those who are possibly involved. The principle of democracy results from a corresponding specification for those action norms that appear in legal form. Such norms can be justified by calling on pragmatic, ethical-political, and moral reasons—here justification is not restricted to moral reasons alone.' Focusing on the democratic principle, he states: 'The

of validity if achieved in an ideal speech situation.[34] This author recognizes
that the ideal speech situation cannot be realized, given the realistic constraints of time and space.[35] Still, it provides a critical standard; that is, it
functions as a counterfactual to test actual consensus.[36] Habermas affirms
the possibility of establishing institutional measures, such as legislative and
judicial procedures,[37] in order to approximate the conditions for rational
discourse.[38] Others have pursued this strand of deliberative democracy and
have continued to expand upon Habermas's discursive framework in somewhat diverging directions.[39] Several scholars have advocated forms of dialogue or deliberation as the source of law's legitimacy, without necessarily
embracing Habermas's views about a universal consensus reached in an ideal
speech situation, which are at the core of his philosophical account of the
'correctness' of norms. Broadly speaking, deliberative democracy opposes
an aggregative notion of democracy and claims that 'democratic legitimacy
should be sought...in the ability of all individuals subject to a collective
decision to engage in authentic deliberation about that decision. These individuals should accept the decision only if it could be justified to them in
convincing terms.'[40] Finally, some authors concerned about the legitimacy
of international governance claim to apply Habermas's discourse theory to
the analysis of processes of communication and deliberation as the source

principle of democracy should establish a procedure of legitimate lawmaking....The democratic principle states that only those statutes may claim legitimacy that can meet with the assent
of all citizens in a discursive process of legislation that in turn has been legally constituted.'

[34] Habermas quoted in ROBERT ALEXY, A THEORY OF LEGAL ARGUMENTATION. THE THEORY OF
RATIONAL DISCOURSE AS THEORY OF LEGAL JUSTIFICATION 119 (Clarendon Press 1989), defined
the ideal speech situation as a situation in which 'communication in it is hampered neither by
external contingent factors, nor by constraints which are internal to the structure of communication itself'.

[35] JÜRGEN HABERMAS, MORAL CONSCIOUSNESS AND COMMUNICATIVE ACTION 92 (MIT Press
1990).

[36] Habermas in Alexy, *supra* n 34, at 122, claimed that the ideal speech situation 'provides a
critical standard for questioning and testing whether any actual consensus is a sufficient indica-
tor for a well-founded consensus'.

[37] Habermas, *supra* n 32, at 234: 'Like democratic procedures in the area of legislation,
rules of court procedure in the area of legal application are meant to compensate for the fal-
libility and decisional uncertainty resulting from the fact that the demanding communicative
presuppositions of rational discourses can only be approximately fulfilled.'

[38] Habermas, *supra* n 35, at 92.

[39] See, among others, CARLOS SANTIAGO NINO, THE CONSTITUTION OF DELIBERATIVE
DEMOCRACY (Yale University Press 1996); JON ELSTER (ed.) DELIBERATIVE DEMOCRACY
(Cambridge University Press 1998); Dryzek, *supra* n 25.

[40] *Id.*, at v.

of legitimacy for international law. Jens Steffek argues that the prevailing mechanism of legitimation in international governance consists of a process of communication and asserts that 'the legitimacy of international governance is established and challenged through a rational discourse'.[41] Others explore how '[Habermas's] "discourse ethics" might be employed to construct a legitimate international order'.[42] In spite of anchoring their approaches in Habermas, these authors tend to focus on the benefits of deliberation as a rational exchange of arguments from the standpoint of the outcome's legitimacy, without necessarily embracing Habermas's larger political-philosophical theory. In this work, the turn to dialogue as a source of legitimacy is associated with the particular pluralist structure of the EU—neither a single state nor a mere constellation of sovereign states. The ideal of dialogue seeks to provide a conceptual model for the normative authority of ECJ fundamental rights' adjudication in this unprecedented mode of polity.

3   Dialogue in the European Union. A variety of claims

The term 'dialogue' and a variety of related words such as 'conversation', 'discussion', and 'discourse' are employed interchangeably and extensively in EU academic literature. Such a prolific and ambiguous use has worked to mystify the meaning of 'dialogue'. The dialogic claim might be descriptive, explanatory, or normative. In a descriptive sense, dialogue depicts the interaction between the ECJ and state courts through the preliminary reference, the mechanism through which state courts may send a question to the ECJ regarding the validity or interpretation of EU law.[43] This literature has focused on ECJ doctrinal outputs and the implications for the national legal systems. Broadly, in the political science literature, dialogue plays a central role in explaining the 'constitutionalization' of the EU legal system.[44] Landmark outcomes for the EU constitutional system, such as

---

[41]   Steffek, *supra* n 4, at 271.

[42]   Rodger A. Payne & Nayef H. Samhat, Democratizing Global Politics 19, 24 (State University of New York Press 2004).

[43]   Eric Stein, *Lawyers, Judges, and the Making of a Transnational Constitution*, 75 American Journal of International Law 1 (1981).

[44]   Alec Stone Sweet, *Constitutional Dialogues in the European Community*, in The European Court and National Courts, Doctrine and Jurisprudence. Legal Change in its Social Context 305 (Anne-Marie Slaughter, Alec Stone Sweet & Joseph H.H. Weiler eds. 1998): 'The construction of a constitutional, "rule of law" Community has been a participatory process, a set of constitutional dialogues between supra-national and national judges.'

the acceptance of the supremacy principle of EU law over ordinary state law by domestic courts[45] or the judicial development of a catalogue of EU fundamental rights,[46] are the result of dialogue between supranational and national courts. This literature has articulated varying accounts of judicial behaviour that attempted to explain the patterns of resistance and compliance within such judicial interaction. These accounts might be classified as neo-realist, which portray courts as delegates of state governments voicing national interests,[47] or neo-functionalist, which focus on judicial self-empowerment[48] or other judicial interests.[49] With regard to fundamental rights, the analyses tend to be limited to early cases and to explain the reasons why the ECJ elaborated a catalogue of fundamental rights through its case law (after initially resisting this).[50] The most common explanation relies on the ECJ interest in protecting the supremacy of EU law against the threats posed by several state constitutional courts.[51] Political science

[45] See Marta Cartabia, *The Italian Constitutional Court and the Relationship Between the Italian Legal System and the European Union*, in THE EUROPEAN COURT AND NATIONAL COURTS, DOCTRINE AND JURISPRUDENCE. LEGAL CHANGE IN ITS SOCIAL CONTEXT 133, 135–137 (Anne-Marie Slaughter, Alec Stone Sweet & Joseph H. H. Weiler eds. 1998); Stone Sweet *supra* n 44.

[46] In this field, the main interactions occurred between the ECJ and German courts, see Juliane Kokott, *Report on Germany*, in THE EUROPEAN COURT AND NATIONAL COURTS, DOCTRINE AND JURISPRUDENCE. LEGAL CHANGE IN ITS SOCIAL CONTEXT 77 (Anne-Marie Slaughter, Alec Stone Sweet & Joseph H.H. Weiler eds. 1998).

[47] Geoffrey Garrett, *International Cooperation and Institutional Choice: The EC's Internal Market*, 46 INTERNATIONAL ORGANIZATION 533 (1992); Geoffrey Garret, *The Politics of Legal Integration in the European Union*, 49 INTERNATIONAL ORGANIZATION 171 (1995); MARY L. VOLCANSEK, JUDICIAL POLITICS IN EUROPE (Peter Lang 1986).

[48] Weiler, *supra* n 19, at 523; Anne-Marie Burley & Walter Mattli, *Europe Before the Court: A Political Theory of Legal Integration*, 47 INTERNATIONAL ORGANIZATION 41 (1993); Mattli & Slaughter, *supra* n 16, at 253, 258, offering a more refined notion of 'judicial empowerment'.

[49] Karen Alter, *Explaining National Court Acceptance of European Court Jurisprudence: A Critical Evaluation of Theories of Legal Integration*, in THE EUROPEAN COURT AND NATIONAL COURTS, DOCTRINE AND JURISPRUDENCE. LEGAL CHANGE IN ITS SOCIAL CONTEXT 227, 241–246 (Anne-Marie Slaughter, Alec Stone Sweet & Joseph H.H. Weiler eds. 1998); Alter, *supra* n 16, at 45: 'Judges are primarily interested in promoting their independence, influence and authority.' She differentiates herself from neo-functionalists, redefining the content of judicial interests and emphasizing the competition between lower and higher courts within the same judicial system to explain the patterns of acceptance and resistance to EU law.

[50] *Friedrich Stork & Cie v High Authority of the European Coal and Steel Community*, C-1/58; *Präsident Ruhrkolen-Verkaufsgesellschaft mbH, Geitling Ruhrkohlen-Verkaufsgesellschaft mbH, Mausegatt Ruhrkohlen-Verkaufsgesellschaft mbH and I. Nold KG v High Authority of the European Coal and Steel Community*, C-36, 37, 38, and 40/59.

[51] Joseph H. H. Weiler, *Eurocracy and Distrust: Some Questions Concerning the Role of the European Court of Justice in the Protection of Fundamental Rights within the Legal Order on the European Communities*, 61 WASHINGTON LAW REVIEW 1103, 1118–1119 (1986).

studies provide enlightening accounts regarding the evolution of the EU legal order. This literature reminds us of the need to be aware of factors external to the law shaping judicial behaviour. There is no agreement in the literature, however, about how best to explain judicial behaviour in the EU, and the several existing accounts remain contested. In addition, these analyses occasionally oversimplify the terms of the interaction between national and supranational courts. Several critics have claimed that they are limited in their scope and unable adequately to depict judicial interaction in the EU.[52] It is further argued that in order to understand how the legal system evolves on the basis of dialogue between courts, there is a need to shift the focus from the ECJ to state courts since the actual reception of ECJ rulings by state courts remains very much unknown.[53] The mere number of preliminary references is taken by some studies as a measure of the willingness to co-operate and accept EU law, but this is not necessarily the case.[54] In any event, it is not the goal here to supply a theory that explains EU integration by the judiciary, nor to conduct an empirical study of the interaction between national courts and the ECJ regarding fundamental rights, but rather to establish a normative basis for the ECJ's authority in managing fundamental rights conflicts.

Political science studies tend to leave aside the normative dimension of dialogue and avoid engaging questions of legitimacy. The following pages will claim that, and explore how, the ideal of dialogue might provide a normative account for the legitimacy of court-based fundamental rights norms. Some scholars have pointed out the legitimating potential of dialogue, but these accounts have remained underdeveloped, under-theorized, limited in their scope.[55] The legitimating potential of dialogue cannot simply be

[52] Kilpatrick, *supra* n 15, at 145–146: 'Close analysis of a particular substantive area seriously challenges the explanatory capacity of intergovernmentalism and various neofunctionalist inspired integration theories—both empirically and normatively.'

[53] The compilation of national reports by ANNE-MARIE SLAUGHTER, ALEC STONE SWEET, JOSEPH H. H. WEILER (eds.), THE EUROPEAN COURT AND NATIONAL COURTS, DOCTRINE AND JURISPRUDENCE. LEGAL CHANGE IN ITS SOCIAL CONTEXT (Hart Publishing 2000), first published in 1998, is still the reference text.

[54] Kilpatrick, *supra* n 15, at 128, claiming: 'Without examining in more detail what courts do when they do make a reference in the context of the development of a specific policy area, it is difficult to know whether a reference straightforwardly represents a willingness to co-operate and accept EC law.'

[55] Miguel Poiares Maduro, *Las Formas del Poder Constitucional de la Unión Europea*, 119 REVISTA DE ESTUDIOS POLÍTICOS 11, 31, 27 (2003). Maduro's account deserves attention. He argues that dialogue may well be the basis for the legitimacy of the European legal order. He uses dialogue in both senses, explanatory and normative, sometimes conflating both uses.

derived from the observation of instances of communication between the ECJ and national courts, as this happens to be the way in which certain doctrines have evolved in the EU. There is a need for a theoretical account demonstrating how the ideal of dialogue might provide the grounds for the legitimacy of ECJ adjudicative decisions. Such a theory of normative legitimacy would serve as a model to assess the activity of the ECJ, that is, as a tool to critique institutional practices as well as to guide judicial action.

4 Dialogue as the source of the ECJ's legitimacy in adjudicating fundamental rights

The contention of judicial dialogue as the regulative ideal supporting the ECJ's normative authority in the interpretation of fundamental rights requires justification. How can the ideal of dialogue potentially render ECJ judicial decisions interpreting fundamental rights legitimate? This analysis adopts a constructivist approach to rights interpretation. The legitimacy of norms protecting rights cannot be verified through correspondence with something 'out there'.[56] As such, the meaning of fundamental rights is not a

---

Maduro argues that the EU's legitimacy is found in a bottom-up construction, not just because the ECJ needs the collaboration of national courts for the enforcement and efficacy of EU law, but also because national courts and other actors have the chance to shape the interpretation and application of EU law. In this way, the interpretive outcome is the result of the collaboration of different participants in the community, and not just the ECJ. The notion that participation in the interpretive process legitimates EU law intuitively has merit, but he does not elaborate fully on this. In addition, the principles that constitute his framework are formulated at a very abstract level and their application to actual judicial practice is utopian. Thomas de la Mare, *Article 177 in Social and Political Context*, in THE EVOLUTION OF EU LAW (Paul Craig & Gráinne de Búrca eds. 1999), indicates the normative force of dialogue through the preliminary reference and examines some insights from discourse theory. The ideal of dialogue also appears in seminal form in Neil Walker, *Flexibility within a Metaconstitutional Frame: Reflections on the Future of Legal Authority in Europe*, in CONSTITUTIONAL CHANGE IN THE EU. FROM UNIFORMITY TO FLEXIBILITY? 9, 26–29 (Gráinne de Búrca & Joanne Scott eds. 2000). He argues that constitutional pluralism can open for a dialogic approach and fuller processes of legitimation. However, it is not clear what this dialogue would consist of. Anne-Marie Slaughter, *A Typology of Transjudicial Communication*, 29 UNIVERSITY OF RICHMOND LAW REVIEW 99 (1994), refers to the function of judicial communication as enhancing legitimacy, but she does not further elaborate.

[56] Habermas, *supra* n 32, at 226: 'One cannot explain the rightness of normative judgments along the lines of a correspondence theory of truth, for rights are a social construction.'

truth to be discovered through a process of individual reasoning.[57] This view implies the rejection of objectivism (or determinism) since the correctness of an interpretation does not depend on the discovery of a universal truth. This view, however, does not compel one to accept that the interpretation of rights cannot be constrained and that interpreters are free in their activity (subjectivism).[58] This dichotomy between determinism and subjectivism, pervasive in political and moral philosophy as well as in debates concerning legal interpretation, needs to be overcome.[59] Hence, the role of the ECJ in the interpretation of EU fundamental rights does not consist in finding the truth about the meaning of fundamental rights, nor is the ECJ free to attribute any meaning to these rights. Thus, the question is how adjudicative decisions on fundamental rights can be justified. In other words, what are the grounds for the legitimacy of the supranational adjudication of fundamental rights norms? It should be kept in mind that the quest for legitimacy refers to the project of building (and justifying) norms that contain fundamental rights for a supranational community whose constituting members are democratic states. Each member state interprets these rights on the basis of the state constitution and the corresponding state constitutional sources. Given the EU political structure, the ECJ should engage in dialogue with state courts in an attempt to fashion an interpretation that all could rationally agree upon (not that they actually do at the moment). To ground legitimacy in the participatory nature of a dialogic process in order to reach the best-reasoned interpretation reflects equal respect for the community members' constitutional identities. To be more specific, dialogue among national and supranational courts might provide legitimacy for interpretive decisions because argumentative communication based upon the exchange of reasons furthers better-reasoned outcomes for the community as a whole. Also, dialogue enhances participation by all members in the interpretive process in such a way that the interpretation given might be regarded as a shared outcome. Additionally, dialogue benefits the building

---

[57] Paul W. Kahn, *Interpretation and Authority in State Constitutionalism*, 106 HARVARD LAW REVIEW 1147, 1147–1148 (1993), claims that 'constitutionalism is not a single set of truths, but an ongoing debate about the meaning of the rule of law in a democratic political order'.

[58] Fiss, *supra* n 21, at 183–184: 'The interpretive process—whether it be of a specific clause or a highly general one, like equal protection—is neither wholly determined nor wholly free, but it is constrained.'

[59] Gardbaum, *supra* n 23, at 706: 'The communitarian view seeks to transcend the traditional epistemological dichotomy of either objectivism or subjectivism; that is, either values are "out there" or else they are simply personal preferences. It does so by means of the notion of the intersubjective constitution of value.'

of a common identity and is the most consistent form of interaction within a pluralist framework.[60]

Obviously, the ECJ cannot enter into simultaneous dialogue, at the same time and in the same place, with all member state courts for an unlimited period of time until a consensus is reached. The argument for dialogue as a regulative ideal is not made from the standpoint of an 'ideal speech situation', which can never be realized. Instead, dialogue needs to be conceived as evolving over time. Judicial dialogue in the EU will develop in a fragmented manner since the exchanges of arguments among supranational and national courts occur case by case. Dialogue should be viewed diachronically, rather than synchronically, ie, as a single occasion of interaction. As dialogue unfolds among courts from other states and new arguments are brought to the floor, the interpretation of fundamental rights will be tested and refined continuously. The interpretive outcome is never fixed. Since discourse develops in a fragmented form under conditions that are not ideal, there is always the opportunity to review previous interpretations in light of better arguments.[61] Only over time, as more conversations take place, will it be possible to reach a broad consensus. Dialogue cannot determine the substantive outcome in advance. It will always depend on the particular community in which it takes place.

The obvious shortcoming of a dialectical model is the persistence of a certain degree of indeterminacy, but this is not necessarily dysfunctional. Dialogue is actually driven by the potential for conflict, which furthers the exchange of arguments in order to reach better-reasoned outcomes for the community as a whole. As Sunstein emphasizes, 'In law, as in politics, disagreement can be a productive and creative force, revealing error, showing gaps, moving discussion and results in good directions.'[62] Dialogue does not work to eliminate conflict, but rather it manages conflict over time in a process of constant 'mutual accommodation'.[63] Properly managed through dialogue, the potential for conflict offers the opportunity to reach interpretive outcomes at

---

[60] These arguments are further developed below.

[61] De la Mare, *supra* n 55, n 127: 'Results are always reviewable, since factual reality and the imperfections inherent in legal discourse make them essentially contestable.'

[62] CASS R. SUNSTEIN, LEGAL REASONING AND POLITICAL CONFLICT 58 (Oxford University Press 1996).

[63] Damian Chalmers, *The Dynamics of Judicial Authority and the Constitutional Treaty*, in Jospeh H. H. Weiler & Christopher L. Eisgruber (eds), ALTNEULAND: THE EU CONSTITUTION IN A CONTEXTUAL PERSPECTIVE, Jean Monnet Working Paper 5/04, http://www.jeanmonnet program.org/papers/04/040501–14.html.

the supranational level that can better accommodate the values and sensibilities of all participants. It is enough for the purposes of managing conflict and reaching common understandings in the EU that there is agreement on the outcome. Participants may arrive at the same conclusion for different reasons, as long as the reasons can stand up to deliberative scrutiny.[64] The reasons of others might be acknowledged, but not shared, in order to reach mutually accepted outcomes.[65] Given the presence of pluralism and diversity in the EU, this kind of agreement permits commonality 'without producing unnecessary antagonism'.[66] Finally, the best-reasoned outcome is not necessarily a uniform interpretation. In some instances, the best outcome would entail deferring the interpretive decision to the states. For reasons delineated in the previous chapter, diversity should not just be obliterated. Exchanging arguments over time might work as a source of convergence, without excluding diversity.

4.1 *The case for judicial dialogue*

As argued, interpreting fundamental rights does not include finding universal truths. Instead, their meanings should be woven into the fabrics of established communities. Consistently, the legitimating potential of dialogue mainly resides in two features. First, judicial dialogue, as an ongoing exchange of arguments, is a means to reach better-reasoned outcomes for the community as a whole. Secondly, judicial dialogue promotes participation in interpretive activity so that the outcome emerges from a collective communicative enterprise. In addition, from a broader perspective, dialogue contributes to building a common 'constitutional identity' for this

---

[64] Dryzek, *supra* n 25, at 48.

[65] A Habermasian consensus requires not only agreement on a certain outcome, but also agreement on the reasons supporting it. Habermas, *supra* n 32, at 166: 'Rationally motivated consensus rests on reasons that convince all parties *in the same way*'. In contrast, the Rawlsian overlapping consensus does not require agreement on the reasons supporting it; the consensus about the political conception is endorsed by different reasonable doctrines 'each from its own point of view'. John Rawls, Political Liberalism 134 (Columbia University Press 1995).

[66] Sunstein, *supra* n 62, at 5, argued that in a context of disagreement and pluralism, judges try to produce what he called 'incompletely theorized agreements', in the sense that 'the relevant participants are clear on the result without agreeing on the most general theory that accounts for it'. The possibility of reaching agreements on particular outcomes without agreeing on the general theory has advantages for reaching social stability and demonstrates mutual respect, civility, and reciprocity. Cass R. Sunstein, *Incompletely Theorized Agreements*, 108 Harvard Law Review 1733, 1746–1751 (1995), claimed that incompletely theorized agreements were a 'device for producing convergence despite disagreement, uncertainty, limits of time and capacity and heterogeneity'.

supranational community through an ongoing discussion on the meaning of shared fundamental rights. Ultimately, given the EU pluralist framework, dialogue provides the best regulative model for the dynamic interaction between national and supranational systems regarding fundamental rights adjudication.

4.1.1 *Better-reasoned interpretive outcomes*

Dialogue is a form of communication consisting of an exchange of arguments in order to reach common understandings. Some features, endogenous to the practice of dialogue, work to improve the quality of the decisions and obtain better-reasoned outcomes for the general community. First, dialogue brings to the fore information about the views and concerns of the participants.[67] Communication between national and supranational courts thus promotes knowledge and sustains a better understanding of competing interests and values at different levels of governance. Usually, fundamental rights norms reflect the essential political and social values of the community in which they are applied. Thus, by entering into dialogue with national courts, the ECJ might better understand their claims and underlying motivations.[68] This is relevant since the ECJ aims to put forward an interpretation upon which all could agree. Achieving this goal would be difficult if differing views were ignored or wrongly understood. In this vein, as the interlocutors have the possibility to check the arguments expounded by others, dialogue facilitates detecting mistakes or misunderstandings about factual or normative claims.[69] At the same time, courts contrasting their claims with those of other courts enhance self-understanding of their respective interpretations, thus permitting them to revise these interpretations with added insights.

Secondly, dialogue brings together distinct voices and enriches the debate with participants adding arguments not thought of by others.[70] By coming together, they might come up with new possibilities and solutions.[71] The exchange of arguments expressing distinct views furthers innovation. In the

---

[67] James D. Fearon, *Deliberation as Discussion*, in DELIBERATIVE DEMOCRACY 44 (Jon Elster ed. 1998).
[68] Nino, *supra* n 39, at 119.   [69] *Id.* at 124.
[70] Kahn, *supra* n 57, at 1155, favouring state-federal dialogue in the US regarding the interpretation of the constitution, writes: 'When there is only a single view of the possibilities of law, the meaning of the constitutional order is impoverished.'
[71] Fearon, *supra* n 67, at 49–50, Diego Gambetta, *'Claro!:' An Essay on Discursive Machismo*, in DELIBERATIVE DEMOCRACY 19, 22 (Jon Elster ed. 1998).

EU, the voices coming from state and supranational courts reflect different experiences and viewpoints, which are grounded in their different institutional roles and positions in the overall system. Thus, judicial dialogue enriches the debate regarding the meaning of fundamental rights by bringing a plurality of voices and, more importantly, differing national and supranational perspectives to the debate.

Thirdly, engaging in dialogue forces courts to justify the sustained interpretation and respond to the arguments advanced by others. The need to give reasons and the fact that all participants' assertions are subject to scrutiny promotes a particular mode of justification, which might dilute self-interested claims and advance impartiality.[72] Although courts might have their own policy interests, they are compelled to present their views in the form of legal principles and arguments to persuade others that a particular interpretation is the best outcome for the community as a whole.[73]

4.1.2 *Participation*

Dialogue contributes to the normative legitimacy of the outcome because it gives participants the opportunity to offer input on the interpretive decision and to regard the interpretation as a shared result. The right to have a say before a decision is rendered is generally regarded as a condition ensuring the fairness of binding norms. In the EU, state courts are given the possibility to talk directly to the ECJ regarding the interpretation of rights through the preliminary reference. The possibility of participation is a necessary condition for the legitimacy of the outcome, but it is not sufficient. The ECJ could merely ignore national judicial voices in the interpretation of EU rights. For the sake of the legitimacy of its interpretive decisions, the ECJ ought to be responsive to the different arguments brought before this Court, signalling to the participants that 'they have been heard and recognized as important participants in the debate whose arguments must be answered'.[74] ECJ judgments need to show how the competing arguments are weighed and how

---

[72] Jon Elster, *Strategic Uses of Argument*, in BARRIERS TO CONFLICT RESOLUTION 237, 250 (Kenneth Arrow et al. eds. 1995); Fearon, *supra* n 67, at 53–54; Gambetta, *supra* n 71, at 23. This argument will be further developed below.

[73] Payne & Samhat, *supra* n 42, at 20–21 (State University of New York Press 2004): 'The veracity of self-interested claims can be challenged by any participant in a dialogue, which should encourage everyone to offer ideas and arguments geared toward achieving communicative consensus.... Because deliberations are inclusive, public, and oriented towards consensus, at least some participants in a discussion should be able to provide good reasons to challenge and reject deceptive or self-serving arguments.'

[74] Helfer & Slaughter, *supra* n 17, at 321.

the interpretive decision is justified. In the words of Joseph H. H. Weiler, 'Especially in its Constitutional jurisprudence it is crucial that the Court demonstrate in its judgments that national sensibilities were fully taken into account.'[75]

In addition, the intersubjective construction of meaning through dialogue allows participants to see the outcome as the result of a collective enterprise.[76] In this vein, the importance of a real dialogue between national and supranational courts, as opposed to a monological reflection by the ECJ, can be appraised. The inquiry about the interpretation of fundamental rights at the supranational level does not adopt the perspective of a Rawlsian original position, in which the participants are unaware of their identities and positions in society.[77] The members of the EU supranational community are constitutional polities with their own constitutional identities and cultures. State courts enter into the debate with this baggage. Dialogue allows them to voice their claims and see if their arguments are answered in convincing terms. In turn, dialogue allows the ECJ to better accommodate the claims of a diverse community and offer an interpretation that state courts might embrace as reasonable, even if not coincident with their originally preferred outcome.[78]

Hence, if participation is guaranteed, those affected by EU fundamental rights norms might be inclined to support the interpretive results as fair. In this way, participation through dialogue in interpreting fundamental rights

[75] Joseph H. H. Weiler, *Epilogue: The Judicial Après Nice*, in THE EUROPEAN COURT OF JUSTICE 215, 225 (Gráinne de Búrca & Joseph H.H. Weiler eds. 2001).

[76] Habermas, *supra* n 35, at 67: 'What is needed is a "real" process of argumentation in which the individuals concerned cooperate. Only an intersubjective process of reaching understanding can produce an agreement that is reflexive in nature; only it can give the participants the knowledge that they have collectively become convinced of something.'

[77] In that situation, there is not such a need for a 'real' dialogic interaction because the principles of justice can be reached through individual reflection. Habermas, *supra* n 35, at 66: 'Rawls wants to ensure impartial consideration of all affected interests by putting the moral judge into a fictitious "original position"...Rawls operationalizes the standpoint of impartiality in such a way that every individual can undertake to justify basic norms on his own.' In this vein, Dryzek, *supra* n 25, at 15, also notes the lack of a thick interactive communication in Rawls's conception of public reason: 'Rawls downplays the *social* or interactive aspect of deliberation, meaning that public reason can be undertaken by the solitary thinker. This is deliberation of a sort—but only in terms of the weighing of arguments in the mind, not testing them in real political interaction.'

[78] Fearon, *supra* n 67, at 62, explained: 'Discussion rather than private deliberation would be necessary to "put on the table" the various reasons and arguments that different individuals had in mind, and thus to ensure that no one could see the end result as arbitrary rather than reasonable and justifiable, even if not what he or she happened to see as *most* justifiable.'

not only contributes to the legitimacy of the interpretive outcome, it also helps to generate a perception of legitimacy among those bound by these decisions. This perception, as argued before, is relevant for the effectiveness of norms. Hence, the participatory nature of the process of interpretation and the synthetic nature of outcomes may well enhance compliance.[79] To conclude, co-operation in the construction of supranational rights through dialogue would contribute to the legitimacy of the ECJ's interpretive decisions. As such, the interpretive outcome is not a sole product reached in solitude by the ECJ and imposed through a top-down process. Rather, the interpretive outcome is the product of the community, built through a bottom-up process that gives voice to state courts.[80]

4.1.3 *Identity building*

Several scholars have explored dialogue's potential for individual as well as community identity building.[81] As James A. Gardner put it, 'Any type of discourse is a means of debating the identity—the internal roles, relations and ethos—of the community in which it occurs.'[82] In particular, fundamental rights make up part of the constitutional identity of a polity. These rights encapsulate the values that are deemed to be basic in every society. The meaning attributed to them reflects and, at the same time, is constitutive of the identity of individuals and the polity itself.

In the EU context, dialogue's potential for identity building is predicated on a supranational community whose constitutive parts are constitutional polities. For the purposes of building a supranational common identity, it is not enough to create a supranational catalogue of rights. Rather, the key is how these rights are to be interpreted. The authoritarian imposition of supranational uniformity might have a divisive potential, fostering resistance and the reassertion of national identity. In contrast,

---

[79] De la Mare, *supra* n 55, at 242, asserted: 'From a compliance or loyalty perspective, discourse theory helps explain why results mediated through such a participatory and embracing procedure may have a normative pull. It is the synthetic and participatory nature of the resulting norms (for instance fundamental rights based on common constitutional traditions that are recognizable in part to every participant...) that is one of the strengths of EC law.'

[80] Maduro, *supra* n 55, at 27, 31.

[81] Kahn, *supra* n 31, at 5: 'We create and maintain our personal identity in the very same process by which communal identity is created and maintained. Thus, the historically specific discourse...simultaneously created the individual and the community.'

[82] James A. Gardner, *The Failed Discourse of State Constitutionalism*, 90 MICHIGAN LAW REVIEW 761, 769 (1992).

dialectical interaction aimed at reaching agreement would facilitate the forging of common understandings in a non-hierarchical way while, when the case so warrants, accommodating diversity. Hence, judicial dialogue might contribute to building a common EU identity around shared rights at the supranational level, while respecting the constitutional identities of the member states. In this way, dialogic interaction among national and supranational courts becomes the driving force for the articulation of fundamental rights at both levels of governance. The participation of supranational and national courts in dialogue generates mutual influence. EU rights law draws from national constitutional law. Thus, state courts contribute to the articulation of EU rights. It should be noted that the more state courts engage in dialogue, the more influence they might have in defining the meaning of supranational rights. In turn, EU rights law might have an impact in the interpretation of state constitutional rights, even in areas outside EU law's field of application (in which EU fundamental rights are not binding upon the states). Both supranational and national courts have an active and a passive role, influencing and being influenced by other courts. Hence, this mutual influence might be a source for greater convergence.

4.1.4 *Respecting the pluralist framework*

As argued in Chapter 3, there is no hierarchy between national and supranational norms protecting rights. In each system, there is a court with the ultimate authority to interpret the respective rights. As Damian Chalmers contends, 'The regime is able to develop provided it does not significantly disrupt the egalitarian relations enjoyed between national courts and the Court of Justice.'[83] Dialogue provides a regulative model of horizontal interaction between the judicial authorities from different levels of governance. Hence, dialogue offers a model to manage potential conflicts consistent with the EU political structure. In a pluralist framework, judicial dialogue provides a fuller form of legitimacy for supranational rights' adjudication because this model acknowledges the plurality of voices, enhances participation in the interpretive process, and is able to better accommodate the claims from diverse levels of governance.

---

[83] Damian Chalmers, *Judicial Preferences and the Community Legal Order*, 60 THE MODERN LAW REVIEW 164, 180 (1997).

4.2 *Prerequisites for dialogue*

For an effective dialogue to develop with the capacity to ground the normative legitimacy of ECJ fundamental rights adjudication, minimally, the
following prerequisites need to be fulfilled. Dialogue obtains (i) when there
are competing viewpoints about the meaning of law, and at the same time
(ii) there is common ground for mutual understanding. For dialogue to
develop, (iii) neither of the participants should have complete authority
over the other, and yet (iv) they should see themselves as part of a common
enterprise in which members mutually recognize and respect each other.
Finally, (v) all should have equal opportunity to participate (vi) in dialogue
over time. As will be demonstrated, these prerequisites are met in the EU or,
at least, the political structure of the EU allows for them to be fulfilled—not
that they are necessarily fulfilled in each and every case.

4.2.1 *Differing viewpoints*

Differences among the participants do not preclude dialogue. On the contrary, the opportunity for dialogue is created precisely when the systems
involved represent different viewpoints.[84] As Robert M. Cover and Alexander Aleinikoff asserted, one of the main preconditions for dialogue is
'two distinct voices'.[85] Therefore, competing, or at least distinct viewpoints
regarding a common issue are prerequisites for dialogue to be effective.
Differing viewpoints among courts might derive from diverse legal or institutional perspectives.[86] In the EU, the different natures and goals of national
and supranational legal systems (constitutional nation-states, on the one
hand, and a supranational organization created with the goal of establishing a common market, on the other) might entail differing approaches to
fundamental rights adjudication. In particular, national and supranational
courts might sustain differing viewpoints arising from their respective institutional roles (and the self-perception of those roles), their positions in the
legal system, and the law being applied.

---

[84] Robert M. Cover & T. Alexander Aleinikoff, *Dialectical Federalism: Habeas Corpus and the
Court*, 86 THE YALE LAW JOURNAL 1035, 1049–1050 (1977), arguing that 'a dialogue is created
when the two systems in fact represent different viewpoints'; Lawrence Friedman, *The Constitutional Value of Dialogue and the New Judicial Federalism*, 28 HASTINGS CONSTITUTIONAL LAW
QUARTERLY 93, 114 (2000).
[85] Cover & Aleinikoff, *supra* n 84, at 1049.
[86] Robert B. Ahdieh, *Between Dialogue and Decree: International Review of National Courts*, 79
NEW YORK UNIVERSITY LAW REVIEW 2029, 2095–2096 (2004).

In this vein, since the ECJ was created to secure that 'in the implementation of the common market the law is observed',[87] it might possess a bias favouring the success of the integration process.[88] For example, EU law's efficacy, the protection of the basic freedoms of movement, or the success of the common market might shape the ECJ's approach to fundamental rights adjudication. Thus, the ECJ might develop a pragmatic viewpoint in interpreting rights. As several scholars suggested, at its outset, the main purpose of the ECJ's case law protecting fundamental rights was to secure the supremacy of EU law.[89] This does not necessarily mean that the ECJ is not going to 'take rights seriously',[90] but it confirms the ECJ's pragmatic approach to fundamental rights.

In turn, state constitutional courts were specifically created for the sake of securing national constitutions. They are committed to guaranteeing constitutional fundamental rights against public authorities. Constitutional courts are the ultimate interpreters of constitutional rights within the state and their interpretive decisions are binding upon all other courts. Hence, given this position, they aim to delineate a coherent and comprehensive system of constitutional rights. Consequently, they might adopt a more 'utopian' approach to fundamental rights interpretation. Particularly, in the context of the EU integration process, they have seen themselves as the protectors of constitutional values in front of the expansion of the common market. To some extent, it was the 'rebellion' of the German and Italian Constitutional Courts that fostered the protection of fundamental rights by the ECJ.[91] The EU system has come to threaten their authority, and, as a consequence, some have been reluctant to engage with EU law. For example, the Spanish Constitutional Court declared that its function was to interpret the Spanish Constitution and protect state constitutional rights against public authorities, regardless of whether state authorities acted

---

[87] Ex article 164 EEC Treaty (now article 220 EC Treaty).

[88] G. Federico Mancini & David T. Keeling, *Democracy and the European Court of Justice*, 57 THE MODERN LAW REVIEW 175, 186 (1995), wrote: 'The preference for Europe is determined by the genetic code transmitted to the court by the founding fathers, who entrusted to it the task of ensuring that the law is observed in the application of a Treaty whose primary objective is an "ever closer union among the peoples of Europe".'

[89] Weiler, *supra* n 51.

[90] Joseph H. H. Weiler & Nicolas J. S. Lockhart, *'Taking Rights Seriously' Seriously: The European Court of Justice and its Fundamental Rights Jurisprudence*, 32 COMMON MARKET LAW REVIEW 51, 71 (1995).

[91] See Weiler, *supra* n 51; ALEC STONE SWEET, GOVERNING WITH JUDGES. CONSTITUTIONAL POLITICS IN EUROPE 170–172 (Oxford University Press 2000); Cartabia, *supra* n 45; Kokott, *supra* n 46.

within the field of application of EU law.[92] It is more difficult to appraise the ordinary courts' approach to fundamental rights' interpretation from the standpoint of their institutional role. Ordinary state courts have a double dimension since they take part in both the national and the supranational systems of governance, and they are bound to apply both constitutional and EU fundamental rights.[93] Given the lack of EU lower courts, they are in charge of the enforcement of EU law within the state. At the same time, they must check that state authorities comply with the state constitution (in collaboration with the constitutional court in centralized systems of judicial review). They play a key role because they decide whether to submit a question to the constitutional court, a preliminary reference to the ECJ, or to resolve the case without further reference. On the one hand, allegiance to the respective national legal and constitutional cultures might be expected. On the other hand, collaborating with the ECJ might contribute to their self-empowerment, vis-à-vis other courts in the system or other political actors.[94] Therefore, a variety of viewpoints might emerge, depending, for instance, on the hierarchical position within the judicial system,[95] the state to which they pertain, or the kinds of rights at stake. For example, German courts have been very active in advancing individuals' constitutional rights before the ECJ; whereas, on occasion, English courts have been reluctant to protect rights in the workplace. Generally, ordinary courts are the ones in charge of actually deciding cases. They enjoy the best knowledge of the facts, and they can assess the impact of different interpretations to the case at hand. Instead of concern for a comprehensive system of rights protection, their actions might be guided by the everyday needs of judicial decision-making.

A thorough analysis of how national and supranational courts' perceptions of their institutional roles might be characterized and how these perceptions might shape their approaches to fundamental rights exceeds the scope of this work. At this point, the goal is to demonstrate no more than the contention that judicial viewpoints might differ as a consequence of diverse legal or institutional perspectives, which creates the opportunity for dialogue.

---

[92] STC, 64/1991, 22 March 1991.

[93] Kilpatrick, *supra* n 15, at 145.

[94] Several theories have been advanced to explain the willingness of national courts to collaborate with the ECJ, even in circumstances in which constitutional principles were ignored, such as the prohibition of judicial review of legislation by ordinary courts. See Alter, *supra* n 16.

[95] *Id.*

Kilpatrick points out how the differences among courts further dialogue in the EU:

Instead of a European *community* of courts and law, it is the need to mediate differences between European *communities* of courts and law which produces the possibility for dialogue, structures how those dialogues take place and change over time, and pinpoints when dialogue will be smooth or difficult.[96]

In sum, diversity is the substratum of dialogue. As long as a basic ground of communication and understanding exists, as will be shown in the next section, the possibility of an intelligible dialogue on the meaning of rights will be secured.

4.2.2 *Common ground of understanding*

For an intelligible, inter-systemic dialogue to develop, the participants need to share collective understandings and experiences that provide them with a common ground of communication. It might be questioned whether there is enough commonality for a meaningful dialogue to develop in the EU; even more so after the accession of twelve countries from Eastern Europe (in 2004 and 2006), whose democratic regimes were established in the 1990s only after the collapse of the Soviet empire. To some extent, the diversity of cultures, languages, history, and legal traditions among the member states might shape differing understandings of the basic values encapsulated in fundamental rights and thereby hinder communication.[97] In turn, the EU legal system has its own goals and culture regarding the realization of liberal, common market values at the supranational level.

At the same time, as European countries, EU member states share an historical and cultural past. Their common features are more salient when opposed to other geopolitical areas of the world, such as the US, the Middle East, or Asia. As for their legal systems, all EU member states are constitutional democracies and are committed to the protection of fundamental rights. Most of them have parliamentary systems of government and

---

[96] Kilpatrick, *supra* n 15, at 129.

[97] HOWARD CHARLES YOUROW, THE MARGIN OF APPRECIATION DOCTRINE IN THE DYNAMICS OF EUROPEAN HUMAN RIGHTS JURISPRUDENCE (Martinus Nijhoff Publishers 1996), writing about the European Convention, held: 'The "Nordic" and "Mediterranean" mentalities are powerful factors conditioning diversities among European national legal systems.' Also, he affirmed that the incorporation of Central and Eastern European states may occasion new 'East-West' fault lines.

constitutional courts with the power of judicial review of legislation.[98] It is contended that their common experiences and values, furthered by the project of EU integration, provide a common ground for communication regarding fundamental rights. As members of the EU, at a minimum, all national and supranational legal systems share the same basic principles. These are encapsulated in article 6.1 EU Treaty: 'The Union is founded on the principles of liberty, democracy, respect for human rights and fundamental freedoms, and the rule of law, principles which are common to the Member States.' Accession and continued membership in the EU are conditional upon compliance with these principles. To be more specific, article 49 EU Treaty establishes that only the states that respect the principles set out in article 6.1 may apply for accession. Also, article 7 contains a mechanism that allows suspending some state membership rights in case of a 'serious and persistent breach' or a 'clear risk' of a serious and persistent breach of the principles mentioned in article 6.1. In addition, article 6.2 establishes that the EU shall respect fundamental rights as they result from the constitutional traditions common to the member states. The drafting of the EU Charter of fundamental rights was an occasion for representatives of state parliaments and governments, the EU Parliament, and the Commission to deliberate about a set of rights common to all in the EU.

Regarding the newest members from Eastern Europe, the conditions for accession required guaranteeing general democratic stability and human rights.[99] When these states joined the EU, the Charter had already been proclaimed (2000). This Charter, in spite of lacking binding force, gave specificity to the general commitment to the protection of fundamental rights as a condition of accession.[100] Still, fundamental rights allow for diverging interpretations. There might have been some suspicions concerning the 'depth and sincerity of democratic transformations in Central and Eastern parts of the continent'.[101] Wojciech Sadurski claims that Western countries should not fear or adopt a paternalistic approach towards the participation

---

[98] *Id.* at 3.

[99] Wojciech Sadurski, *Accession's Democracy Dividend: The Impact of the EU Enlargement upon Democracy in the New Member States of Central and Eastern Europe*, 10 EUROPEAN LAW JOURNAL 371, 374 (2004), claiming that membership to the EU might help to make the democratic transition irreversible.

[100] For the interrelation between the Charter and EU enlargement, see Wojciech Sadurski, *Charter and Enlargement*, 8 EUROPEAN LAW JOURNAL 340, 344–345 (2002), arguing that the Charter might be seen as closing the gap between the human rights standards applied within the EU and those required to candidate states.

[101] *Id.* at 344, 360–366.

of Eastern European countries in the dialogue on fundamental rights. He argues that catalogues of rights in these countries are not substantially different from those in Western European countries.[102] Fundamental rights are regarded as higher order values, and they are protected by constitutional courts with the power of judicial review. The communist past of these countries does not imply that individual values are always subordinated to collective goals. There is a mix of classic liberal rights and socio-economic rights, as in the constitutions of Western Europe. Sadurski concludes the following:

There are unlikely to be any major frictions or clashes between Member States and candidate states—certainly no more than the tensions within the actual group of Member States, which display a wide variety of constitutional traditions regarding such issues as constitutionalisation of socio-economic rights or justiciability of rights through a process of judicial review.[103]

In addition, all EU members are also members of the European Convention and are bound by the ECtHR's decisions. Also, the ECJ held that, in the interpretation of EU fundamental rights, it would draw inspiration from the European Convention.[104] This obligation has been entrenched in article 6.2 EU Treaty. Also, according to article 52.3 of the Charter, the European Convention sets a minimum standard for the interpretation of EU fundamental rights. Thus, there is a common way of talking about fundamental rights prompted by the European Convention as interpreted by the ECtHR. In sum, as well-ordered democratic societies, EU member states agree on certain basic principles and rights that need to be protected. Although fundamental rights norms, given their abstract formulation and essential contestability, allow for diverse interpretations, there is common ground among member states permitting the development of a meaningful dialogue and the attainment of common understandings.

4.2.3 *Lacking complete authority over the other*

For an inter-systemic judicial dialogue to occur and be effective, none of the participants should have complete authority over the others.[105] In the words of Cover and Aleiknikoff, a model of dialogue obtains when 'neither system can claim total sovereignty'.[106] Each court should have the capacity

---

[102] *Id.* at 351.   [103] *Id.* at 359.
[104] *Liselotte Hauer v Land Rheinland-Pfalz*, C-44/79.
[105] Ahdieh, *supra* n 86, at 2088–2095.
[106] Cover & Aleinikoff, *supra* n 84, at 1048.

to exercise some pressure over other systems' courts, but not to impose its will. Hence, there will be incentives to co-operate and to try to find paths of common understanding, while maintaining a measure of autonomy.[107] In the EU, as argued in Chapter 3, none of the interacting legal systems enjoys absolute sovereignty. Notwithstanding the rhetoric about supremacy in the judicial opinions of both the ECJ and state constitutional courts, neither can supersede the others.[108] Thus, there is no hierarchy between national and supranational courts. In particular, there is no appellate review by the ECJ over cases decided by national courts. They pertain to different judicial structures within distinct legal systems. Furthermore, the ECJ is deprived of coercive power to enforce its decisions within the states. In this context, no system has exclusive voice as to the prevailing values. Thus, a degree of autonomy for the interpretation of rights is acknowledged.

At the same time, the EU political structure provides incentives to co-operate in this interpretive endeavour. Since the ECJ does not have coercive power over the states, it needs the collaboration of state courts for the enforcement of EU law. In this sense, it is said that national courts have a '*de facto* veto power'[109] over the development of the EU legal order. In other words, state courts have the capacity to frustrate the application and real-ization of integration goals.[110] Moreover, since individuals cannot appeal state court decisions before the ECJ, the ECJ lacks control over the applica-tion of previous interpretations to future cases that arise in national legal systems. Therefore, the ECJ has reasons to engage in dialogue and try to accommodate, to some extent, the claims from state courts regarding funda-mental rights protection.[111] In turn, the ECJ interprets fundamental rights that are common to all member states and that are to be applied in future cases. By engaging in dialogue with the ECJ, state courts might have input regarding the articulation of supranational fundamental rights. In addition, state courts are aware that consistent rejection of ECJ rulings interpreting rights might undermine the efficacy of EU law and impair the integration project.[112] After all, given its position, the ECJ has the capacity to com-bine national and supranational approaches to particular legal controversies

---

[107] Ahdieh, *supra* n 86, at 2090: 'Neither court can impose its will on the other, producing a degree of incident autonomy within an overall pattern of systemic dependence.'

[108] Chalmers, *supra* n 63, at 40.

[109] Chalmers, *supra* n 83, at 180.   [110] *Id.*

[111] *Id.*: 'The formal freedom of the Court of Justice is thus necessarily tempered by the social reality of having to accommodate national judicial concerns.'

[112] *Id.* at 179.

better than single state courts.[113] Hence, state courts also have incentives to collaborate and pay due regard to ECJ interpretive decisions.

In sum, given the shared interest in the functioning of the overall system, there are reasons to acknowledge the claims from other courts and attempt to satisfy the most reasonable demands. Although the absence of an ultimate authority for the resolution of conflicts might make the system seem precarious, at the same time, it prepares the ground and fosters a dialogic type of interaction.[114] Therefore, the lack of absolute authority between national and supranational courts in the EU might indeed be an incentive to co-operate and enter into dialogue, which offers a flexible way to manage fundamental rights' conflicts.

4.2.4 *Mutual recognition and respect*

For a normative exchange about the meaning of rights to be possible, the participants must mutually recognize each other.[115] Hence, the participants need to acknowledge others, notwithstanding their differences, as part of a common enterprise.[116] In this common enterprise, all participants' viewpoints need to receive equal respect.

In the EU, national and supranational courts mutually recognize each other in their judicial capacity. As courts, they are committed to defining the rule of law. Part of this activity consists of constructing the meaning of fundamental rights protected against public authorities. It has been suggested that mutual recognition among courts in the EU is fostered by a common

---

[113] Helfer & Slaughter, *supra* n 17, at 325.

[114] Walker, *Supra* n 55, at 26, remarked: 'The absence of a final trans-systemic authority and a definitive framework for dispute resolution also stimulates the pursuit of a type of relation between legal orders quite different from the hierarchical and authoritative or strategic. Space opens up for a more heterarchical and dialogic approach, and this is positively reinforced by the close function interdependence of different constitutional and metaconstitutional sites and the significant overlap of their key officials.'

[115] In the words of Michelman, *supra* n 30, at 32–33, mutual recognition 'makes possible normative interchange that is at the same time: (i) mutually intelligible, (ii) potentially critical of any participant normative visions, and (iii) free of a priori privileged status for any vision'; Thomas Risse, *'Let's Argue!': Communicative Action in World Politics*, 54 INTERNATIONAL ORGANIZATION 1 (2000), listing among the preconditions for argumentative rationality 'the mutual recognition of speakers as equals in a nonhierarchical relationship'.

[116] Slaughter, *supra* n 55, at 127, holding that awareness of a common enterprise would only require 'a sense of confrontation of common issues or problems....Recognition of this commonality does not obviate cultural differences, but it assumes the possibility that generic legal problems such as the balancing of rights and duties, individual and community interests, and the protection of individual expectations may transcend those differences.'

legal methodology and language.[117] Furthermore, they are aware of being part of a common political project of integration, reinforced by the institutional framework established by the EU Treaty.[118] From this broader perspective, all members are committed to the goal of developing a functioning structure of political action at the supranational level. As a consequence, the EU and the constituting member states are under a mutual obligation of loyalty.[119] At the same time, mutual recognition does not imply renouncing their respective identities. Indeed, the duty of the EU to respect member states' national and constitutional identities is encapsulated in article 6.3 EU Treaty.

Hence, mutual recognition between national and supranational courts, while respecting diverging opinions, secures a fair dialogue. Although mutual recognition is regarded as a prerequisite for dialogue, at the same time, the development of a dialogic interaction itself reinforces recognition and respect among the participants. In the words of Robert B. Ahdieh, 'A pattern of repeat participation in the relevant dialogue can be expected to build trust and confidence among the judicial parties to the exchange' and 'receptivity to alternative perspectives... may grow'.[120]

4.2.5 *Equal opportunity to participate*

For dialogue to fulfil its legitimating role, all members of the community must be granted the opportunity to have a voice. All participants ought to be able to put forward an interpretation as well as to challenge the interpretations of others (and eventually revise their own). No claim should be free from criticism.[121] In the EU, all state courts have equal access to dialogue.

---

[117] *Id.* at 126; Weiler, *supra* n 19, at 521, referring to the compliance pull of dialogue conducted between courts in 'legalese' and to the legitimacy of ECJ opinions deriving from 'legal language itself: the language of reasoned interpretation, logical deduction, systemic and temporal coherence'.

[118] Slaughter, *supra* n 55, at 128.

[119] Deirdre Curtin & Ige Dekker, *The Constitutional Structure of the European Union: Some Reflections on Vertical Unity-in-Diversity*, in Convergence and Divergence in European Public Law 60, 70 (Paul Beaumont, Carole Lyons & Neil Walker eds. 2002), arguing that the duty of co-operation of the member states to secure the achievement of EU goals established in article 10 EC Treaty should be understood more broadly as a 'mutual obligation' of loyalty. In their own words, '[article 10] has evolved from a duty of co-operation on the part of the member states to a multi-sided duty of loyalty and good faith in the vertical relationship between the Union and its member states and also among the member states themselves'.

[120] Ahdieh, *supra* n 86, at 2100.

[121] Habermas in Alexy, *supra* n 34, at 120: 'All participants in discourses must have an equal opportunity to put forward interpretations, assertions, recommendations, explanations, and justifications and to problematize, justify, or refute their respective claims to validity

They all have the possibility of engaging in conversation with the ECJ through the preliminary reference.[122] In the course of a case before a state court, this procedure allows state judges to refer a question to the ECJ about the interpretation or validity of EU provisions applicable to the case. Article 234 EC Treaty establishes that 'any court or tribunal of a Member State' may make a reference. The notion of 'court or tribunal' allowed to make a reference[123] has been interpreted by the ECJ in broad terms to include any institution that enjoys official status and exercises a judicial function.[124] This notion would include institutions that are not described as courts or tribunals in their own countries.[125] Therefore, any court from any member state may file a preliminary reference. What is more, courts of last resort are obliged to do so when they have a doubt about the interpretation or validity of EU law.[126] Obviously, the possibility of dialogue requires that a case is initiated before a state court. Courts cannot initiate judicial processes on their own motion. Such a limitation is often read under a democratic light. Given that they are not elected and accountable bodies, they can only exercise their power when a process is initiated by those who are granted standing.[127] Through the preliminary reference, courts can call into question a previous interpretation by the ECJ or let the ECJ know about the potential for conflict between EU law and state constitutional rights.[128] In practice, imbalances of participation and strength might occur. Some states, such as Germany, tend to refer more questions to the ECJ than others. The more questions are referred, the greater the possibility to have input in the interpretive outcome.[129]

in such a way that no opinion can remain permanently free from thematization and criticism.'

[122] De la Mare, *supra* n 55, at 241.

[123] See DAVID W.K. ANDERSON, REFERENCES TO THE EUROPEAN COURT 29–43 (Sweet & Maxwell 1995); Brown & Jacobs, *supra* n 18, at 223–227.

[124] *Politi S.A.S v Ministry for Finance*, C-43/71; *Katarina Abrahamsson and Leif Anderson v Elisabet Fogelqvist*, C-407/98.

[125] *Vaasen v Beambtenfonds voor het Mijnbedriff*, C-61/65; *Pretore di Salo v Persons Unknown*, C-14/86.

[126] Regarding the obligation to submit a preliminary reference, see Anderson, *supra* n 123, at 154–217; Brown & Jacobs, *supra* n 18, at 227–232.

[127] Cappelletti, *supra* n 19, at 31–32.

[128] The potential and shortcomings of the preliminary reference as a channel for dialogue about the meaning of fundamental rights will be discussed in more detail below.

[129] There are several reasons that might explain the varied number of references sent by each state. See de la Mare, *supra* n 55, at 243–244.

In addition, the preliminary reference furthers participation of a broad range of actors in the process of interpreting fundamental rights.[130] First of all, individuals are given the opportunity to make their voices heard in the process of giving content to fundamental rights norms. Courts are far more accessible than EU legislative bodies. Only powerful actors with great economic power have the resources for their voices to reach Brussels and the opportunity to influence decision-making processes. Although individuals have no standing before the ECJ against the action of state authorities, this limitation is partly overcome through the preliminary reference. The preliminary reference offers individuals an avenue to reach the ECJ by bringing cases before state courts. In the course of a case, individuals might try to convince state courts about the need to refer a question to the ECJ. Then, individuals are entitled to submit written observations and to appear at the oral hearing before the ECJ.[131] The preliminary reference has been defined as 'the principal avenue whereby individuals may make use of the rights (and duties) bestowed upon them by the EC legal order'.[132] Thus, by means of the interaction between national and supranational courts, individuals might participate in the interpretation of fundamental rights at the supranational level.[133] To secure equal opportunities of participation through the judicial process, access to justice should be guaranteed for those who cannot afford it. The parties in proceedings before the ECJ may apply for legal aid in case of insufficient means.[134] Legal aid might also be available according to domestic law.[135] Furthermore, the preliminary reference allows for national governments and European institutions to intervene in the debate. National governments, whether of the same country as the referring court or of other

---

[130] Cappelletti, *supra* n 19, at 44: 'The judicial process is so structured as to be, at the same time, the most "participatory" and yet the least "partisan" of all law-making processes.'

[131] For the role of private parties, see Anderson, *supra* n 123, at 224–226.

[132] Jean Paul Jacqué & Joseph H. H. Weiler, *On the Road to European Union—A New Judicial Architecture: An Agenda for the Intergovernmental Conference*, 27 COMMON MARKET LAW REVIEW 185, 187 (1990).

[133] RONALD DWORKIN, A MATTER OF PRINCIPLE (Harvard University Press 1985), pointed out the advantages of courts over the legislative for advancing the democratic ideal of equality of political power, giving voice to minorities that cannot reach the legislative. Also, MARTIN SHAPIRO, FREEDOM OF SPEECH: THE SUPREME COURT AND JUDICIAL REVIEW 32 (Prentice-Hall 1966).

[134] Article 76 of the Rules of Procedure. Jacqué & Weiler, *supra* n 132, at 240–241; Brown & Jacobs, *supra* n 18, at 229–231.

[135] It should be kept in mind that the preliminary ruling occurs in the course of a domestic judicial process. In many member states, legal aid for those who cannot afford it is deemed to be a constitutional right. Anderson, *supra* n 123, at 193, 240.

member states, may intervene in the proceedings. National governments might be prone to intervene for a variety of reasons.[136] On occasions, they have been very influential.[137] Moreover, the Commission may also participate in the procedures before the ECJ. The Council and the EU Parliament may participate when the question refers to measures emanating from them.[138] All participants may make submissions regarding the admissibility of the preliminary reference, the interpretation of EU law, or any other issue. Member states and EU institutions 'often take the opportunity to annex relevant documents and to inform the Court of their own law, policy, or practice on a particular point'.[139] In this way, national, supranational, and individual inputs are brought to the process of ECJ decision-making. The potential intervention of a wide range of actors allows for a variety of interests and viewpoints to be represented before the ECJ.

4.2.6 *Continuity over time*

The equal opportunity to participate in dialogue needs to be understood over a period of time. In the real world, it is not possible for all participants to engage in a debate at the same time and in the same place until an agreement is reached. Thus, a prerequisite for an effective judicial dialogue is the guarantee of its continuity over time.[140] In the EU, the institutional framework established by the Treaties secures the continuity of dialogue among courts over a period of time. Particularly, the preliminary reference allows for subsequent cases to be brought before the ECJ by courts from the several member states regarding common issues. After the ECJ issues a preliminary ruling interpreting an EU fundamental right, domestic courts from that state (including the same court) or from other states might submit subsequent references expounding new arguments. In this way, state courts might challenge past ECJ interpretations. Such a challenge should not necessarily be regarded as a rebellion against the ECJ, but instead as an attempt to convince the ECJ to reconsider its previous interpretation. Dialogue not only entails a pleasant conversation, but also a passionate discussion, which is actually driven by conflict. The so-called banana saga can illustrate this dynamic.[141] The ECJ, in spite of the opinion of ordinary courts

---

[136] *Id.* at 231–233.   [137] *Id.* at 233–234.
[138] Article 23 of the Statute of the Court of Justice (March 2008).
[139] Anderson, *supra* n 123, at 227.
[140] Ahdieh, *supra* n 86, at 2098.
[141] *Federal Republic of Germany v Council of the European Communities*, C-280/93; *Atlanta Fruchthandelsgesellschaft mbH and others v Bundesamt für Ernährung und Forstwirtschaft*, C-465

to the contrary, initially held that the EU regulation regarding the banana market did not violate the right to property and the freedom to pursue a professional or trade activity. The German Constitutional Court, instead, allowed for provisional measures in case of risk of bankruptcy. In a subsequent preliminary reference brought by an ordinary court, the ECJ rejected the jurisdiction of state courts to order provisional measures, but declared that the Commission was required to take the necessary transitional measures when fundamental rights were impaired. Eventually, an outcome that could be accepted by all was reached. Other examples of an ongoing judicial dialogue regarding a particular right are found in the succession of cases on the equality principle with regard to affirmative action measures[142] and the legal treatment of transsexuals.[143] In sum, the extended nature of judicial dialogue in the EU allows for the gradual evolution of judicial norms in a process of collective deliberation.

5 Objections to judicial dialogue

The feasibility of a robust judicial dialogue might be opposed for a variety of reasons. A general objection claims that courts, as political actors, act strategically. Consequently, dialogue, as an exchange of arguments with the goal of reaching common understandings, cannot develop between national and supranational courts. More specifically, the preliminary reference might not be considered adequate for a robust dialogue regarding the interpretation of fundamental rights to develop. The next section will consider these objections in order to reassert the model of judicial dialogue as the source of legitimacy of ECJ adjudicative decisions protecting rights.

5.1. *Strategic vs dialogic action*

It might be argued that there cannot be dialogue among courts because dialogue, by definition, employs argumentative action to reach the

---

and 466/93; *T. Port GmbH & Co. KG v Bundesanstalt für Landwirtschaft und Ernährung*, C-68/95; German Constitutional Court decisions of 25 January 1995 and 7 June 2000.

[142] *Eckhard Kalanke v Freie Hansestadt Bremen*, C-450/93; *Hellmut Marschall v Land Nordrhein Westfalen*, C-409/95; *Georg Badeck and Others, interveners: Hessische Ministerpräsident and Landesanwalt beim Staatsgerichtshof des Landes Hessen*, C-158/97; *Katarina Abrahamsson and Leif Anderson v Elisabet Fogelqvist*, C-407/98.

[143] *P v S and Cornwall County Council*, C-13/94; *K.B. v National Health Service Pensions Agency and Secretary of State for Health*, C-117/01.

best-reasoned outcome, whereas courts act strategically. In this sense, Karen Alter asserts that judicial interaction in the EU is better described as 'doctrinal negotiation' rather than 'legal dialoguing'.[144] Both dialogic and strategic action (or, respectively, arguing and bargaining) are forms of communication used to reach agreements. They differ in their presuppositions, mode, and goal.[145] In a bargaining process, the interests and preferences of actors are taken as fixed, and it is assumed that they do not change over the process of negotiation.[146] In this kind of communication, which is based on threats and promises, participants try to convince each other with the goal of maximizing their own interests. In contrast, dialogue consists of exchanging rational arguments with the goal of reaching the best-reasoned outcome for all participants. Preferences are not fixed, possibly changing in light of a better argument.[147] It is not denied that courts, as political actors, might have their own agendas and interests. There is no agreement in the literature about the model that best describes what these judicial interests or preferences shaping judicial behaviour comprise. Judicial interests have been defined in a variety of ways. Some view judges as having preferences for substantive policies. Through their decisions, they might strive to promote their policy interests.[148] Judicial preferences have also been characterized as an interest in promoting 'judicial power',[149] and more specifically 'independence, influence, and authority'[150] vis-à-vis other courts or other political branches. According to these accounts, different courts will compete among themselves to satisfy their policy preferences or interests.[151] From

---

[144] Alter, *supra* n 16, at 38: 'A dialogue implies two or more actors talking to each other, using reason to reach a mutually accepted outcome. The notion of a dialogue implies that the outcome reached is the best reasoned outcome, the one that convinces all sides. A negotiation, on the other hand, implies competing interests where parties recognize that they may not be able to have it as they most like it. Negotiations usually lead to compromises that take into account the power of the negotiating parties, the conflicting interests of the different actors, and the intensity of those interests.'

[145] For the distinction of these two kinds of communication see Elster, *supra* n 72; Habermas, *supra* n 25, at 286–287.

[146] Dryzek, *supra* n 25.   [147] Habermas, *supra* n 35, at 89.

[148] Mattli & Slaughter, *supra* n 16, at 258, 262–263; Alter, *supra* n 49, at 242.

[149] Mattli & Slaughter, *supra* n 16, at 258, explaining that 'judicial empowerment' includes the power of judicial review, the pursuit of institutional power and prestige relative to other courts within the same judicial system, and the power to promote certain substantive policies through law. Also, Burley & Mattli, *supra* n 48, at 63.

[150] Alter, *supra* n 16, at 45.

[151] Alter, *supra* n 49, at 241–242 was the first one to propose an 'inter-court competition explanation' to legal integration: 'It is the difference in lower and higher court interests which

a different perspective, judicial interests can also be defined as maximizing the number of 'correct' decisions. For example, Lewis A. Kornhauser treats the judicial system as a team, in which all members share a common goal: 'to maximize the expected number of "correct" answers'.[152] In this vein, the problems courts face are seen as problems of co-ordination and division of labour, rather than competition and strategy. The 'team model' encapsulates the attempt by some scholars to appraise judicial behaviour as understood by the participants in the adjudicative practice.[153] This legal account of judicial behaviour, as an alternative to political models, has gained some acceptance even among political scientists.[154]

The discussion of these alternative accounts of judicial behaviour exceeds the scope of this work. It is not the purpose here to attempt to describe or explain judicial behaviour, but rather to argue for the desirability and feasibility of a dialogic model of interaction among courts. The claim for the legitimating potential of dialogue is not made from the perspective of an 'ideal speech situation'. No action occurs in a pure form in the real world and, as such, it is difficult to separate argumentation from bargaining in actual instances of discourse.[155] The fact that judicial action might be partly strategic does not mean that the claim of dialogue as a model of judicial interaction to construct the meaning of rights should be rejected. Nor does it mean that it cannot be realized. As has been remarked, judicial preferences are not necessarily self-interested and judicial behaviour does not have to be a selfish and competitive enterprise that leads courts to adopt a strategic action vis-à-vis other courts. Indeed, some elements pertaining to the judiciary, such as due process obligations, as well as the self-understanding of the judicial function, might enhance the realization of dialogue in the search

provides a motor for legal integration to proceed.' For a criticism of judicial empowerment accounts and inter-court competition models see Kilpatrick, *supra* n 15, at 127, 128.

[152] Lewis A. Kornhauser, *Adjudication by a Resource-Constrained Team: Hierarchy and Precedent in a Judicial System*, 68 SOUTHERN CALIFORNIA LAW REVIEW 1605, 1606 (1995). This author does not define the notion of correctness. As he argues, a court system might seek to implement an efficient legal system or some conception of corrective justice. What matters for his analysis is not the specific content of this goal, but the fact that it is shared by all members of the team, that is, the courts within a judicial system.

[153] Francisco Ramos, JSD manuscript on file with the author, 27 (NYU 2003).

[154] At least, it is regarded as an alternative worthy of being investigated. See the research project by Charles Cameron, Lee Epstein & Jeffrey A. Segal, *Strategic Defiance of the US Supreme Court* (Funded by the National Science Foundation, SES-007996), description available at <http://www.artsci.wustl.edu/polisci/epstein/research/defiance.html>.

[155] Jon Elster, *Introduction*, in DELIBERATIVE DEMOCRACY 1, 5–8 (Jon Elster ed. 1998); Gambetta, *supra* n 71; Risse, *supra* n 115, at 18–19.

for the best-reasoned outcome. According to their judicial role, judges need to be impartial. Impartiality requires that judges do not decide on the basis of personal, subjective preferences, or partisan ends.[156] In this vein, judges must give reasons to justify their decisions. Mauro Cappelletti refers to the practice of giving reasons as an 'attempt to assure the public that court decisions are not the result of the caprice or the subjective idiosyncrasies and predilections of the judges, but rather the judges' attempt to be faithful to the "community's sense of fairness and justice"'.[157] Although it must be admitted that the obligation to give reasons is not all constraining, 'any decision-maker under an obligation to give reasons may be less prone to arbitrary, capricious, self-interested, or otherwise unfair judgment'.[158] Not all reasons are acceptable, but only those deemed to be valid within the legal framework. The language of law that judges are bound to use might constrain the kind of arguments available to them.

Therefore, the same practice of communication, precisely because it takes place among courts (and they are obliged to be impartial and give reasons) might further a dialogic type of communication. When courts interact in the interpretation of fundamental rights, they do not want to appear as self-interested since this could damage their credibility and hence their persuasive authority. They not only need to be impartial, but also to appear to be so. Irrespective of their internal motives, they need to justify their interpretive decisions on the basis of arguments that have the potential of convincing their interlocutors or, at least, that might be regarded as reasonable. As argued by Jon Elster, argument, even if based on self-interest, has a powerful 'civilizing influence'.[159] Elster explains how engaging in discussion might induce even self-interested speakers to argue in terms of the public interest or the common good. The effort to dress up their interests might positively affect the result.[160] In this way, dialogue is a way of containing selfish interests, since it has a tendency to exclude those positions that cannot be sustained on an impartial basis.[161]

---

[156] Cappelletti, *supra* n 19, at 31–32.   [157] *Id.* at 43.

[158] Martin Shapiro & Alec Stone Sweet, On Law, Politics and Judicialization 232 (Oxford University Press 2002).

[159] See Elster *supra* n 72, at 250; Fearon, *supra* n 67, at 52–55; Gambetta, *supra* n 71, at 19.

[160] Elster, *supra* n 72, at 250, elaborating on the mechanisms that explain how the effort to disguise self-interest with impartial arguments might contribute to more equitable results; see also Jon Elster, *Deliberation and Constitution Making*, in Deliberative Democracy 97, 104 (Jon Elster ed. 1998); Fearon, *supra* n 67, at 54.

[161] Nino, *supra* n 39, at 101.

5.2 Questioninig the preliminary reference as an avenue for dialogue

Some have argued that the preliminary reference (or preliminary question) is not suitable for a real judicial dialogue to develop because it only allows for a 'one-to-one' conversation, and it takes place 'in the distance'.[162] Moreover, the questions are rarely formulated as questions about constitutional matters and constitutional courts have hardly referred any question to the ECJ. Bruno de Witte contends that a true judicial conversation does not exist in the EU and, furthermore, that it would not be possible to develop in the present institutional setting.[163] In theory, the preliminary reference allows state courts to raise a question about the interpretation or validity of an EU provision applicable to a case before them. It is based on a division of tasks between the ECJ and state courts. The ECJ is in charge of interpreting the applicable EU norm, while state courts decide the case at hand.[164] In practice, however, this formal division has not always been as intended or as professed to be.[165] Although the ECJ has repetitively confirmed that under the preliminary reference it has no powers to decide on the validity of state provisions, or even on the compatibility between state and EU law, its decisions leave little doubt about whether the state provision at stake clashes with EU law.[166] The ECJ has used the preliminary ruling to determine the compatibility between state measures and EU law, including EU fundamental rights.[167] For this mechanism to be effective, however, the ECJ needs the

---

[162] Bruno de Witte, *The Closest Thing to a Constitutional Conversation in Europe: The Semi-Permanente Treaty Revision Process*, in CONVERGENCE AND DIVERGENCE IN EUROPEAN PUBLIC LAW 39–41 (Paul Beaumont, Carole Lyons and Neil Walker eds. 2002).

[163] *Id.* at 41: 'A true *judicial conversation* would be made possible in an entirely different, and yet-to-be-created, institutional setting.'

[164] RENAUD DEHOUSSE, THE EUROPEAN COURT OF JUSTICE 136 (St. Martin's Press 1998).

[165] GERHARD BEBR, DEVELOPMENT OF JUDICIAL CONTROL OF THE EUROPEAN COMMUNITIES 391 (Brill 1981).

[166] Jeffrey C. Cohen, *The European Preliminary Reference and U.S. Supreme Court Review of State Court Judgments: A Study in Comparative Judicial Federalism*, 44 AMERICAN JOURNAL OF COMPARATIVE LAW 421, 429–430 (1996): 'The Court's confinement to the role of interpretation, however, is not as pure as its rhetoric suggests.'

[167] Francis G. Jacobs & Kenneth L. Karst, *The 'Federal' Legal Order: The U.S.A. and Europe Compared—A Juridical Perspective*, in INTEGRATION THROUGH LAW: EUROPE AND THE AMERICAN FEDERAL EXPERIENCE—METHODS, TOOLS, AND INSTITUTIONS 169, 233 (Mauro Cappelletti et. al. eds. 1986): 'The Court of Justice has not limited itself in the exercise of its article 177 jurisdiction, to ruling on interpretation alone, but has had occasion to deal also with the effects of Community law.'

collaboration of state courts:[168] state courts are the ones to decide whether to file a preliminary reference, and, ultimately, they are in charge of resolving the case after the preliminary ruling has been issued. As demonstrated before, national and supranational courts have incentives to co-operate through dialogue.[169]

The intervention of national courts is not limited to the formulation of a question. Additionally, they are expected to submit a 'statement of case'.[170] State courts should provide information about the points of fact and law relevant to the interpretation of the EU provision at stake.[171] They need to define the legal context in which the question should be placed.[172] In particular, the ECJ requires national courts, when making a preliminary question, to explain 'why they consider that a reply to their questions is necessary to enable them to give judgment'.[173] Hence, the preliminary question offers state courts the opportunity to inform the ECJ about the potential conflict with constitutional rights, as they have been interpreted by the state constitutional court.[174] State courts could offer reasons for adopting state understandings at the EU level or simply for respecting them through the exercise of deference. This is not to suggest that the preliminary reference in most cases is used (or should be used) in confrontational terms.[175] This is pointing out, instead, that this procedure affords the opportunity to state

---

[168] As Cappelletti, *supra* n 19, at 367, points out, 'In practice, however, much more than in the United States, the Community system of review requires the co-operation and goodwill of the courts of the member states. The need for this co-operation arises from two limitations of the Community system: the Community litigants' lack of standing to bring appeals from national judicial decisions to the Court of Justice, and the Court's lack of coercive powers to enforce its judgments.'

[169] See *supra* 4.2.3.

[170] See Anderson, *supra* n 123, at 185–186.

[171] *Irish Creamery Milk Suppliers Association v Ireland*, C-36 and 71/80.

[172] *Union Laitière Normande v French Dairy Farmers Ltd.*, C 244/78.

[173] *Pasquale Foglia v Mariella Novelo*, C-244/80.

[174] For instance, in *Anacleto Cordero Alonso v Fondo de Garantía Salarial (Fogasa)*, C-81/05, in its question to the ECJ, the referring court pointed out the existence of diverging interpretations between the ECJ and the Spanish Constitutional Court regarding the equality principle: 'when applying directive [2002/74] and the provisions of national law transposing the content thereof, are the Spanish administrative and judicial institutions bound by the principle of equality before the law and the prohibition of discrimination deriving from Community law, as defined by the interpretation thereof given by the [ECJ] ..., notwithstanding that that interpretation does not coincide with the interpretation in the case-law of the Spanish Constitutional Court of the equivalent fundamental right which is enshrined in the Spanish Constitution?'

[175] De la Mare, *supra* n 55, at 241–242, distinguishing a weak or inquisitive form of discourse from a strong or confrontational one.

courts to engage in a robust dialogue with the ECJ, beyond the mere formulation of a question. Moreover, after a preliminary ruling is issued, the
same national court might refer another question to the ECJ. This re-referral
keeps dialogue alive.[176] In particular, as assessed by several commentators,
national courts re-refer questions when they are not satisfied with ECJ
answers and invite this Court to reconsider previous interpretations.[177] For
instance, domestic courts might think that the ECJ failed to understand
the implications of a particular interpretation for state constitutional law
and re-refer the question to clarify the potential for conflict.[178] This gives
the ECJ the opportunity to refine its interpretations. Re-referrals evidence
a critical attitude of some state courts towards the ECJ.[179] In addition, the
ECJ asks state courts to report back as to the outcome of the national case
after a preliminary ruling has been issued. The report from state courts is
voluntary. Such feedback offers a further opportunity for national courts to
speak to the ECJ, but these voluntary reports tend to be missing.[180] In short,
although the preliminary reference might not have been used to its fullest
potential, it offers a procedural setting allowing for a direct and robust dialogue among courts.

  As for the constitutional dimension of these dialogues, it has been claimed
that constitutional courts very rarely refer questions to the ECJ[181] and that

[176] *Id.* at 241.

[177] Spiros Simitis, *The Complexities of Living with an Interpretation Prerogative—Some Observations on an Imperfect Dialogue*, in LABOUR LAW IN THE COURTS. NATIONAL JUDGES AND THE
EUROPEAN COURT OF JUSTICE 291, 294 (Silvana Sciarra ed. 2001); Kokott, *supra* n 46, at 112; Claire
Kilpatrick, *Gender Equality: A Fundamental Dialogue*, in LABOUR LAW IN THE COURTS. NATIONAL
JUDGES AND THE EUROPEAN COURT OF JUSTICE 31, 47 (Silvana Sciarra ed. 2001): 'The reason for
repeated references is to put pressure on the ECJ to change its mind about a previous decision on
a similar issue because the referring court does not agree with what the ECJ decided.'

[178] Dehousse, *supra* n 164, at 75: 'German courts often choose to resubmit further questions to
the ECJ when it has in their view failed to understand the legal background of the problem.'

[179] Kokott, *supra* n 46, at 113.

[180] It could be thought that state courts fail to report back to hide non-compliance with ECJ
rulings. Others have suggested that state courts do not usually report to the ECJ because they
are overburdened, irrespective of actual compliance or non-compliance with ECJ judgments.
Again, the lack of empirical studies regarding the behaviour of state courts does not allow reaching a conclusion about the reasons for the lack of feedback.

[181] Until now, only a few constitutional courts have referred preliminary questions to
the ECJ: the Belgian Court of Arbitration, which is the equivalent of a constitutional court,
Federation Belge des Chambers de Médicins v Flemish Government, C-93/97; later on, the same
Court submitted a preliminary reference asking the ECJ about the validity of the European
Arrest Warrant framework decision, with relevant constitutional implications, *Advocaten voor
der Wereld VZW v Leden van de Ministerraad*, C-303/05; *Government of the French Community,
and Walloon Government v Flemish Government*, C-212/06. Also, the Austrian Constitutional

references brought by ordinary judges are not formulated as questions about constitutional matters.[182] Given their function and place in the system, constitutional courts do not usually deal with the application of EU law. Ordinary courts are the ones in charge of enforcing EU law and the ones that are most likely to face a potential conflict between the application of EU law and the state constitution. This is not to deny, however, that cases with a European dimension might reach constitutional courts. For example, this would be the case when constitutional courts review state measures enacted within the field of application of EU law. In any event, constitutional courts have proven to be very reluctant to file a preliminary reference.[183] It has even been questioned whether constitutional courts are allowed to do so, since in many countries they are not formally part of the judiciary. Their special status notwithstanding, there is no legal obstacle to their filing a preliminary reference. As argued above, the ECJ interprets very broadly what 'court or tribunal' is allowed to send a reference. Indeed, the ECJ has admitted questions coming from constitutional courts without having their status as courts called into question.[184] In the case brought by the Lithuanian Constitutional Court, Advocate General Kokott declared that constitutional courts fall within the definition of court for the purposes of article 234 EC Treaty. She further argued that a constitutional court, when reviewing the constitutionality of a legislative act, is called upon to make a decision of a judicial nature.[185] The ECJ admitted the preliminary question without further examination.[186] A referral from a constitutional court would allow a

---

Court, *Adria-Wien Pipeline GmbH and Wietersdorfer & Peggauer Zementwerke GmbH v Finanzlandesdirektion für Kärnten*, C-143/99, *Österreichischer Rundfunk and Others*, C-465/00; the Lithuanian Constitutional Court, *Julius Sabatauskas and Others*, C-239/07; and the Italian Constitutional Court (102/08, 3 February 2008), in which case the ECJ decision is still pending.

[182] De Witte, *supra* n 162, at 41.

[183] For instance, STC 64/1991, 22 March 1991, declared that it was not its function to enforce EU fundamental rights, but rather the protection of fundamental rights entrenched in the Spanish Constitution. EU fundamental rights would only be taken into consideration for interpreting state constitutional rights (article 10.2 Spanish Constitution).

[184] See *supra* n 181.

[185] Opinion of Advocate General Kokott, *Julius Sabatauskas and Others*, C-239/07, paras 15–19.

[186] *Id.*, at para. 15: 'when examining whether a law is constitutional, [the constitutional court] decides a dispute between the person or persons bringing the action and the institution which has adopted the contested law, namely the Lithuanian Parliament. Its decisions are not subject to appeal.'

direct conversation between the ultimate interpreters of rights in each legal system, with the discussion focusing on the contested fundamental right.[187]

In any event, a dialogue with a constitutional dimension might develop, even if state constitutional courts do not bring questions directly before the ECJ. On occasion, ordinary courts have been a conveyance between state constitutional courts and the ECJ. For instance, the preliminary ruling in *Internationale Handelsgesellschaft*,[188] one of the first cases in which the ECJ declared that fundamental rights were part of the EU legal order, was issued as a reply to the reference brought by an administrative court in Frankfurt. Not satisfied with the ECJ judgment, in which the ECJ held that the fundamental right at stake had not been violated, the Frankfurt court referred a constitutional question to the German Constitutional Court. The reply was encapsulated in the famous *Solange I* decision, which is regarded as the 'rebellion' that spurred the ECJ case law protecting fundamental rights. In this example, the same ordinary court referred subsequent questions to both the ECJ and the state constitutional court, which is rather unusual. Still, state courts can always refer a question to the ECJ regarding the interpretation of an EU fundamental right or the validity of a EU measure (particularly when its implementation within the state territory might impair fundamental rights). State courts should inform the ECJ about the constitutional scope of protection and the potential for conflict. For example, this was the case in *Wachauf*.[189] In its referral to the ECJ, a German ordinary court indicated that the implementation of a 1985 EC regulation by state authorities could challenge the constitutional right to property.[190] For a dialogue with a constitutional dimension to develop, it is enough that the content of the question has constitutional implications, which is usually the case when fundamental rights are involved. Yet, to make the ECJ aware of potential conflicts and

[187] In fact, it seems that the ECJ tends to pay more attention to the voice of constitutional courts. In the banana saga, not until the German Constitutional Court issued its decision did the ECJ reconsider its previous interpretation regarding the right to property and the freedom to pursue an economic activity. Dieter Grimm, *The European Court of Justice and National Courts: The German Constitutional Perspective after the Maastricht Decision*, 3 COLUMBIA JOURNAL OF EUROPEAN LAW 229, 238 (1997), claimed that a direct reference by a constitutional court would increase the awareness of the case and hopefully foster the participation of other states through the submission of their opinions, providing information to both the ECJ and the constitutional court involved.

[188] *Internationale Handelsgesellschaft mbh v Einhfuhr- und Vorratsstelle für Getreide und Futtermittel*, C-11/70.

[189] *Hubert Wachauf v Bundesamt für Ernährung und Forstwirtschaft*, C-5/88.

[190] See also *Anacleto Cordero Alonso v Fondo de Garantia Salarial (Fogasa)*, C-81/05, regarding diverging interpretations of the equality principle.

to develop a full dialogue, state courts should emphasize the constitutional implications of their questions. The fact that they fail to do so on many occasions shows that the preliminary reference's potential for dialogue is not fully realized.

Finally, it has been argued that 'a real dialogue, with mutual exchange of arguments, requires a series of subsequent references in different cases raising similar problems, which is rather cumbersome and rarely happens'.[191] Nevertheless, there are already examples of this sort of robust dialogue taking place, such as the succession of cases about the admissibility of affirmative action measures,[192] the myriad cases regarding sex equality in the workplace,[193] and the banana saga about the interpretation of the right to property and the freedom to pursue a commercial activity.[194] Hence, such a robust dialogue is not unfeasible. The number of occasions in which an ongoing dialogue develops on the interpretation of a particular fundamental right might be greater than thought, but the empirical research in this field is incomplete. Usually, the scope of existing works is limited to seminal decisions by the ECJ or its interaction with the courts of a single state, thus failing to undertake an analysis of case law evolution regarding a particular right over time and across countries.[195] Obviously, a situation in which all participants could join an open-ended discussion about the interpretation of rights until reaching a universal consensus is unattainable in the real world. Dialogue will take place over time, as courts from different states bring new arguments before the ECJ, and the interpretive outcomes keep being refined. This procedural mechanism provides a

[191] De Witte, *supra* n 162, at 41.
[192] *Eckhard Kalanke v Freie Hansestadt Bremen*, C-450/93; *Hellmut Marschall v Land Nordrhein-Westfalen*, C-409/95; *Georg Badeck and Others, interveners: Hessische Ministerpräsident and Landesanwalt beim Staatsgerichtshof des Landes Hessen*, C-158/97; *Katarina Abrahamsson and Leif Anderson v Elisabet Fogelqvist*, C-407/98.
[193] Kilpatrick, *supra* n 15, analysing the dialogue between the ECJ and English courts concerning the interpretation of sex equality; also Kilpatrick, *supra* n 177, expanding the analysis to other countries.
[194] *Federal Republic of Germany v Council of the European Communities*, C-280/93; *Atlanta Fruchthandelsgesellschaft mbH and others v Bundesamt für Ernährung und Forstwirtschaft*, C-465/93; *T. Port GmbH & Co. KG v Bundesanstalt für Landwirtschaft und Ernährung*, C-68/95; German Constitutional Court decisions of 25 January 1995 and 7 June 2000. Christoph U. Schmid, *All Bark and No Bite: Notes on the Federal Constitutional Court's 'Banana Decision'*, 7 EUROPEAN LAW JOURNAL 95 (2001); Ulrich Everling, *Will Europe Slip on Bananas? The Bananas Judgment of the Court of Justice and National Courts*, 33 COMMON MARKET LAW REVIEW 401 (1996).
[195] Kilpatrick, *supra* n 15, pointed out the input to dialogues between the ECJ and English courts coming from the ECJ's answers to other state courts.

procedural mechanism particularly well suited to channel judicial dialogue in a non-hierarchical way.[196] The preliminary reference links state and supranational courts with regard to overlapping areas in which neither system can claim total sovereignty. Hence, the preliminary reference is fit for a robust dialogue about the interpretation of fundamental rights between courts pertaining to different levels of governance.

[196] Dehousse, *supra* n 164, at 136–137: 'On paper, Article 177 [now 234] preliminary references...could have given rise to two distinct models of relationships: a hierarchical model, in which the ECJ would have tried to affirm its own superiority, or a co-operative model, based on goodwill and mutual respect. Yet, one element clearly militated in favor of the co-operative model, namely the fact that Article 177 is entirely dependent on the goodwill of national courts.'

6

Comparative Constitutional Reasoning: Recasting its Justification and Operation

In the previous chapter, it was argued that dialogue provides a regulative model to ground the legitimacy of European Court of Justice (ECJ) fundamental rights' adjudication in its interaction with state courts. Judicial dialogue contributes to conflict management in a process of mutual accommodation over time. What are the implications of this dialogic ideal for the mode of judicial reasoning? This chapter focuses on the interpretation of European Union (EU) fundamental rights itself. In the context of legal theory, interpretation consists of attributing meaning to a norm. Given the claim of authority attached to any judicial decision, the attribution of meaning to norms needs to be justified.[1] Interpretive theories offer methods to justify the attribution of meaning to a text. Legal justification consists in giving (good) reasons.[2] 'Good legal reasons are not "good reasons in all possible worlds" as reasons in ethics ideally are, but rather reasons that fit into a legal system. Thus reasons in legal justification are more relative, more context-bound, than reasons in moral justification.'[3] What kinds of reasons might justify the attribution of meaning by the judiciary to a legal text in a given political context? In answering this question with regard to EU

---

[1] ROBERT ALEXY, A THEORY OF CONSTITUTIONAL RIGHTS (Oxford University Press 2002): 'The legal problem of constitutional rights is first and foremost a problem of the interpretation of authoritative formulations of positive law'; Paul W. Kahn, *Interpretation and Authority in State Constitutionalism*, 106 HARVARD LAW REVIEW 1147, 1164 (1993): 'An authority that no longer considers itself bound by interpretation becomes merely a power to coerce.'

[2] JOXERRAMON BENGOETXEA, THE LEGAL REASONING OF THE EUROPEAN COURT OF JUSTICE. TOWARDS A EUROPEAN JURISPRUDENCE 159 (Clarendon Press 1993).

[3] *Id.*

fundamental rights, we need to take into account the supranational nature of the law being interpreted and the institutional position of the ECJ in this supranational community.

The methods of constitutional interpretation are several, and there is no agreement about how to choose among them. It will be argued that given that the EU constitutes a particular kind of overarching community, embracing a plurality of constitutional self-governing polities, there is a need to recognize and respect the diverse constitutional approaches in building supranational fundamental rights. As will be demonstrated, the comparative analysis of state constitutional law provides good reasons to justify the interpretation of EU rights. Therefore, in adjudicating EU rights, the ECJ ought to pay due regard to state constitutional law as the main source of interpretation and seek to build common understandings through the comparative method. In this vein, comparative reasoning for interpreting EU rights might be regarded as a form of extending the dialogic ideal for the interaction between national and supranational courts to the process of intellectual interpretation within the ECJ. Some academics refer to the practice of comparative reasoning, in which judges from one legal system cite the judgments from other jurisdictions, as dialogue.[4] Broadly, the term 'dialogue' has been used to refer to the increasing worldwide interaction among courts at multiple levels.[5] In this work, however, the term 'dialogue' receives a much more restrictive use. The mere borrowing or citation of foreign judicial decisions, without other jurisdictions necessarily being aware of such actions, does not amount to dialogue in the sense delineated in the previous chapter. Although some have insisted that there is a move from mere reception or borrowing to dialogue in the way comparative materials are used,[6] still, dialogue in the EU has a different nature and structure.[7] In

---

[4]   Claire L'Heureux-Dubé, *The Importance of Dialogue: Globalization and the International Impact of the Rehnquist Court*, 34 TULSA LAW JOURNAL 15 (1998); Anne-Marie Slaughter, *A Typology of Transjudicial Communication*, 29 UNIVERSITY OF RICHMOND LAW REVIEW 99 (1994); Anne-Marie Slaughter, *A Global Community of Courts*, 44 HARVARD INTERNATIONAL LAW JOURNAL 191 (2003).

[5]   Slaughter, *A Typology of Transjudicial Communication, supra* n 4, points out that one can distinguish different degrees of reciprocal engagement among courts involved in comparative reasoning; yet she conceives all forms of interaction as part of a common phenomenon of transjudicial communication.

[6]   L'Heureux-Dubé, *supra* n 4, at 17; Slaughter, *A Global Community of Courts, supra* n 4, at 198.

[7]   Slaughter, *A Typology of Transjudicial Communication, supra* n 4, at 113, referring to the interaction between national and supranational courts in the EU, declared: 'The key distinguishing feature between this type of dialogue and other forms of judicial communication is the awareness on the part of both participants of whom they are talking to and a corresponding willingness to take account of the response.'

the EU, dialogue between national and supranational courts occurs within an established institutional framework set up as part of a broader integration project. These legal systems are closely interdependent: instead of a court citing decisions from a foreign court to interpret domestic rights, the ECJ is interpreting rights that are going to be applied to the legal systems that provide the sources of interpretation. National and supranational courts are aware of being part of a common enterprise, and there are incentives for them to engage in an exchange of arguments over time to reach the best reasoned outcome for the community as a whole. In this context, judicial dialogue (complemented by comparative reasoning) aims at fostering a collective deliberation about the meaning of fundamental rights and ultimately enhancing the legitimacy of supranational interpretive outcomes.

Indeed, the ECJ has repeatedly declared that EU fundamental rights should be interpreted in accordance with the constitutional traditions common to the member states,[8] which implies the use of the comparative method.[9] The actual use that the ECJ has made of these sources and method, however, has been the object of persistent criticism in the literature. It is not clear whether the ECJ is actually interpreting according to what this court declares (and would be normatively desirable) and, in any event, it is not clear what this method of interpretation entails. Although the criticism of the actual practice is well taken, given the lack of systematic inter-state comparisons in ECJ decisions, this does not mean that the comparative method should be rejected or that it cannot be properly applied. First, a normative justification for the comparative method will be articulated. Thereafter, this chapter will expand on how the ECJ should operationalize this method.

---

[8] For instance, *Hoechst AG v Commission of the European Communities*, C-46/87 and 227/88: 'The Court has consistently held that fundamental rights are an integral part of the general principles of law the observance of which the Court ensures, in accordance with constitutional traditions common to the Member States'; *Omega Spielhallen- und Automatenayfstellungs-GmbH v Oberbürgermeisterin der Bundesstadt Bonn*, C-36/02: '[F]undamental rights form an integral part of the general principles of law the observance of which the Court ensures, and...for that purpose, the Court draws inspiration from the constitutional traditions common to the Member States.'

[9] As former ECJ Justice Pierre Pescatore, *Le Recours, dans la Jurisprudence de la Cour de Justice des Communautés Européennes, a des Normes Déduites de la Comparaison des Droits des Etats Membres*, 2 REVUE INTERNATIONALE DE DROIT COMPARÉ 337, 341 (1980), put it, the reference to the 'common constitutional traditions' evidently implied a whole programme of constitutional comparative law.

1 Comparative constitutional reasoning in fundamental rights interpretation

1.1 *Sources and methods of constitutional interpretation*

Generally speaking, the term 'sources of law' is ambiguous. It can be used in a broad variety of ways.[10] For the purposes of this discussion, we will distinguish among sources of law, sources of interpretation, and methods of interpretation, notwithstanding the fact that these concepts are intimately related. 'Sources of law' are narrowly understood as the written norms or unwritten principles that constitute binding law. Within state legal systems, the main source of fundamental rights law is traditionally the constitution. Given the open texture and indeterminacy of the language of fundamental rights clauses, their meanings are essentially contested.[11] 'Sources of interpretation' provide the arguments upon which the interpreter justifies the attribution of meaning to a legal text. There are multiple sources for interpreting fundamental rights. The source of interpretation that will be relied upon depends on the relevant 'method of interpretation'. Methods of interpretation direct how to ascertain the meaning of a legal provision on the basis of the corresponding sources. The function of the methods of interpretation is to justify the attribution of meaning to a text. These methods offer ways in which legal reasoning needs to be cast in order to fulfil this function.[12]

Written state constitutions tend to include a catalogue of fundamental rights. In systems of judicial review, these rights are employed by the judiciary to ascertain the validity of state legislation. Given the uniqueness of the constitution and its function as the supreme norm of the legal system, the methods of constitutional interpretation are distinguished from the methods for interpreting general legislation.[13] Most of these methods might yet coincide. Generally, the traditional methods of constitutional

---

[10]   Bengoetxea, *supra* n 2, at 64–65.

[11]   Jeremy Waldron, *Vagueness in Law and Language: Some Philosophical Issues*, 82 CALIFORNIA LAW REVIEW 509 (1994).

[12]   ROBERT ALEXY, A THEORY OF LEGAL ARGUMENTATION. THE THEORY OF RATIONAL DISCOURSE AS THEORY OF LEGAL JUSTIFICATION 234, 250 (Clarendon Press 1989).

[13]   Jed Rubenfeld, *Legitimacy and Interpretation*, in CONSTITUTIONALISM. PHILOSOPHICAL FOUNDATIONS 194, 205–209 (Larry Alexander ed. 1998): 'Constitutional interpretation cannot be derived from the bare fact that the Constitution is an object of interpretation, or from the only

interpretation rely on sources that are internal to the legal system. Among the most common methods of interpretation employed by the judiciary, we can include the following:[14] textual, originalist, dynamic, structural, and natural law. First, the textual method requires that fundamental rights be interpreted according to the plain meaning of the text.[15] Thus, the source of interpretation is the text of the norm. If the text is clear, there is no need to consult other sources. Due to the indeterminacy of human rights provisions, however, the language of the text tends to leave room for differing interpretations. In connection with the textual method, intratextualism establishes that other provisions contained in the same legal document as the clause being interpreted might enlighten the meaning of this clause.[16] Secondly, originalism dictates that constitutional rights should be interpreted according to the intent of the framers.[17] The sources to ascertain the framers' intent usually encompass the constitution-drafting debates and the ratification history.[18] Thirdly, according to the dynamic (also referred to as 'evolutionary') method, the interpretation of constitutional rights should take into consideration current understandings of the place and time in which those rights are to be applied. The source of this method is fairly vague, sometimes encompassing social opinion or constitutional culture.[19] Fourthly, the structural method states that constitutional provisions should be interpreted according to the basic normative structures established by the constitution. As defined by Philip Bobbitt, 'Structural arguments are inferences from the existence of constitutional structures and the relationships which the

---

slightly less bare fact that the Constitution is law. We are obliged, instead, to say what mode of interpretation is appropriate to this particular kind of text, this particular kind of law.'

[14] For other categorizations, see Richard Fallon, *A Constructivist Coherence Theory of Constitutional Interpretation*, 100 HARVARD LAW REVIEW 1189 (1987); PHILIP BOBBITT, CONSTITUTIONAL FATE 1–119 (Oxford University Press 1982).

[15] Fallon, *supra* n 14, at 1195–1198; Michael J. Perry, *The Authority of Text, Tradition, and Reason: A Theory of Constitutional 'Interpretation'*, 58 SOUTHERN CALIFORNIA LAW REVIEW 551, 554–555, 568 (1985).

[16] Akhil R. Amar, *Intratextualism*, 112 HARVARD LAW REVIEW 747, 748 (1999).

[17] Fallon, *supra* n 14, at 1198–1199; Bobbitt, *supra* n 14, at 9–24; Michael S. Moore, *A Natural Law Theory of Interpretation*, 58 SOUTHERN CALIFORNIA LAW REVIEW 277, 338–358 (1985).

[18] Originalism does not seem to be as popular in Europe as it is in some circles in the United States. Robert Bork, *Neutral Principles and Some First Amendment Problems*, 47 INDIANA LAW JOURNAL 1 (1971).

[19] Robert C. Post, *Foreword: Fashioning the Legal Constitution: Culture, Courts and Law*, 117 HARVARD LAW REVIEW 4, 8 (2003), defining 'constitutional culture' as 'the beliefs and values of nonjudicial actors about the substance of the constitution'.

Constitution ordains among these structures.'[20] This method relies on the purpose and function of the provision interpreted within the constitutional design. Finally, natural law requires that fundamental rights be interpreted according to universal principles (or moral values). The source is a universal conception of justice or morality. According to this method, fundamental rights provisions, to some extent, incorporate natural law into the legal system. Therefore, their interpretation ought to be justified by reference to the principles of natural law.[21]

This enumeration does not aim at completeness. Generally, courts do not restrict themselves to the use of one single method, but instead they combine several. Different legal systems, during different periods of time, have preferred some methods over others. With the exception of natural law, whose source is a universal standard, the sources of interpretation attached to these methods have a common element: they are 'internal' to a given legal order. To be clear, they are found within the boundaries of the state legal system: the constitutional text, the drafting history and the framers' intent, the constitutional culture of that specific society, and the constitution's structure and purpose. At the same time, courts might also engage in comparative reasoning as a method for interpreting fundamental rights. Comparative reasoning consists of referring to foreign judicial decisions or legal texts to justify the interpretation of one's own laws. In contrast to the above methods, the sources of interpretation are external to the interpreter's legal system.[22] They are not external in the sense of being universal, as natural law is, but rather they pertain to foreign legal systems. For this reason, comparative reasoning might pose particular problems of legitimacy, especially regarding constitutional interpretation. In addition, as a result of the increasing development of international human rights law, international treaties on human rights have also become a source for constitutional rights' interpretation. Furthermore, when the states are parties to these treaties, their provisions are not just sources of interpretation, but binding norms according to domestic rules governing the incorporation and hierarchy of international law.

---

[20] Bobbitt, *supra* n 14, at 74.

[21] Ronald Dworkin, *The Model of Rules*, 35 UNIVERSITY OF CHICAGO LAW REVIEW 14 (1967); RONALD DWORKIN, LAW'S EMPIRE (Harvard University Press 1986).

[22] This idea has been expressed with the notion of 'hetero-integration' as opposed to 'auto-integration'. See ALEJANDRO SAIZ ARNAIZ, LA APERTURA CONSTITUCIONAL AL DERECHO INTERNACIONAL Y EUROPEO DE LOS DERECHOS HUMANOS. EL ARTÍCULO 10.2 DE LA CONSTITUCIÓN ESPAÑOLA (Consejo General del Poder Judicial 1999).

1.2 Comparative constitutional interpretation: the debate

The use of comparative reasoning by courts, particularly for interpreting fundamental rights, has been steadily increasing around the world.[23] As Christopher McCrudden asserts, 'It is now a commonplace in many...jurisdictions...for courts to refer extensively to the decision of the courts of foreign jurisdictions when interpreting human rights guarantees.'[24] The growing use of comparative reasoning in judicial interpretation is regarded as a part of a larger phenomenon: the globalization of the practice of modern constitutionalism.[25] Yet, as the use of comparative reasoning has been expanding, both the legitimacy and efficacy of this method have raised some concerns. There is an open debate about the appropriateness of using comparative reasoning in judicial interpretation,[26] particularly in the domain of constitutional law.[27]

1.2.1 Arguments supporting comparative reasoning

Some academics have sought to justify the use of comparative reasoning or, at least, to describe the normative justifications offered by courts when they use it. Comparative reasoning might be used in different ways, and the question of legitimacy might be different for each of these uses.[28] Basically, foreign sources might be advanced, first, as an independent argument for the interpretation of domestic law. In this vein, a reason to interpret that a specific constitutional right means X is that courts in a foreign system interpreted an analogous right to mean X.[29] This is not to say, however, that foreign interpretations are binding as precedent. Instead, the fact that these

---

[23] Slaughter, *A Typology of Transjudicial Communication*, *supra* n 4, at 99; Anne-Marie Slaughter, *Judicial Globalization*, 40 VIRGINIA JOURNAL OF INTERNATIONAL LAW 1103 (2000); L'Heureux-Dubé, *supra* n 4; Sujit Choudhry, *Globalization in Search of Justification: Toward a Theory of Comparative Constitutional Interpretation*, 74 INDIANA LAW JOURNAL 819, 820 (1999); Christopher McCrudden, A Common Law of Human Rights?: *Transnational Judicial Conversations on Constitutional Rights*, 20 OXFORD JOURNAL OF LEGAL STUDIES 499 (2000).

[24] *Id.*, at 506.

[25] Choudhry, *supra* n 23, at 821.

[26] McCrudden, *supra* n 23, at 507–510.

[27] Choudhry, *supra* n 23, at 821: 'The globalization of the practice of modern constitutionalism generally, and the use of comparative jurisprudence in particular, raise difficult theoretical questions because they stand at odds with one of the dominant understanding of constitutionalism: that the constitution of a nation emerges from, embodies, and aspires to sustain or respond to that nation's particular history and political traditions.'

[28] Jens C. Danmann, *The Role of Comparative Law in Statutory and Constitutional Interpretation*, 14 ST. THOMAS LAW REVIEW 513, 519–520 (2002).

[29] *Id.*, at 521; McCrudden, *supra* n 23, at 516.

interpretations are authoritative in a foreign state is regarded as a reason to attribute the same interpretation to a domestic right.[30] These are called 'authority-based comparisons'.[31] Additionally, foreign sources might also be used in a 'non-authoritative' way to enlighten the interpreter by providing information about foreign constitutional experiences,[32] or to better ascertain the traditional methods of interpretation.[33] The reasons provided by the literature supporting the use of authority-based comparisons are basically the following:

1. *Genealogical.* The use of foreign sources might be justified when there is a relationship of descent and history between the constitutions of different legal systems. Sujit Choudhry explains how 'those relationships are sufficient justification to import and apply entire areas of constitutional doctrine'.[34] This author distinguishes genealogical relationships from genetic relationships. A genetic relationship exists when one constitution influences the framing of another, whereas a genealogical relationship 'describes a rather different phenomenon—literally, the birth of one constitutional order from another'.[35] Understood in the latter, the reach of this mode of comparative reasoning would be very limited in its scope. Indeed, a mere genetic relationship might be regarded as a good reason to borrow foreign constitutional law, even though it does not provide such a strong basis for justifying authority-based uses of comparative law.

2. *Procedural.* According to a 'procedural argument', there are reasons to borrow from other constitutional democracies since these polities follow procedures set to guarantee the fairness of outcomes. As Jens Danmann put it, 'If one assumes that democratic and legal procedures meeting a certain standard of fairness are apt to lead to desirable laws, then...the fact that a variety of such procedures have produced a certain rule can indicate the desirability of this rule.'[36]

---

[30] Carlos F. Rosenkrantz, *Against Borrowings and Other Nonauthoritative Uses of Foreign Law*, 1 International Journal of Constitutional Law 269, 270 (2003), explains that in these cases: 'The decision to use foreign law is based, at least in part, upon the authority that foreign law has in its original jurisdiction.'

[31] Danmann, *supra* n 28, at 521.   [32] Rosenkrantz, *supra* n 30, at 286–287.

[33] Danmann, *supra* n 28, at 520–521.

[34] Choudhry, *supra* n 23, at 825, 838–839; Rosenkrantz, *supra* n 30, at 278.

[35] Choudhry, *supra* n 23, at 838.

[36] Danmann, *supra* n 28, at 527; Rosenkrantz, *supra* n 30, at 280.

3. *Universalist*. The use of comparative reasoning might be justified on the basis of natural law.[37] The argument for comparative reasoning premised upon natural law assumes that there is a universal standard of justice and that all legal systems are aimed at interpreting legal provisions according to this universal standard. Therefore, if several countries have adopted the same interpretation, there are reasons to adopt it as an approximation to the universal standard of justice.[38] This justification is, nonetheless, highly contested, in part because the existence of natural law is controversial and clearly opposed by cultural relativists.[39] Even if the existence of natural law were accepted, empirical convergence would not necessarily imply that the outcome approximates the content of natural law,[40] as multiple examples demonstrate, such as the widespread legal discrimination of women over time around the world.

The most common underlying justifications for non-authoritative uses of comparative law are the following:

1. *Legal innovation*. To consult the law of other systems might provide new insights and ideas to interpret one's own law.[41] Foreign experiences enrich and broaden our horizons. Comparative reasoning might help to see one's own law in a new light and to reach outcomes that would not have been possible otherwise.[42] In this vein, knowledge of foreign interpretations might be a source of legal innovation.[43]

2. *Self-understanding*. Engaging in comparative analysis might help to better understand one's own constitutional system.[44] In the words of Choudhry, 'Courts identify the normative and factual assumptions underlying their own constitutional jurisprudence by engaging with comparable jurisprudence of other jurisdictions.'[45] This use of comparative reasoning might show striking similarities with underlying constitutional principles of other systems and then favour the reception of foreign interpretive outcomes. Conversely, it might contribute to an

---

[37] Kathryn A. Perales, *It Works Fine in Europe, so Why not Here? Comparative Law and Constitutional Federalism*, 23 VERMONT LAW REVIEW 885, 904–905 (1999); Choudhry, *supra* n 23, at 833–835, Danmann, *supra* n 28, at 526.

[38] Choudhry, *supra* n 23, at 825.   [39] *Id.* at 891.

[40] Danmann, *supra* n 28, at 527; Choudhry, *supra* n 23, at 890.

[41] Perales, *supra* n 37, at 902; Mark Tushnet, *The Possibilities of Comparative Constitutional Law*, 108 YALE LAW JOURNAL 1225, 1236 (1999).

[42] *Id.*, at 1236–1237.   [43] Rosenkrantz, *supra* n 30, at 288.

[44] Tushnet, *supra* n 41, at 1228–1229, 1285.

[45] Choudhry, *supra* n 23, at 825.

awareness of constitutional distinctiveness.[46] In any event, comparative constitutional interpretation is an 'important stimulus to legal self-
reflection',[47] which contributes to self-understanding.

3. *Avoiding failure*. Knowledge of foreign constitutional experiences might
help to avoid others' mistakes.[48] In this case, engaging in comparative
reasoning provides information about failed constitutional schemes and
thus borrowing is avoided.

1.2.2 *Objections to comparative reasoning*

The fact that the sources of interpretation are external to the interpreter's
own legal system casts doubts about the legitimacy and effectiveness of the
comparative method for interpreting fundamental rights.[49] There are normative and pragmatic reasons against the use of comparative reasoning as a
method of judicial interpretation. The first objection applies to authority-
based uses of foreign sources. The rest might apply to both.

1. *Democracy as popular sovereignty*. The use of foreign judicial opinions
on the basis of their authoritativeness in the country of origin for the
interpretation of one's own constitutional rights gives rise to a democratic concern from the perspective of popular sovereignty. According
to this principle, law's legitimacy is ultimately derived from the 'people'.
Arguably, interpreting constitutional clauses according to what foreign
legislators and courts have decided detracts from this principle.[50] Underlying this argument, there is a notion of popular sovereignty that conceives the constitution as the expression of the values and commitments
of a certain national community ('the people'). It is incompatible with
this principle to interpret the content of one's own constitution according to the views expressed by 'other peoples'. To put it differently, the
choices and values of others cannot be imposed upon a national people
through the constitution.[51] The use of foreign sources to give meaning to

---

[46] Gunter Frankenberg, *Critical Comparisons: Re-Thinking Comparative Law*, 26 HARVARD
INTERNATIONAL LAW JOURNAL 411 (1985); MARY ANN GLENDON, ABORTION AND DIVORCE IN
WESTERN LAW 142 (Harvard University Press 1987).

[47] Choudhry, *supra* n 23, at 835–838, denominated this mode of comparative constitutional
interpretation 'dialogical' and argued: 'courts that take this interpretive approach engage in
dialogue with comparative jurisprudence in order to better understand their own constitutional
systems and jurisprudence'; Rosenkrantz, *supra* n 30, at 291–292.

[48] *Id.*, at 289–290; Perales, *supra* n 37, at 902.

[49] Choudhry, *supra* n 23, at 825.   [50] Danmann, *supra* n 28, at 529.

[51] In his dissenting opinion in *Thompson v Oklahoma* 487 US 815 (1987), at 869, n 4, Justice
Scalia argued: 'We must never forget that it is a Constitution for the US of America that we are

constitutional provisions betrays the promise of a democratic constitution: self-government by the people.[52]

2. *Irrelevancy.* It has been argued that foreign sources, if not illegitimate, are irrelevant to the interpretation of one's own constitution. Constitutions encapsulate the values of a particular society and are inextricably interwoven with the political and social context in which they operate; therefore, the argument goes, the experience of other nations says little or nothing of relevance about one's own constitution.[53]

3. *Constitutional identity and culture.* What is worse, reliance on foreign law might hinder the development of a national constitutional identity and culture.[54] For a constitutional culture to develop, constitutional law ought to be experienced as a unique and final source for the resolution of conflicts.[55] The emergence and promotion of one's own constitutional identity is hindered if courts constantly refer to foreign systems for the interpretation of constitutional law.

4. *Arbitrariness.* Also, scholars have voiced concerns regarding the arbitrary use of comparative reasoning. Judges have been accused of 'cherry picking' the jurisdictions from which they cite, so that the 'jurisdictions chosen will be those which are likely to support the conclusion sought, leading to arbitrary decision-making, not legitimate judging'.[56] As such, it has been claimed that the use of comparative law is result-driven. Once the court has reached a decision about the meaning of the right to be interpreted, it will look for those jurisdictions that reached the same conclusion to support that interpretation. There are no clear criteria about which countries should be consulted and with what consequences.

5. *Misunderstanding.* Additionally, there is a risk of misunderstanding when consulting foreign sources. There are several reasons that make

expounding. The practices of other nations, particularly other democracies, can be relevant to determining whether a practice uniform among our people is not merely a historical accident, but rather "so implicit in the concept of ordered liberty" that it occupies a place not merely in our mores but, text permitting, in our Constitution as well....But where there is not first a settled consensus among our own people, the views of other nations, however enlightened the Justices of this Court may think them to be, cannot be imposed upon Americans through the Constitution.'

[52] Rosenkrantz, *supra* n 30, at 285: 'If we accept the idea that we are supposed to comply with the law only when it is the result of the collective choices of the political entity to which we belong, then we might object to constitutional borrowing simply because borrowing essentially consists of deferring to the collective choices taken by others.'

[53] Perales, *supra* n 37, at 897, 900–901.

[54] Rosenkrantz, *supra* n 30, at 293–294.

[55] *Id.* at 294–295.   [56] McCrudden, *supra* n 23, at 507.

it difficult to fully understand foreign norms, from language barriers to cultural differences. It is easy to misrepresent the purpose or meaning of a foreign principle.[57] The true understanding of a foreign legal system 'requires knowledge not only of the foreign law, but also of its social, and, above all, its political context'.[58]

6. *Transplantation.* Furthermore, even if foreign law is correctly appraised, there might be yet another difficulty in transplanting a particular legal norm to a different legal order. Certain legal concepts might work in a given system, but not in others.[59] As Mirjan Damaska has metaphorically put it, 'The music of the law changes... when the musical instruments and the players are no longer the same.'[60]

7. *Preponderance of internal sources.* Finally, the comparative law method is seen as illegitimate if it contradicts the interpretive results reached through other methods that make use of domestic sources, such as text or history. At most, comparative reasoning is recognized to have a purely auxiliary use.[61] Thus, the use of the comparative method should be limited to cases in which the traditional methods have failed. The comparative method should be discarded, however, if the interpretive outcome contradicts the one reached on the basis of any of the traditional methods of interpretation.

1.3 *The case for comparative reasoning in the European Union*

It is not the aim here to offer a general theory demonstrating the legitimacy of comparative reasoning as an independent method of interpretation. Instead, an argument justifying the (even authority-based) use of comparative law by the ECJ for interpreting EU fundamental rights on the basis of state constitutional law will be articulated. Indeed, it will be shown that this is an adequate method to give reasons for the interpretation of EU fundamental rights. Furthermore, it will be argued that the EU supranational nature and the particular framework in which judicial interpretation takes place change the premises underlying the foregoing arguments against the comparative method.

---

[57] Perales, *supra* n 37, at 901.
[58] Kahn-Freund, quoted in *id.*
[59] Rosenkrantz, *supra* n 30.
[60] Mirjan Damaska, *The Uncertain Fate of Evidentiary Transplants: Anglo-American and Continental Experiments*, 45 AMERICAN JOURNAL OF COMPARATIVE LAW 839, 840 (1997).
[61] Danmann, *supra* n 28, at 555, 557.

1.3.1 *Justifying the comparative method*

The justification of any judicial interpretation requires giving reasons. The methods of interpretation indicate the kinds of reasons that should be given to justify the attribution of meaning to a text, according to the corresponding sources. As shown above, there are several methods of interpretation. They do not indicate unambiguous results, and sometimes they lead to contradictory interpretations. Despite the efforts to reconcile and rank them, there is no widespread agreement within scholarly literature about how to choose among them.[62] The choice of a concrete method of interpretation (and the correlative sources) as opposed to another method usually depends on the grounds for the legitimacy of judicial adjudication in the broader constitutional-political system, and also on the kind of law being interpreted.[63] The claim here is that given the supranational nature of EU fundamental rights and the view of dialogue as providing the grounds for the normative legitimacy of ECJ adjudication, the comparative analysis of state constitutional law provides the most adequate reasons to justify the attribution of meaning to EU rights. Comparative reasoning as a method for interpreting fundamental rights complements and follows the dialogic model delineated in the previous chapter. Comparative reasoning allows continuing the dialogic ideal in the process of interpretation that takes place within the ECJ, and enhances the same values underlying dialogue: participation and the reasoned-quality of the decisions. First, comparative reasoning furthers participation since it brings as many viewpoints as possible to the interpretive process. Also, the comparative method might contribute to overcome limitations to direct participation by bringing the views of member states not directly intervening in the proceedings before the Court. By welcoming participation and assessing a variety of viewpoints stemming from diverse political and social values judicial decision-making itself becomes a form of collective deliberation.[64] Secondly, the ability to gather diverse approaches in the process of interpretation enhances the quality of the decision. Being aware of competing viewpoints enlightens the ECJ and allows for innovative decisions, tailored to the specific needs of this supranational community. Also, problems of particular interpretations might be detected. As asserted, the comparative method is justified on the basis of the

---

[62] Alexy, *supra* n 1, at 234; Fallon, *supra* n 14; McCrudden, *supra* n 23, at 502.
[63] Rubenfeld, *supra* n 13, at 208–211.
[64] Laurence R. Helfer & Anne-Marie Slaughter, *Toward a Theory of Effective Supranational Adjudication*, 107 YALE LAW JOURNAL 273, 322 (1997).

'enhanced quality of the decisions resulting from the likelihood that cross-national research will either turn up potential errors in and problems with a particular legal solution or open the door to innovation based on a wider range of potential models'.[65]

In this context, a sort of genealogical argument might have some bite regarding the choice of sources and method in the EU. Since EU fundamental rights are rooted in state constitutional rights, interpretation according to these sources is warranted. This relationship is confirmed by article 6.2 EU Treaty,[66] which consecrated judicial doctrine. This is not to deny the autonomy of EU fundamental rights. The ECJ has insisted that state constitutional rights are not binding upon EU institutions. This simply means that state constitutional rights cannot determine the validity of EU law, but not that the ECJ may ignore them in ascertaining the meaning of supranational fundamental rights. Indeed, the ECJ has recognized that it is 'bound to draw inspiration' from the constitutional traditions common to the member states.[67] As Weiler asserted, 'The constitutional traditions of the Member States are the obvious place to seek this inspiration...because it will be there that one may be able to find a European content to human rights.'[68] In this way, the ECJ interpretive freedom to build supranational, common rights would be partly constrained by the constitutional understandings of the members (and creators) of this supranational community. A further reason that justifies the consultation of state constitutional law is the fact that all member states are constitutional democracies (procedural argument). All member states have set internal procedures to guarantee the protection of rights. Almost all recognize the power of judicial review of legislation, usually centralized in a constitutional court. This does not mean that there are no failures of protection. Given these internal checks and balances, however, if a majority of states coincide upon a specific interpretation, there are good reasons to adopt the same interpretation at the supranational level.

---

[65] *Id.*, at 325.

[66] Article 6.2 EU Treaty (article 6.3 Lisbon Treaty): 'The Union shall respect fundamental rights...as they result from the constitutional traditions common to the Member States, as general principles of community law.' Markku Kiikeri, Comparative Legal Reasoning and European Law 112 (Kluwer Academic Publishers 2001).

[67] *Liselotte Hauer v Land Rheinland-Pfalz*, C-44/79.

[68] Joseph H. H. Weiler, *Eurocracy and Distrust: Some Questions Concerning the Role of the European Court of Justice in the Protection of Fundamental Rights within the Legal Order on the European Communities*, 61 Washington Law Review 1103, 1125 (1986).

From a more pragmatic perspective, inter-state comparisons facilitate the elaboration of interpretations that can be extended to the community as a whole.[69] The interpretation that the ECJ reaches in a certain case is going to be applied not only to that case, but also to future cases involving other states. Being aware of diverse national sensibilities and essential moral and political values would allow the ECJ to foresee the implications of a particular interpretation for the several states and to strive for a synthesis that all could assume. Thus, the use of this method would contribute to the avoidance of conflicts. Former Justice Pescatore affirms that thanks to the comparative analysis of national constitutions, it is possible to give response to two exigencies: the development of solutions adapted to the needs and logic of building the European community as well as the avoidance of conflicts with the constitutional rules of particular states.[70]

1.3.2 *Responding to general objections to the comparative method*

Academic literature tends to refer to the phenomenon of comparative reasoning very broadly. The use of foreign decisions in judicial interpretation, however, can occur in very different settings and with different degrees, functions, and purposes.[71] In the EU, the ECJ is not just borrowing from a foreign legal system to interpret rights of a separate system. The ECJ interprets supranational rights that, in turn, are binding upon the state legal systems that provide the sources of interpretation. In addition, the legal systems consulted are not totally foreign since member states are the constitutive parts of the EU. Given the particular political structure in which comparative reasoning takes place, the general objections formulated above become inapplicable.

Foreign sources are regarded by some as illegitimate because in a constitutional democracy all authority is derived from *the people*. Therefore, the argument goes, state constitutional rights should not be interpreted according to the will of other nations. In the EU, however, there is no single 'European people'. To the contrary, this is an overarching community embracing a plurality of European 'peoples'. Given the supranational nature of EU fundamental rights, these rights should reflect the common understanding of the European peoples. In this context, the democratic objection to authority-based comparisons fades away. Also, reliance on state constitutionalism for the interpretation of EU rights would not undermine the

---

[69] Pescatore, *supra* n 9, at 341.   [70] *Id.* at 355–356.
[71] Slaughter, *A Typology of Transjudicial Communication*, *supra* n 4.

development of a *European constitutional culture*. Indeed, a European constitutional culture should develop from the member states. This is not to say that it should replicate national constitutional cultures, which would not be possible because each member state enjoys its distinctive culture. At the same time, the EU supranational community encompasses its own values and interests. National and supranational constitutional cultures influence one another in a process of dialogic interaction.

Moreover, the *relevancy* of member states' constitutional laws as the sources for shaping EU rights becomes evident since the states are the constitutive parts of the supranational community whose common values are being defined. State constitutional sources do not properly belong to the EU legal system, but they are not purely 'foreign' either since they are found within the state legal orders constituting the EU. Furthermore, national and supranational courts participate in a broader common project of integration.[72] This does not mean that the ECJ cannot consult other legal systems, but those sources do not carry the same relevance for the interpretation of EU rights as state constitutional law.[73] Because the relevant systems are those of the member states, there are some guidelines to control the *arbitrary use* of the comparative method. If the ECJ arbitrarily picked those jurisdictions that favoured a certain interpretation, while ignoring others, state courts from those states would have reasons to challenge those interpretive outcomes. In this guise, the dialogic framework provides state courts with a check upon the arbitrary use of the comparative method.

Although the *risk of misinterpretation* does not disappear in the EU, it can be significantly reduced thanks to the dialogic framework. In the event of misinterpretation in a certain case, state courts are encouraged to speak to the ECJ. As has been observed, state courts might re-submit a question to the ECJ, or courts from other states could provide further information to the ECJ in future preliminary references. Moreover, state governments may also provide information in the process before the ECJ. In addition, the same composition of the ECJ might contribute to avoid misinterpretations

---

[72] McCrudden, *supra* n 23, at 521–522, argued that a deliberate alliance might be the basis for citing foreign sources: 'The common alliance impulse will be strongest...when the integration is set out explicitly as a political program, with institutional characteristics, such as in Europe.'

[73] Former ECJ Justice Pescatore, *supra* n 9, at 350, asserted that the comparative trend in the EU naturally found its framework and limit within the circle of the member states and declared that this is a pretty restricted dimension, if compared to what one usually calls 'comparative law' in the scientific sense of the term.

since there is one judge from each member state. Former ECJ Justice Everling declared: 'Each Judge has the important function of introducing the legal thinking and basic concepts of the Member State to which he belongs into the Court's consideration. Each Judge must also ensure that the decision and the reasoning on which it is based are expressed in such a way that they may be understood in his home country.'[74] The *dangers of transplantation* do not purely disappear either, since the interpretation given to a particular right within a member state might not work in the EU legal system, in which other interests and values might need to be balanced. Comparative analysis, however, does not entail automatic borrowing from another system. Rather, it offers the possibility to get to know and compare different solutions given by different member states to the same problem. The shortcomings or benefits of different interpretations can be assessed in light of the needs and goals of the EU legal system itself. In this way, the scope of protection granted to EU rights can be adapted to the structure of the EU.

Finally, should the EU Charter of fundamental rights enter into force, it would make available some of the *traditional methods of interpretation*, such as text or intent. Until the drafting of the Charter (2000), still deprived of binding force, there was no written catalogue of rights in the EU. Hence, the textual method lacked its source. For the same reason, original intent was not available either. Also, since there is no single and unitary European civil society, social understandings might vary across the states. The dynamic method would need to be applied by means of a comparison of the diverse cultural and social understandings. The drafting of a written catalogue of rights for the EU might have been regarded as creating the opportunity to cut the umbilical cord linking EU rights and state constitutionalism. Instead, the text of the Charter explicitly acknowledges, and even emphasizes, the role of constitutional traditions as sources for interpreting EU rights (article 52.4).[75] Some authors argue that the Charter could actually increase the influence of state constitutional traditions.[76] Ultimately, even

---

[74] Ulrich Everling, *The Court of Justice as a Decisionmaking Authority*, 82 MICHIGAN LAW REVIEW 1294, 1296 (1984). It should be borne in mind, however, that they very rarely sit in plenary sessions.

[75] Also, the Preamble declares: 'This Charter reaffirms, with due regard for the powers and tasks of the Union and the principle of subsidiarity, the rights as they result, in particular, from the constitutional traditions and international obligations common to the member states.'

[76] Ricardo Alonso García, *The General Provisions of the Charter of Fundamental Rights of the European Union*, 8 EUROPEAN LAW JOURNAL 492, 511 (2002), argues that the Charter would enhance influence of the common constitutional traditions. See also JUAN IGNACIO UGARTEMENDIA ECEIZABARRENA, EL DERECHO COMUNITARIO Y EL LEGISLADOR DE LOS DERECHOS

if the Charter were granted legal force, after the eventual ratification of the Lisbon Treaty, this would not justify abandoning state constitutional law as a relevant source for interpreting EU rights.

In sum, the general objections to comparative constitutional reasoning do not seem to be applicable in the EU context. This is not to say that state constitutional rights are binding at the supranational level, but that the ECJ should justify the interpretation of EU fundamental rights by referencing them.[77] At the same time, this does not mean that EU rights must replicate state constitutional rights. In the process of synthesizing different approaches, the ECJ might come up with innovative solutions better adapted to the EU legal system. In any case, a bottom-up construction of the meaning of EU fundamental rights, on the basis of a cross-national comparison of state constitutional law, is responsive to the supranational nature of these rights and the legitimacy of the ECJ's adjudication within the EU pluralist structure.

2 The operation of the comparative method

The question one needs to address now is not whether state constitutional law should be a source for interpreting EU rights, but rather how state constitutional law should function as a source for interpreting EU fundamental rights. The use that the ECJ has made of the comparative method has been sharply contested throughout the literature. The scholarly objections go from criticizing the ECJ's use (or non-use) of the comparative method to questioning the ECJ's ability to properly apply it. The analysis of the case law demonstrates that rarely, if at all, does the ECJ engage in a thorough comparative examination of the member states' constitutional orders.[78] Nor does the ECJ specify the sources of interpretation examined.[79] Consequently,

---

FUNDAMENTALES. UN ESTUDIO DE LA INFLUENCIA COMUNITARIA SOBRE LA FUNDAMENTALIDAD DE LOS DERECHOS FUNDAMENTALES 120 (IVAP 2001).

[77] Former ECJ Justice Pescatore, *supra* n 9, at 341, asserted that with the formula referring to the common constitutional traditions, the ECJ recognized that the guarantees granted by the fundamental rights of the several national constitutions constituted a source of inspiration and, more than that, an obligatory directive in and of itself. C. N. Kakouris, *Use of the Comparative Method by the Court of Justice of the European Communities*, 6 PACE INTERNATIONAL LAW REVIEW 267, n 25 (1994).

[78] *Id.*, at 275–273; Pescatore, *supra* n 9, at 338.

[79] Fabrice Picod, *Les Sources*, in RÉALITÉ ET PERSPECTIVES DU DROIT COMMUNAUTAIRE DES DROITS FONDAMENTAUX 125, 148 (Frédéric Sudre & Henri Labayle eds. 2000).

the use of the comparative method has been regarded as discretionary[80] and superficial.[81] Moreover, some critics have even claimed that this method is not workable because 'common' constitutional traditions do not exist among 'all' the member states.[82] Hence, even if the ECJ were committed to applying the comparative method, it would be very difficult to do so in practice,[83] given the increasing number of states and their existing differences.[84] Arguably, there were strategic reasons for the ECJ to refer to the constitutional traditions common to the member states. The Court might have been employing this formula as a tool to calm the anxieties of those member states that feared a lowering of the standards of constitutional protection as well as to reassure them that their constitutions would be taken into consideration when interpreting EU fundamental rights. If this were the case, the reference to the common constitutional traditions would merely be an exercise in empty rhetoric in order to create an appearance of legitimacy. Regardless of the internal motives that might have led the ECJ to refer to constitutional traditions as sources of interpretation, an improper use of the comparative method would be a reason to criticize the ECJ activity, but not necessarily to discard this method. Admitting the difficulties in applying it, and that there are powerful reasons to criticize the ECJ's current practices, it is contended that these are not sufficient grounds for rejecting this interpretive method or the possibility of its successful application. Having established its normative justification already, we will now proceed to explore how it should operate.

2.1 *Between lowest and highest standard approaches*

The use of comparative law in the EU context has prompted a discussion about the standard of interpretation that the ECJ should follow when faced

[80] ANDREW CLAPHAM, I HUMAN RIGHTS AND THE EUROPEAN COMMUNITY: A CRITICAL OVER-VIEW 50 (Nomos Verlagsgesellschaft 1991). Olivier Dord, *Systèmes Juridiques Nationaux et Cours Européennes: De l'Affrontement a la Complémentarité?*, 96 POUVOIRS. REVUE FRANÇAISE D'ETUDES CONSTITUTIONNELLES ET POLITIQUES 5, 12 (2000).

[81] Constance Grewe, *Les Conflits de Normes entre Droit Communautaire et Droits Nationaux en Matière de Droit Fondamentaux*, in L'UNION EUROPÉENNE ET LES DROITS FONDAMENTAUX 57, 70 (Stéphane Leclerc, Jean François Akandji-Kombé & Marei-Joelle Redor eds. 1999) ; Bruno de Witte, *The Past and Future of the European Court of Justice in the Protection of Human Rights*, in THE EU AND HUMAN RIGHTS 859, 878 (Philip Alston ed. 1999).

[82] Luis María Díez Picazo, *¿Una Constitución sin Declaración de Derechos? (Reflexiones Constitucionales sobre les Derechos Fundamentales en la Comunidad Europea)*, 32 REVISTA ESPAÑOLA DE DERECHO CONSTITUCIONAL 135, 150–151 (1991); Clapham, *supra* n 80, at 50.

[83] Kakouris, *supra* n 77, at 276.

[84] Kiikeri, *supra* n 66, at 301; Grewe, *supra* n 81, at 71, emphasizing how northern and southern member states' approaches to economic and social rights differ.

with divergent state interpretations. It will be concluded that neither lowest nor highest standard models provide satisfactory answers and they should not be pursued.[85]

2.1.1 *Lowest common denominator*

One available option is to establish that EU rights should be interpreted according to the lowest common denominator for all states. Let us imagine, for example, that the lowest common denominator is X. Hence, all states would agree that, at least, a specific right protects X. Some states, however, might expand the scope of this right to protect Y as well. If the ECJ mandated X, this standard of protection could fall below the standard of protection granted by states protecting X and Y. Since the ECJ interpretation sets a floor and a ceiling, some states would be precluded from protecting Y when acting within the field of application of EU law.[86]

This approach has been expressly rejected by the scholarly literature and by several ECJ judges. Among the academics, Leonard F. M. Besselink opposed the ECJ's adjudication according to the lowest common standard.[87] Also, Francis G. Jacobs asserted that the common constitutional traditions' formula 'cannot be taken to mean that the Court will apply the lowest common denominator'.[88] In academic writings, ECJ Justices have confirmed

[85] ANNA BREDIMAS, METHODS OF INTERPRETATION AND COMMUNITY LAW 126 (North-Holland Publishing Company 1978): 'The use of the comparative law method is not an *a priori* intent to find the highest common factor...nor the theory of the lowest common denominator but an intent to trace elements from which legal rules can be built for the Communities.'

[86] It should be realized that interpreting according to the lowest common denominator is different from saying that the ECJ interpretation sets a floor of protection. To grasp this difference, one should distinguish 'norm construction' from 'conflict resolution'. Interpreting according to the lowest common denominator refers to the process of norm construction. To be clear, it refers to how the ECJ should interpret a fundamental right when there is divergence among the member states. Once the ECJ finds which the lowest common denominator is, and passes to construct a supranational norm, that norm then operates as both a floor and a ceiling. In contrast, the minimum floor of protection is a rule for the resolution of conflicts between norms applicable to the same case. It does not speak to the specific method of interpretation. Irrespective of how an EU fundamental right has been interpreted, that interpretation sets a floor below which states cannot fall (but they are free to go above). This rule for conflict resolution was examined in Chapter 3.

[87] Leonard F. M. Besselink, *Entrapped by the Maximum Standard: On Fundamental Rights, Pluralism and Subsidiarity in the European Union*, 35 COMMON MARKET LAW REVIEW 629, 679 (1998): 'The enormous disadvantage of this common minimum standard...is that national courts will resist it whenever this standard provides less protection than other relevant standards would.'

[88] Francis G. Jacobs, *The Uses of Comparative Law in the Law of the European Communities*, in LEGAL HISTORY AND COMPARATIVE LAW 99, 106 (Richard Plender ed. 1990).

that the ECJ does not, and should not, follow a lowest common denominator approach. Former ECJ Justice Rodríguez Iglesias, elaborating on how the ECJ proceeds to define the EU standard of protection, explained that 'it is clear that this standard is not built upon the basis of a "common minimum standard"'.[89] Justice Skouris, in a hearing before the Constitutional Convention in charge of drafting the failed European Constitution, was asked about the ECJ's approach to common constitutional traditions of member states. He stated, 'It is not the Court's duty to discern, and, as it were, mechanically transpose into the community legal order, the lowest common denominator of constitutional traditions common to the member states.'[90] The lowest common denominator was clearly ruled out by the drafters of the Charter. The *Explanations* to the article commanding the use of common constitutional traditions as sources of interpretation (article 52.4) were clear: 'Rather than following a rigid approach of a "lowest common denominator", the Charter rights concerned should be interpreted in a way offering a high standard of protection which is adequate for the law of the Union and in harmony with the common constitutional traditions.'[91]

2.1.2 *Highest standard of protection*

An alternative approach to state divergences would require that the ECJ identify the state interpretation that offered the highest level of protection to the individual. This approach is contested in the literature. On the one hand, according to Besselink, if the ECJ interpreted rights according to this standard, this would guarantee an optimal human rights protection, while securing respect for the uniformity and supremacy of EU law.[92] On the other hand, others reject this approach.[93] It is argued that it would be very hard for the ECJ to decide which legal order offers the best level of protection in every case, particularly when several rights conflict with each other.[94] Even if easily identifiable, the highest level of protection would

---

[89] Gil C. Rodríguez Iglesias & Alejandro Valle Gálvez, *El Derecho Comunitario y las Relaciones entre el Tribunal de Justicia de las Comunidades Europeas, el Tribunal Europeo de Derechos Humanos y los Tribunales Constitucionales*, 1 REVISTA DE DERECHO COMUNITARIO EUROPEO 336 (2000).

[90] *Hearing of Judge Mr. Vassilios Skouris*, Working Document 19, 8 (Brussels, 27 September 2002).

[91] *Updated Explanations Relating to the Text of the Charter of Fundamental Rights*, CONV 828/1/03 (Brussels, 18 July 2003).

[92] Besselink, *supra* n 87, at 670–674, supporting a maximum standard approach.

[93] JOSEPH H. H. WEILER, THE CONSTITUTION OF EUROPE 109–116 (Cambridge University Press 1999).

[94] *Id.* at 111.

not necessarily be the most desirable solution at the supranational level. If the ECJ followed this approach, it would be captured by the interpretation reached in a particular member state.[95] The specific standard of protection granted in a particular member state might not be the most suitable in the context of the EU legal order or in other member states.[96]

When article 53 of the Charter, entitled 'levels of protection', establishes that 'Nothing in this Charter shall be interpreted as restricting or adversely affecting human rights...as recognized...by the Member States' constitutions', this could be read as indicating the need to construct EU rights according to the highest standard. In other words, interpreting EU fundamental rights according to the highest national level of protection would 'not restrict or adversely affect' constitutional rights. However, compelling the ECJ to identify and apply the highest national standard in each and every case, even if feasible, would hinder the development of an EU catalogue of rights best suited for the community as a whole.[97] Instead, as further explored below, this article is better understood as suggesting the possibility of being deferential to state courts. As Bruno de Witte once said, 'It is wise for the Court not to adapt the "maximum standard" of protection but to exercise some judicial restraint in applying fundamental rights.'[98]

2.2 Reaching synthetic outcomes while accommodating diversity

2.2.1 Access to sources of interpretation

In order to conduct a comparative analysis, the ECJ should proceed to look into the constitutional laws of the member states. The ECJ might obtain the information needed for an inter-state comparison from several sources.[99] These sources refer not only to the constitutional law of single states, but some also provide the ECJ with extensive comparative law analyses. These sources may be grouped in (i) sources in the domain of the ECJ: Advocate General Opinions, the ECJ Service of Research, and deliberations among judges coming from different countries; (ii) non-judicial actors in

---

[95] *Id.* at 110; de Witte, *supra* n 81, at 881, asserted: 'Following a "maximum standard" approach the ECJ would be actually privileging the approach of one particular state over the others, and there is no obvious reason why this should be so.'

[96] Weiler, *supra* n 93, at 110–112.

[97] See also Francisco Rubio Llorente, *Mostrar los Derechos sin Destruir la Unión (Consideraciones sobre la Carta de Derechos Fundamentales de la Unión Europea)*, 64 REVISTA ESPAÑOLA DE DERECHO CONSTITUCIONAL 13, 44 (2002), against the interpretation of this article as indicating a highest standard approach.

[98] De Witte, *supra* n 81, at 882.   [99] Jacobs, *supra* n 88, at 110.

procedures before the ECJ: Commission, member state governments, and parties; and (iii) judicial actors: state courts and the European Court of Human Rights (ECtHR).

The Opinions of Advocates General (AGs)[100] often carry out studies of national constitutional law in order to interpret EU fundamental rights.[101] The ECJ tends to follow AG opinions, although the ECJ rarely brings the comparative analysis to the judgment.[102] For example, in *Transocean Marine*,[103] AG Warner undertook a comparative analysis of all member states law to determine the status of the right to a hearing before the administration takes a decision adversely affecting the individual. He concluded that the right existed in all countries except Italy and the Netherlands, and he recommended that the ECJ embrace it. In spite of not explicitly referring to state constitutional traditions in the judgment, the ECJ enforced this right. In *Hauer*,[104] which is often cited by those who accuse the ECJ of selectively and discretionarily choosing certain states,[105] AG Capotorti examined the constitutional laws and the regime of expropriation of all member states to determine the scope of the right to property. In cases regarding the equal protection of transsexuals,[106] the respective AG conducted extensive comparative studies covering all member states.[107] Also, the ECJ has a Service of Research and Documentation comprised of 27 lawyers covering every legal system of the member states.[108] The ECJ often calls upon the Service to carry out comparative studies relevant to cases before the ECJ.[109] Former

[100] The duty of Advocates General is to assist the ECJ in an impartial and independent way. Their opinions are not binding, but they are considered with great care by the ECJ.

[101] Kakouris, *supra* n 77, at 277.

[102] Pescatore, *supra* n 9, at 346–347.

[103] *Transocean Marine Paint Association v Commission of the European Communities*, C-17/74.

[104] *Liselotte Hauer v Land Rheinland-Pfalz*, C-44/79.

[105] In that case, only Germany, Italy, and Ireland were mentioned in the ECJ judgment.

[106] *P v S and Cornwall County Council*, C-13/94; *K.B. v National Health Service Pensions Agency and Secretary of State for Health*, C-117/01.

[107] In *P v S*, AG Tesauro identified a tendency, since the 1980s, towards wider recognition of transsexuality, both in the legislative and judicial decisions of the member states. The AG indicated the countries that had adopted special legislation on transsexuality, and identified others in which the problem had been resolved by the courts or at the administrative level. In *K. B.*, AG Ruiz-Jarabo Colomer surveyed the legal treatment given to the marriage of transsexuals in their acquired sex in all member states. He concluded that only the UK and Ireland did not allow marriage after sex reassignment and that this fact was 'not a bar to identifying a sufficiently uniform legal tradition capable of being a source of a general principle of community law'.

[108] Jacobs, *supra* n 88, at 110.

[109] Kakouris, *supra* n 77, at 277; Pescatore, *supra* n 9, at 349; Kiikeri, *supra* n 66, at 149: 'In 1995, for example, there were at least 20 extensive comparative surveys made in the preliminary

Justice Pescatore asserted that these studies actually have an influence in the decisions, in spite of the lack of any reference in the judgment.[110] In addition, the same composition of the ECJ might facilitate the comparative analysis since there is one judge from each member state. As a consequence, there is a diversity of legal traditions represented within the ECJ,[111] bringing a variety of viewpoints to the discussion. As Kakouris pointed out: 'The comparative method is underlying in all cases due to each judge's different legal training, knowledge, approach, and reasoning, which reflects the legal system of his country. The deliberations are enriched by the diversity of the contributions made by the judges. The Court's deliberations constitute a living comparative law in action.'[112] At the same time, despite the fact that judges come from different legal backgrounds, this does not automatically mean that they engage in systematic comparative law analyses covering all the member states on a regular basis. Moreover, it should be kept in mind that judges usually sit on three- or five-member panels. Thirteen-member panels are convened only when required by the parties or an EU institution, or when the complexity of the case requires it. Plenary sessions are very rare.[113] In any event, even with reduced panels, judges with diverse legal perspectives need to engage in deliberation to reach a decision.[114] The deliberative nature of discussions within the ECJ and the Court's diverse composition contribute to comparative judicial reasoning.

Other participants in proceedings before the ECJ might provide information that facilitates the comparative inquiry. Often, the Commission submits comparative law studies, particularly in the course of preliminary rulings.[115] Sometimes, the ECJ has expressly asked the Commission to draw up a comparative law study, such as in *Miss M. v Commission*.[116]

---

preparation of a case. The studies seem to have had a tremendous use and impact. The studies are not necessarily reflected in the explicit judgments.'

[110] Pescatore, *supra* n 9, at 349; Everling, *supra* n 74, at 1302.

[111] Jacobs, *supra* n 88, at 110; Everling, *supra* n 74, at 1296.

[112] Kakouris, *supra* n 77, at 277.   [113] Article 16 of the ECJ Statute.

[114] Everling, *supra* n 74, at 1304–1305, emphasized the deliberative nature of the discussions within the Court: 'This is done by mutual discussion and influence, a process that requires a high degree of understanding of the basic tenets of other legal systems and that will lead to a successful outcome only if all sides possess a willingness to arrive at common conclusions'; Pescatore, *supra* n 9, at 349, pointed out the 'comparative attitude and philosophy' of the judges during the course of the deliberations.

[115] *Id.*, at 348.

[116] *Miss M. v Commission*, C-177/78. In this case, the ECJ explicitly referred to the findings of the Comission's comparative law study.

Justice Pescatore manifested a very positive opinion regarding the Commission's contribution in this field. He explained that the Commission is in an advantageous position to elaborate comparative law studies because it has a legal service with lawyers from all member states and, in the course of its function, enjoys broad access to knowledge regarding national legal systems.[117] Thus, the Commission's reports are often taken into consideration in the decision-making process.[118] As explained in the previous chapter, state governments might also intervene in the preliminary reference. Hence, they may possibly bring information about the scope of protection of the right at stake in that national legal system, as well as about the implications of different interpretations. Although such reports are not necessarily comparative in nature, they offer information to the ECJ to develop inter-state comparisons. Sometimes, comparative studies are submitted, but it is quite rare.[119] The parties in the case might also provide arguments based on comparative studies for or against a particular interpretation.[120] Obviously, they argue from the perspective of their own interests, a fact the ECJ is aware of.[121] For instance, in *AM & S Europe*,[122] the ECJ invited the parties and other interveners to submit comparative materials in order to obtain further clarification on questions of comparative law. These materials were discussed in open court.[123]

State courts, as the main interlocutors of the ECJ through the preliminary reference, might (and should) bring information about the constitutional interpretation of the right at stake in their respective legal systems. Although they do not perform comparative studies, they might refer to other legal systems in submitting their questions to persuade the ECJ. Finally, the European Convention on Human Rights (ECHR) and, more importantly, the ECtHR case law are an important source for finding evidence of comparative

---

[117] Pescatore, *supra* n 9, at 348, stating that the major contributions about comparative law come from the Commission.

[118] Kiikeri, *supra* n 66, at 150–151.   [119] *Id.*, at 150.

[120] *Id.*: 'It is not rare that the parties produce comparative studies.... The studies produced by the parties are taken into account.'

[121] AG Darmon, in *Orkem v Commission*, C-374/87, declared: 'The law of the member states concerning the right not to give evidence against oneself has been extensively described by the parties in their written submissions. However, those submissions give me the impression that in making that comparison of national laws each of them found not what it was looking for but rather what it had decided to find.'

[122] *AM & S Europe v Commission*, C-155/79.

[123] Thijmen Koopmans, *Comparative Law and the Courts*, 45 INTERNATIONAL AND COMPARATIVE LAW QUARTERLY 545, 548 (1996).

law regarding fundamental rights. The ECtHR tends to engage in comparative analyses to determine whether there is a European consensus about the
scope of protection of a particular right. In the past, the ECJ rarely cited
decisions of the ECtHR but presumably did take them into account in reaching a decision. At least, AG opinions and parties' submissions often refer to
ECtHR decisions.[124] Over time, specific references to ECtHR judgments
are becoming more frequent. For instance, regarding the interpretation of
the right to equal protection of transsexuals, the ECJ explicitly referred to
decisions of the ECtHR that included surveys of national law.[125] In sum, the
availability of all the above sources secures the possibility for the ECJ to get
enough information about state constitutional laws to apply the comparative
method in interpreting fundamental rights.[126]

2.2.2 *Toward synthesis at the supranational level*

From these inter-state comparative analyses, the ECJ should derive interpretations adequate for the community as a whole. The ECJ should aim
at synthesizing different national sensibilities and approaches and offering
interpretations that reflect or might promote a consensus among the states,
in the sense that these interpretations can be reasonably accepted. In this
context, the notion of consensus does not require an actual pre-existing
agreement by all states upon certain interpretations.[127] In other words, the
use of the comparative method does not require that all states agree upon a
particular interpretation before it can be legitimately incorporated at the
supranational level.[128] If a majority of states interpret a particular right in a

---

[124] Helfer & Slaughter, *supra* n 64, at 324–325.
[125] *P v S and Cornwall County Council*, C-13/94; *K.B. v National Health Service Pensions Agency and Secretary of State for Health*, C-117/01.
[126] In fact, the ECJ might be relying on comparative law in the intellectual process of inter-
pretation more than is acknowledged by the academic literature. Former Justice Everling, *supra*
n 74, at 1302, stated the following: 'The comparison of laws [is] a process which is used in the
Court to a far greater extent than its expression in the judgments would indicate.' In the same
sense, former ECJ Justice Pescatore, *supra* n 9, asserted that the comparative method is used all
the time, even if the results are absorbed in the interpretation of a right that appears common
and autonomous.
[127] Leonard F. M. Besselink, *The Member States, the National Constitutions and the Scope of the
Charter*, 8 MAASTRICHT JOURNAL OF EUROPEAN AND COMPARATIVE LAW 68, 75 (2001): 'It would
be inconsistent to be very strict in not respecting constitutional rights except those protected in
all Member States.'
[128] Discussing the 'principle of no-fault Community liability', AG Poiares Maduro rejected
a 'mechanistic superimposition of the law of each Member State and the retention of only
the elements that match exactly' to discover a 'general principle common to the laws of the

certain way, this might be a reason for the ECJ to follow that interpretation. Admittedly, the convergence among states does not necessarily secure better protection. Within the EU, however, all member states are constitutional democracies committed to the protection of fundamental rights, which have established internal democratic and procedural guarantees. Under these circumstances, the fact that a majority of member states converge upon a specific interpretation might indicate the desirability of that interpretation for this supranational community. When it is not clear whether there is an actual majority of states in favour of a particular interpretation, the fact that over time more and more states protect certain rights through domestic reforms can signal an emerging consensus. Given this trend, the ECJ could push it further. As such, comparative analysis would help to identify trends of convergence.[129] Still, one might ask why a majority or a common trend toward a particular interpretation justifies adopting this interpretation over competing ones held by other member states. The answer has to do with the unique kind of community the EU constitutes. All member states mutually recognize and respect each other as participants of this common project of integration. After all, they are part of an overarching community immersed in the process of defining itself. Part of this process entails engaging in a search for common principles and establishing common rights at the supranational level. There cannot be an absolute equivalence between state and EU rights in all cases. On certain occasions, some states will have to accept an interpretation they do not prefer. The dialectical framework ensures the possibility for all to participate in the interpretive process. Hence, all participants are allowed to submit their views and to challenge those of others. The ECJ, which is committed to building the rule of law for this supranational community, should reveal how varying perspectives are systematically considered and how the interpretive outcome is reached in order for this outcome to be regarded as reasonable and justifiable.[130]

To be clear, the comparative method should not be understood as limited to identifying a common interpretation to a majority of states. It should be aimed at better understanding the values informing the meanings

Member States', *Fabbrica italiana accumulatori motocarri Montecchio SpA (FIAMM) v Council of the European Union, Commission of the European Communities*, C-120/06, 121/06, para. 55.

[129] Ulrich Scheuner, *Fundamental Rights in European Community Law and in National Constitutional Law*, 12 COMMON MARKET LAW REVIEW 171, 185 (1975): 'The comparative analysis...must follow the general trend of the evolution of legal prescriptions; it must lead to a result acceptable in all member states.'

[130] See *infra* 2.2.4.

attributed to fundamental rights across the states. This inter-state comparison would help to transcend superficial differences and to strengthen common understandings, while fostering an in-depth appraisal of pervasive particularities.[131] In this way, the ECJ should seek to capture elements of commonality and assess elements of divergence in order to articulate an interpretation that reflects a synthetic understanding. This interpretive outcome will not necessarily be identical to the law of any particular state. As the comparative analysis brings different viewpoints to bear, it allows for combining national and supranational approaches and arrives at innovative solutions appropriate to the EU legal order. As Ulrich Scheuner held, '[The comparative method's] object must be to find the rules best suited to express a common tradition and compatible with the structure of the Community.'[132] On the whole, through the comparative method, the ECJ should consider the scope of protection granted within each state and strive for a synthesis that all states could partly recognize or, at least, reasonably accept.

2.2.3 *Judicial self-restraint*

Given the supranational nature of the EU system, comprised of a plurality of constitutional polities interpreting their respective fundamental rights, the ECJ should not seek to impose a uniform interpretation in each and every case. On certain occasions, the best way to proceed would be to accommodate diversity by deferring the interpretation of fundamental rights to state courts. Broadly speaking, deference is a doctrine that governs the extent to which courts will exercise their power of review upon state action or will restrain themselves. At the state level, underlying the doctrine of deference is a democratic concern. Given that laws are enacted by the representatives of the people, the power of judges to strike them down should be limited to cases in which the unconstitutionality is clear.[133] Otherwise, if different interpretations are permitted under the constitution, courts should refrain from exercising control and defer to

---

[131] Paolo G. Carozza, *Uses and Misuses of Comparative Law in International Human Rights: Some Reflections on the Jurisprudence of the European Court of Human Rights*, 73 NOTRE DAME LAW REVIEW 1217, 1236 (1998).

[132] Scheuner, *supra* n 129, at 185.

[133] James B. Thayer, *The Origin and Scope of the American Doctrine of Constitutional Law*, 7 HARVARD LAW REVIEW 129 (1983); Post, *supra* n 19, at 43–44; VÍCTOR FERRERES COMELLA, JUSTICIA CONSTITUCIONAL Y DEMOCRACIA (Centro de Estudios Políticos y Constitucionales 1997), regarding the notion of 'presumption of constitutionality'.

the legislative branch. At the supranational level, the doctrine of deference reflects a democratic concern as well since supranational courts review decisions taken by democratic states.[134] The doctrine of deference is well established in the ECtHR case law, known as the 'margin of appreciation' doctrine.[135] Through this doctrine the ECtHR decides upon the scope of discretion granted to state authorities to interpret specific rights. Therefore, this doctrine responds to the adjudicative question (what institution is responsible for defining the scope of rights), rather than the interpretive one (what is the method of judicial interpretation). The use of this doctrine by the ECtHR is very much debated. While some reject its legitimacy, others worry about the lack of coherent application and clear criteria guiding its functioning.[136] At the same time, it has been pointed out that this is a flexible mechanism that has helped to avoid clashes with member states, while signalling national authorities 'the risk that particular policies might one day be regarded as violations',[137] as the saga of cases regarding the treatment of transsexuals in the UK illustrates. The debate regarding the margin of appreciation within the Convention system might provide some insights to address a judicial policy of deference in the EU. One should keep in mind, however, that since the European Convention and the EU differ in their natures, goals, and institutional structures, the margin of appreciation doctrine cannot be transplanted automatically to the EU. As seen before, the ECtHR interpretation sets a minimum floor of protection that the states can freely improve upon. In contrast, since the ECJ interpretation sets a floor and a ceiling, deference might be granted to allow for higher standards of protection.

With regard to the ECJ's decision-making, the doctrine of deference would indicate when a decision about the meaning of rights is better taken at the state level, as a matter proper for each state community to decide, or when an interpretive decision at the supranational level is required. In the EU

---

[134] Jeoren Schokkenbroek, *The Basis, Nature and Application of the Margin-of-Appreciation Doctrine in the Case-Law of the European Court of Human Rights*, 19 HUMAN RIGHTS LAW JOURNAL 30, 30–31 (1998); HOWARD CHARLES YOUROW, THE MARGIN OF APPRECIATION DOCTRINE IN THE DYNAMICS OF EUROPEAN HUMAN RIGHTS JURISPRUDENCE 195–196 (Martinus Nijhoff Publishers 1996).

[135] Carozza, *supra* n 131, at 1220.

[136] GEORGE LETSAS, A THEORY OF INTERPRETATION OF THE EUROPEAN CONVENTION ON HUMAN RIGHTS (Oxford University Press 2007).

[137] Nico Krisch, *The Open Architecture of Human Rights Law*, 71 THE MODERN LAW REVIEW 183, 207 (2008); *Rees v United Kingdom*, 17 October 1986; *Cossey v United Kingdom*, 27 September 1990; *Christine Goodwin v United Kingdom*, 11 July 2002.

legal framework, deference finds a legal hook in the so-called 'subsidiarity principle'. The notion of subsidiarity is elusive.[138] Basically, in a strict legal sense, it refers to the exercise of powers in spheres of shared competences. When both the EU and the states have powers over a certain subject matter, the subsidiarity principle indicates that the EU shall take action 'only if and in so far as the objectives of the proposed action cannot be sufficiently achieved by the member states and can, therefore, by reason of the scale or effects of the proposed action, be better achieved by the community'.[139] Article 1 EU Treaty suggests a broader political meaning.[140] This article establishes that decision-making processes should take place 'as closely as possible to the citizen'.[141] In general, this principle speaks to the action of institutions responsible for law-making, namely Commission, Council, and Parliament. Yet, it should be admitted that the ECJ also participates in law-making, broadly understood, through its interpretive decisions. Particularly when adjudicating fundamental rights, the ECJ needs to make policy choices about the scope of its own powers to interpret those rights.[142] Thus, subsidiarity might also speak to the exercise of powers by the ECJ vis-à-vis state courts. Even if the ECJ has jurisdiction, there might be cases in which the interpretive decision would be better taken at a level 'closer to the citizen'. Indeed, one should realize that when adjudicating fundamental rights, the ECJ is taking decisions about both the substantive meaning of those rights and the scope of its own interpretive and supervisory powers. As further argued below, the Charter seems to confirm the application of the subsidiarity principle in the sphere of fundamental rights. In particular, article 53 might be read as indicating to the ECJ the need of being deferential to the constitutional interpretation held by state courts to avoid 'restricting or

---

[138]   Gráinne de Búrca, *The Principle of Subsidiarity and the Court of Justice as an Institutional Actor*, 36 JOURNAL OF COMMON MARKET STUDIES 217, 218 (1998).

[139]   Article 5.2 EC Treaty.

[140]   Article 1 EU Treaty: 'This Treaty marks a new stage in the process of creating an ever closer union among the people of Europe, in which decisions are taken as openly as possible and as closely as possible to the citizens.'

[141]   The Protocol added to the Treaty of Amsterdam (1997) about the subsidiarity principle incorporated both meanings. De Búrca, *supra* n 138, at 219, claiming: 'The fact that subsidiarity is dealt with across a number of different parts of the Treaties, and that it is dealt with rather differently within these various provisions further exacerbates its complexity.'

[142]   Regarding the ECJ as a political actor, see de Búrca, *supra* n 138; Anne-Marie Burley & Walter Mattli, *Europe Before the Court: A Political Theory of Legal Integration*, 47 INTERNATIONAL ORGANIZATION 41 (1993).

adversely affecting' fundamental rights recognized by the member states' constitutions.

The case of *Omega*[143] offers a good example to show how the ECJ might accommodate diverse levels of protection deferring to the states the decision about the interpretation of the right at stake. Omega was a German company that operated an installation known as the 'laserdrome'. This game included hitting sensory tags placed on the jackets worn by players with a kind of laser machine-gun. The German authorities banned this activity because 'playing at killing people' was regarded as violating the principle of human dignity. The question that reached the ECJ was whether banning Omega from pursuing this economic activity clashed with the freedom to provide services. The ECJ acknowledged that human dignity was a general principle of law protected within the EU legal order. At the same time, the ECJ realized that this principle did not receive the same level of protection in all member states. Despite the lack of a common understanding about the meaning of human dignity, the ECJ admitted the possibility for German authorities to restrict the basic freedom to provide services in order to secure the constitutional standard of protection.[144] The ECJ held that the fact that other member states did not recognize such a broad scope to this right did not preclude Germany from doing so. At the same time, the ECJ did not adopt the more protective German standard of protection for the EU legal system. In sum, the ECJ restrained itself from setting the interpretation of this right for the whole community and accommodated diversity.

On other occasions, the ECJ has deferred the application of the proportionality test to state courts. The proportionality test might be applied to decide whether a measure constraining a basic freedom of movement (or a

---

[143] *Omega Spielhallen- und Automatenayfstellungs GmbH v Oberbürgermeisterin der Bundesstadt Bonn*, C-36/02. When asked about the meaning of article 53 and its connection with the subsidiarity principle, ECJ Justice Leanerts referred to *Omega* to illustrate how this article should be understood (Global Constitutionalism Seminar, Yale Law School, 23 September 2005).

[144] *Omega Spielhallen- und Automatenayfstellungs GmbH v Oberbürgermeisterin der Bundesstadt Bonn*, C-36/02, para. 37: 'It is not indispensable in that respect for the restrictive measure issued by the authorities of a Member State to correspond to a conception shared by all Member States as regards the precise way in which the fundamental right or legitimate interest in question is to be protected'; para. 39: 'the prohibition on the commercial exploitation of games involving the simulation of acts of violence against persons, in particular the representation of acts of homicide, corresponds to the level of protection of human dignity which the national constitution seeks to guarantee in the territory of the Federal Republic of Germany'.

fundamental right) is justified. It is usually applied in cases in which a conflict exists between a fundamental right and a basic freedom of movement. In particular, the ECJ has applied the proportionality test to decide whether state measures enacted to protect fundamental rights were compatible with EU basic freedoms of movement.[145] The proportionality test asks whether the contested measure is adequate to achieve the goal pursued and whether there are less restrictive means for free movement (or a conflicting fundamental right) in achieving this goal. Arguably, there might be reasons to defer the specific application of the proportionality test to state courts.[146] State courts are closer to the facts of the case and may reach a more accurate decision. Also, this would be less intrusive to state autonomy and might avoid conflicts in cases in which state measures protecting constitutional rights are at stake. The ECJ could specify the interests to be balanced and even lay down some guidelines for the performance of the proportionality test, while allowing national courts to decide about the scope of protection granted to the specific right in the case at hand. This was the case in *Familiapress*,[147] arising as a consequence of the banning of a German magazine in Austria. The reference brought to the ECJ questioned whether an Austrian law containing a general prohibition on offering consumers free gifts linked to the sale of goods or the supply of services was compatible with free movement of goods and free speech. The Austrian Government alleged that this statute was intended to protect press diversity. The ECJ argued that in order to determine whether the Austrian statute was justified on the grounds of protecting press diversity (as a form of free speech), the proportionality test had to be applied regarding the restriction of both free

---

[145] For example, *Eugen Schmidberger, Internationale Transporte und Planzüge v Austria*, C-112/00. In this case, there was a conflict between the right to free speech and assembly and free movement of goods.

[146] Iris Canor, *Harmonizing the European Community's Standard of Judicial Review?*, 8 EUROPEAN PUBLIC LAW 135, 166 (2002), has identified and criticized a move in the ECJ case law from self-restraint in the application of the proportionality test to an abusive use. She claims that, after a 'minimalist' application of the proportionality test, 'The ECJ started using the proportionality principle as a methodological tool to shape its relations with national courts while extending the limit of its interference into national norms', and asserts that the correct policy would be: 'entrusting national courts with the application of the [proportionality] principle'; Schokkenbroek, *supra* n 134, at 31, referring to the European Convention, claimed that one of the main categories in which the margin of appreciation has been applied is: 'instances where the Convention provision at hand requires a balancing of interests and the performance of a proportionality test'.

[147] *Vereinigte Familiapress Zeitungsverlags- und Vertriebs GmbH v Heinrich Bauer Verlag*, C-368/95.

movement of goods and free speech (since there was a claim of free speech on both sides). The ECJ offered several criteria that had to be taken into consideration in order to perform the proportionality test, but the ECJ deferred the decision to the state court.[148] Note that, in this case, the ECJ left the decision about the compatibility between the state measure protecting press diversity and EU law to the domestic court whereas in *Omega*, the ECJ did decide about the compatibility between dignity and the free provision of services. As seen before, the ECJ ruled that restricting the freedom to provide services in order to protect human dignity was justified.[149] In both cases, the ECJ admitted that, as long as the principle of proportionality was met, free movement might be limited in order to protect fundamental rights, according to the constitutional level of protection. The difference is that, in *Omega*, the ECJ also ruled that the proportionality test had been fulfilled, while in *Familiapress* the ECJ left the final decision to the domestic court. On the whole, in both cases, the ECJ accommodated a higher level of constitutional protection, instead of setting a uniform interpretation for the whole community.

It is not clearly established which criteria should guide the ECJ in the exercise of deference (and the degree of deference might vary). Since the doctrine of deference refers to the level of government at which decisions should be taken, the criteria to guide a judicial policy of deference might derive from the underlying EU structure, ie, the overall distribution of

---

[148] *Vereinigte Familiapress Zeitungsverlags- und Vertriebs GmbH v Heinrich Bauer Verlag*, C-368/95, para. 34: 'Article 30 of the EC Treaty is to be interpreted as not precluding application of legislation of a member state the effect of which is to prohibit the distribution on its territory by an undertaking established in another Member State of a periodical produced in that latter State containing prize puzzles or competitions which are lawfully organized in that State, provided that that prohibition is proportionate to maintenance of press diversity and that that objective cannot be achieved by less restrictive means. This assumes, inter alia, that the newspapers offering the chance of winning a prize in games, puzzles or competitions are in competition with small newspaper publishers who are deemed to be unable to offer comparable prizes and the prospect of winning is liable to bring about a shift in demand. Furthermore, the national prohibition must not constitute an obstacle to the marketing of newspapers which, albeit containing prize games, puzzles or competitions, do not give readers residing in the member state concerned the opportunity to win a prize. It is for the national court to determine whether those conditions are satisfied on the basis of a study of the national press market concerned.'

[149] *Omega Spielhallen- und Automatenayfstellungs GmbH v Oberbürgermeisterin der Bundesstadt Bonn*, C-36/02, para. 39: 'by prohibiting only the variant of the laser game the object of which is to fire on human targets and thus "play at killing" people, the contested order did not go beyond what is necessary in order to attain the objective pursued by the competent national authorities.'

authority between the national and supranational systems. Additionally, from a substantive standpoint, given the potential conflicts between standards of protection, deference could also be an instrument for the ECJ to allow for higher constitutional standards of protection, without imposing that standard to the whole community, in the line of *Omega*.[150]

With regard to the overall distribution of power, the doctrine of deference needs to take into account the scope of judicial and legislative powers[151] allocated to EU institutions, vis-à-vis member states.[152] The scope of the ECJ's power to review state action under EU fundamental rights is obviously limited by its own jurisdiction. According to established judicial doctrine, state acts bound by EU rights are those falling 'within the field of application of EU law'. The determination of the boundaries of the 'field of application of EU law', however, is itself a matter of interpretation.[153] Given the generality of this formula as well as the overarching nature of EU law, a broad range of state acts might fall under it, even when the states exercise their own residual powers.[154] Hence, when the state measures under review do not directly implement EU law or do not have a cross-frontier nature, there are justifiable reasons for being deferential to state courts. In these circumstances, the efficacy of EU law within the territory of the states would not be significantly undermined and the values of self-government,

[150] This is not to say that the ECJ should interpet EU fundamental rights according to the highest standard of protection. Rather, the constitutional standard of protection granted in a specific state is taken into acount as a criterion for the exercise of deference.

[151] It should be noted that the EU has no general powers to regulate fundamental rights. Unlike section 5 of the Fourteenth Amendment of the US Constitution, neither the Treaties nor the Charter grant general powers to legislate on fundamental rights to the 'EU legislator'. On the contrary, article 51.2 explicitly says that the Charter 'does not establish any new power or task for the Union or modify the powers and tasks defined in the other parts of the Constitution'. The Lisbon Treaty reiterates that, 'The provisions of the Charter shall not extend in any way the competences of the Union as defined in the Treaties' (article 6.1). In any event, it cannot be excluded that the Charter might promote an extensive use of powers already granted (articles 13, 95 EC Treaty) in connection with fundamental rights. See Allard Knook, *The Court, the Charter, and the Vertical Division of Powers in the European Union*, 42 COMMON MARKET LAW REVIEW 367, 383–393 (2005).

[152] Paul Mahoney, *Judicial Activism and Judicial Self-Restraint in the European Court of Human Rights: Two sides of the Same Coin*, 11 HUMAN RIGHTS LAW JOURNAL 57, 81 (1990), in the context of the European Convention, declared that the margin of appreciation was a 'natural product of [the] distribution of powers [between the Convention institutions and the national institutions]'.

[153] See Chapter 1.

[154] For the distinction between matters on which the EU is granted powers to legislate and other matters which merely fall 'within the scope of application of EU law', see de Búrca, *supra* n 138, at 221. Also, Alan Dashwood, *The Limits of European Community Powers*, 21 EUROPEAN LAW REVIEW 113 (1996).

constitutional identity, individual liberty, and experimentation might be enhanced. States should enjoy more autonomy when further away from the core of EU law. For example, in *Abrahamsson*,[155] the case regarding a Swedish affirmative action measure concerning certain professors' and research assistants' posts, the ECJ might have deferred the decision about the compatibility of this measure with the equality principle to state courts. That measure did not directly implement the EU directive on equal treatment of men and women, nor did it have a cross-frontier nature. Moreover, the state was exercising its own powers to regulate appointments to state public posts, which, in principle, do not directly implicate EU law. Also, the Treaty of Amsterdam had included the following clause: 'With a view to ensuring full equality in practice between men and women in working life, the principle of equal treatment shall not prevent any Member State from maintaining or adopting measures providing for specific advantages in order to make it easier for the underrepresented sex to pursue a vocational activity or to prevent or compensate for disadvantages in professional careers' (article 141.1 EC Treaty). Hence, accommodating diversity among the states as a result of judicial deference would not have impaired the EU directive on equality in a way that would render it ineffective or threaten the goals of the EU.

Additionally, from a substantive standpoint, the ECJ could defer to state courts the interpretation of fundamental rights to allow for more protective standards.[156] Arguably, as suggested above, article 53 Charter could be interpreted along these lines. Since the Charter was drafted, the interpretation of article 53 has brought about a heated debate. Opinions are divided between those who argue that article 53 excepts or at least weakens the supremacy principle,[157] and those who claim that such an exception is inadmissible, since it would endanger the efficacy of EU law

---

[155] *Katarina Abrahamsson and Leif Anderson v Elisabet Fogelqvist*, C-407/98.

[156] Admittedly, in many circumstances it will be difficult to determine which system gives a better standard of protection, particularly when different rights conflict with each other.

[157] Leonard F. M. Besselink, *The Member States, the National Constitutions and the Scope of the Charter*, 8 MAASTRICHT JOURNAL OF EUROPEAN AND COMPARATIVE LAW 68, 80 (2001), interprets this article as follows: 'This...would mean an official recognition of the exception to Community law supremacy'; Alejandro Saiz Arnaiz, *El Tribunal de Justicia, los Tribunales Constitucionales y la Tutela de los Derechos Fundamentales en la Unión Europea: entre el (potencial) Conflicto y la (deseable) Armonización. De los Principios no escritos al Catálogo Constitucional, de la Autoridad judicial a la Normativa*, in CONSTITUCIÓN EUROPEA Y CONSTITUCIONES NACIONALES 531, 575–576 (Marta Cartabia, Bruno de Witte & Pablo Pérez Tremps eds. 2005).

and deviates from the framers' will.[158] The latter conclude that this is an empty clause.[159] An interpretation that would give content to it, without directly clashing with supremacy, would understand that this provision contains a self-restraint mandate to the ECJ in applying the Charter.[160] In other words, the ECJ should defer to state courts if the level of constitutional protection were higher and there were no other rights or general interests that should prevail in the particular case. In this context, judicial self-restraint would allow for diverse interpretations regarding a specific fundamental right.

To sum up, in the process of rights interpretation, the ECJ should pay due regard to state constitutional rights and engage in comparative reasoning seeking a synthesis at the supranational level. Dialogue with state courts and other participating actors helps finding interpretations better accommodated to the community as a whole and gives reasons to follow the ECJ's fundamental rights adjudication, according to the arguments spelled out in Chapter 5—dialogue enhances better-reasoned interpretive outcomes, participation, identity building, and is consistent with the EU pluralist framework. Admittedly, a model of dialogue does not necessarily lead to deference. A supranational court may engage in meaningful dialogue with state courts and still be expected to settle on a uniform protection of human rights across the states. Yet, the same exercise of dialogue within a pluralist framework (Chapter 3), in which the values underlying state autonomy are acknowledged (Chapter 4), may well indicate, on occasion, the appropriatness of deferring to the constitutional interpretation of the right at stake. Deference relates to the way a court exercises its authority. As argued, the relevant criteria for the exercise of deference relate to the overall power structure and the standards of protection.[161] In this sense, there are good reasons to defer when the constitutional standard of protection is higher and the state measure under review is remotely connected to the field of EU law. Admittedly, these criteria might point in opposite directions. The answer cannot be given in

---

[158]   Rubio Llorente, *supra* n 97, at 43–44.

[159]   Jonas Bering Liisberg, *Does the EU Charter of Fundamental Rights Threaten the Supremacy of Community Law? Article 53 of the Charter: A Fountain of Law or just an Inkblot?*, Jean Monnet Working Paper 4/01.

[160]   This is different from saying that state courts should be free to disregard EU law when the constitutional standard of protection is higher. As such, the decision to defer in cases of higher level of constitutional protection would correspond to the ECJ. See the discussion in Chapter 3 about the 'minimum floor of protection' rule.

[161]   It is acknowledged that the criteria for deference need to be examined in more detail and others might need to be added, but this would exceed the scope of this work.

the abstract, but the circumstances of the case will have to be considered. The exercise of self-restraint might contribute to the ECJ's authority building by respecting constitutional diversity.

2.2.4 *Articulating the comparative reasoning in the judgment*

The legitimacy of ECJ interpretive outcomes would be bolstered if the ECJ expressed the comparative reasoning in the judgment. Otherwise, the failure to articulate with precision the functioning of the comparative method might pose a potential threat to the ECJ's claim to authority. Because ECJ decisions are characterized by their laconic brevity, it might be difficult to see how a particular decision is justified. Instead of such a broad reference to common constitutional traditions, there is a need for a more rigorous approach that systematically discusses the sources and shows how the interpretive outcome is reached. As such, the judicial mode of reasoning articulated in the decision,[162] revealing how diverse constitutional viewpoints are balanced in searching for synthetic understandings, might contribute to the perception of the outcome as a fair one. Along these lines, de Witte stated the following:

[The ECJ] could be less vague about the 'common constitutional traditions' by venturing, when a case so warrants, into a genuine comparative evaluation of Member States constitutions; this would make a rejection of arguments taken from the law of just one State more compelling. . . . Justice must also be seen to be done, particularly in the field of human rights.[163]

Thus, in addition to making use of the comparative method in the internal process of deliberation within the Court, the ECJ needs to show how this method is applied. This is important for enhancing the perception of the outcome as legitimate and for better persuading its interlocutors, particularly state courts. By systematically addressing the competing arguments for the interpretation of a specific right, the ECJ would acknowledge a diversity of viewpoints that often reflect essential societal values. The discussion of the arguments advanced for or against a particular interpretation would allow participants to feel they have been heard. In this way, law would be presented as the 'fabric of a diverse community'.[164] Moreover, making judicial reasoning explicit might also foster dialogue because the Court's arguments

---

[162] Helfer & Slaugher, *supra* n 64, at 321.
[163] De Witte, *supra* n 81, at 882.
[164] Helfer & Slaughter, *supra* n 64, at 322.

could be responded to in future cases.[165] In addition, an explicit and articulate writing of the reasons why certain arguments are adopted or rejected works as a self-check. This might be a corrective measure for preconceptions or misunderstandings.

Nonetheless, others, including several ECJ judges, seem to think there are good reasons to leave the comparative analysis aside. Given the complexity of comparative studies and the difficulties inherent in reaching an agreement among judges within the ECJ, the authority of the Court could be undermined if references to comparative law were explicitly included in the decisions.[166] According to this view, the acknowledgement of a range of competing perspectives rooted in differing values or interests should be avoided. This rationale corresponds to a civil law mentality. It derives from the notion that judges must speak 'the law'. Judicial rulings ought to be presented as incontrovertible interpretations of the text, which is why, for example, dissenting opinions are not admitted in the ECJ. In the domain of fundamental rights, however, it is evident there is room for diverse positions regarding their scope of protection, given the variety of interpretations among member states. Hence, instead of hiding disagreements and the availability of different interpretive choices, the legitimacy and authority of this Court would be better served by engaging in fuller reasoning. Weiler argued that particularly in the constitutional domain, it is crucial that the Court demonstrates in its judgments that national sensibilities are fully taken into account. The ECJ 'must amply explain and reason its decisions if they are to be not only authoritarian but also authoritative'.[167] If reasons are given and the differing arguments at stake are carefully weighed, the interpretive outcome can be seen as reasonable and justifiable rather than arbitrarily reached and imposed.

---

[165] *Id.*; Joseph H. H. Weiler, *Epilogue: The Judicial Après Nice*, in THE EUROPEAN COURT OF JUSTICE 215, 225 (Gráinne de Búrca & Joseph H. H. Weiler eds. 2001).

[166] Pescatore, *supra* n 9, at 346; Everling, *supra* n 74, at 1308.

[167] Weiler, *supra* n 165, at 225.

Concluding Remarks

For the most ambitious, the drafting of a constitutional text for the EU furthered the illusion of a new and united Europe. For the most cautious, it constituted yet another step, more symbolic than profound, in the process towards political integration. The main declared goal of the constitutional process was enhancing democracy and the overall legitimacy of the EU. This goal, expressed in the formula of 'bringing the EU closer to the citizens',[1] was pursued on two levels. First, the deliberative nature of the very process of constitution-making was deemed to contribute to the popular legitimacy of the resulting Constitution. For one thing, the constitutional text was drafted by a convention gathering a broad range of representatives of national and supranational institutions engaged in public discussion. Secondly, the constitutional text was aimed at clarifying the institutional framework and strengthening the transparency, efficiency, and participatory nature of law-making procedures. In addition, the proposed Constitution included the Charter of fundamental rights, which encapsulated the fundamental rights common to all European citizens. In this vein, the ratification of an EU Constitution would arguably have contributed to the replacement of the 'Europe of the states' for the 'Europe of the people'. In the difficult balance between the national and the supranational, an EU constitution would tip the scales in favour of the supranational.

Nevertheless, the same constitutional text fell short of these aspirations. The 'constitution' title was merely symbolic. For the most cynical, it constituted an attempt to appropriate for the EU the legitimating force of such a document. The so-called EU Constitution did not set the ground for a new federal state; neither could it be attributed to a single European people. Its ratification and amendment still required the unanimity of all the states. Furthermore, the Preamble could not avoid keeping the plural form, 'peoples' of Europe. A set of changes was introduced regarding

---

[1] European Council, *Laeken Declaration—The Future of the European Union*, 15 December 2001.

the institutional framework and decision-making procedures, such as the reinforcement of the role of the European Parliament in the legislative procedure, the extension of qualified majority voting within the Council to new fields, the modification of the way qualified majority was determined in order to render it more proportionate to population size, and the new role for national parliaments in monitoring EU institutions' compliance with the principle of subsidiarity. These failed, however, to achieve a far-reaching democratization of the EU internal functioning. In sum, the proposed Constitution did not create much more room for supranational decision-making with links of legitimacy with the population.

Beyond the actual and diverse reasons for the 'no' vote in the French and Dutch referenda, the failure of this constitutional project demonstrates the difficulties of reinforcing an ideal of supranational unity. Specifically, it has been pointed out that the same title 'Constitution' might have helped raise anxieties among the citizenry. The arguments for and against the Constitution remained largely national in their tone and scope. This whole process showed that although a European Constitution was meant to express and promote European unity, national political cultures across the EU remain fairly diverse. Regardless of the nature and content of this particular text, the lesson to be learned from the failed constitutional process is that deeper political integration is a contested path to follow. Instead, the EU should adopt a more pragmatic approach in the future and recognize the benefits of flexibility and decentralization. As such, the rejection of the Constitutional Treaty and the overall difficulties of furthering political integration reinforce the virtues of the dialogic model proposed.

The European Charter of fundamental rights was at the centrepiece of the constitutional project. Remarkably, it has survived the 'de-constitutionalization' effort undertaken by the Treaty of Lisbon, but it has not gone unharmed. The Charter has been granted the same legal value as the Treaties, while it has been expelled from the text of the Treaties itself. Should the Lisbon Treaty be ratified, the Charter would enter the scenario of primary EU law through the back door. In any event, the recognition of its legally binding force would contribute to reinforce the legitimacy of the ECJ's case law on fundamental rights and would put its adjudicative function on a much firmer footing. Still, the debates during the Charter's drafting process and later during its revision by the constitutional convention reflect the anxieties that the Charter provokes from the standpoint of the interaction between legal systems. Some fear that a binding Charter, similar to the US Bill of Rights, might be used as a 'federalizing' instrument to enhance the power and influence of the EU and the ECJ, vis-à-vis the member states. These fears are reflected in the so-called horizontal clauses regulating the Charter's interpretation and application. In particular, they are aimed at reassuring that the Charter would neither extend the scope of application of fundamental rights to state action, nor increase EU law-making powers, or restrict the constitutional standards of protection. According to the Charter, the interpretation of these rights remains heavily grounded in the constitutional traditions common to the member states. In light of current ECJ case law, however, a binding Charter might enhance the expansion of the scope of application of EU rights to the states. An expansive use of the Charter would increase the occasions for overlapping constitutional and EU fundamental rights. Hence, even if the Charter were finally given binding force, the dialogic model would still be relevant as the source of the ECJ's legitimacy in adjudicating fundamental rights, if not bolstered given the increased potential for conflicts between overlapping rights.

A dialogic model for crafting supranational human rights through the interaction between national and supranational courts is consistent with the current pluralist framework. This framework defies traditional statist categories and might seem precarious and unstable. Nevertheless, it should not be regarded as a temporary evil to overcome through the reconstitution of an ultimate sovereign authority at the supranational level. On the contrary, the model of an overarching community constituted by partly separate but interdependent national and supranational legal orders, whose foundational norms are not hierarchically ordered, should be normatively embraced. It constitutes the opportunity to overcome the dangers of exacerbated state sovereignty establishing mutual checks and balances between the national and supranational spheres, as well as to realize the benefits of a dual system of rights protection. The interdependence of functions and goals among the national and supranational orders secures the continuity of this particular kind of community. This is not to deny, however, that instances of overlapping and conflict between norms protecting rights might arise. The emerging pluralist framework requires redefining the basis for institutional legitimacy in the interaction between systems. Given its position, the ECJ is destined to play a central role in managing interpretive conflicts. This does not imply, however, that the ECJ should be unconstrained in exercising its authority. Hence, this inquiry has focused on the normative authority of the ECJ to attribute meaning to supranational fundamental rights norms, which are also binding upon state public authorities. The purpose was to provide a normative model to guide or otherwise critically assess the ECJ

adjudicative function, consistent with the goal of building common understandings without neglecting to accommodate diversity. This work has contended that dialogue provides the source of legitimacy for ECJ fundamental
rights' adjudication.

The same practice of dialogue, as an exchange of arguments, furthers
understanding of the values informing the scope of rights' protection in
other legal systems and promotes better-reasoned outcomes. The need
to give reasons justifying any particular interpretation furthers objectivity, enriches the debate, and allows for innovative solutions adapted to this
supranational community. Also, participation in the interpretive activity
favours legitimacy since it allows all members of the community to contribute and to regard the outcome as a shared product of collective deliberation. The political structure of the EU allows for the prerequisites for an
effective and fair dialogue to be fulfilled. National and supranational courts'
viewpoints regarding fundamental rights differ, and yet there is a common
ground for understanding. Since national and supranational courts mutually recognize each other and no absolute hierarchy between them exists, all
courts have incentives to engage in dialogue. Also, all courts have the opportunity to participate in dialogue, according to the processes established by
law. It is the continuing pattern of judicial dialogue regarding the meaning
of fundamental rights that promotes convergence around solutions adapted
to this supranational community. Therefore, the model of dialogue needs
to be understood over time. One obvious shortcoming attached to this kind
of model is the persistence of some degree of indeterminacy. Hierarchical
models (regardless of whether the supranational or the national system is on
top) put an end to conflicts through the exercise of vertical authority. A model
of dialogue acknowledges intersystemic conflict and uses it as a trigger for
judicial institutions to engage in an exchange of arguments in order to reach
the best-reasoned outcome for the community as a whole. Dialogue does not
work to eliminate conflict, but rather it manages conflict over time in a process of constant, mutual accommodation. The argument for the comparative
method (as the inter-state analysis of national constitutional law) follows and
complements the dialogic model. This method of interpretation is consistent with the view of dialogue as the source of legitimacy for ECJ adjudication
and the supranational nature of EU fundamental rights. EU fundamental
rights, though autonomous, derive from state constitutional rights. Thus,
the main sources for their interpretation are found in the constitutional law
of the member states. At the same time, the legitimacy of the interpretive outcome would be enhanced if the comparative reasoning were reflected in the

decision. As conceived in this work, comparative reasoning does not merely consist of identifying a common interpretation to the majority of states. It is aimed at understanding the values informing the meaning attributed to constitutional rights across the states. Thus, comparative reasoning helps to identify threads of commonality and pervasive divergences. Consistently, the ECJ should articulate the rationale underpinning a supranational inter-pretation to be applied in all states. This interpretation attempts a synthesis that all states can partly recognize or reasonably accept. This interpretive outcome is not necessarily identical to existing interpretations; since in the process of synthesizing different approaches the ECJ might come up with innovative solutions better adapted to the community as a whole. At the same time, given the EU political structure, a single interpretation is not the only desirable outcome. Rather, the best outcome for the community as a whole might be accommodating diversity. From the perspective of ECJ adjudica-tion, this means being deferential to state courts. 'United in diversity' is a recurrent theme in the EU that needs to be given content. This will never be easy because these are two poles in constant tension with each other, and yet neither can be obliterated.

On the whole, the failure of the EU constitutional project, if anything, enhances the virtues of a model of dialogue to ground the legitimacy of ECJ adjudicative decisions interpreting fundamental rights. At the same time, the ratification of the proposed constitutional text, or even a more fully fledged constitution some time in the future, would not render this model obsolete. Supreme courts within federal states, such as the US, also face the tensions between uniformity and diversity in the interpretation of fundamental rights. In a supranational structure like the EU, these tensions are even more pervasive and probably everlasting. Admittedly, a model of dialogue does not determine a particular outcome in advance. This will be shaped by the community in which dialogue takes place. Dialogue allows flexibility and furthers deliberation in a process of mutual accommodation over time. Ultimately, the dialogic process becomes the source of legitimacy of interpretive outcomes.

BIBLIOGRAPHY

BRUCE ACKERMAN, SOCIAL JUSTICE IN THE LIBERAL STATE (Yale University Press 1980)
—— THE FUTURE OF LIBERAL REVOLUTION (1989)
—— *Why Dialogue?*, 86 THE JOURNAL OF PHILOSOPHY 5 (1989)
—— WE THE PEOPLE: FOUNDATIONS (Harvard University Press 1993)
—— *The Rise of World Constitutionalism*, 83 VIRGINIA LAW REVIEW 771 (1997)
—— WE THE PEOPLE: TRANSFORMATIONS (Harvard University Press 2001)
Robert B. Ahdieh, *Between Dialogue and Decree: International Review of National Courts*, 79 NEW YORK UNIVERSITY LAW REVIEW 2029 (2004)
ROBERT ALEXY, A THEORY OF LEGAL ARGUMENTATION. THE THEORY OF RATIONAL DISCOURSE AS THEORY OF LEGAL JUSTIFICATION (Clarendon Press 1989)
—— A THEORY OF CONSTITUTIONAL RIGHTS (Oxford University Press 2002)
Ricardo Alonso García, *The General Provisions of the Charter of Fundamental Rights of the European Union*, 8 EUROPEAN LAW JOURNAL 492 (2002)
—— & DANIEL SARMIENTO, LA CARTA DE LOS DERECHOS FUNDAMENTALES DE LA UNIÓN EUROPEA (Civitas 2006)
PHILIP ALSTON (ed.), THE EU AND HUMAN RIGHTS (Oxford University Press 1999)
Karen Alter, *Explaining National Court Acceptance of European Court Jurisprudence: A Critical Evaluation of Theories of Legal Integration*, in THE EUROPEAN COURT AND NATIONAL COURTS, DOCTRINE AND JURISPRUDENCE. LEGAL CHANGE IN ITS SOCIAL CONTEXT 227 (Anne-Marie Slaughter, Alec Stone Sweet & Joseph H.H. Weiler eds. 1998)
—— ESTABLISHING THE SUPREMACY OF EUROPEAN LAW. THE MAKING OF AN INTERNATIONAL RULE OF LAW IN EUROPE (Oxford University Press 2001)
AKHIL R. AMAR, *Of Sovereignty and Federalism*, 96 YALE LAW JOURNAL 1425 (1987)
—— *The Bill of Rights and the Fourteenth Amendment*, 100 YALE LAW JOURNAL 1136 (1991)
—— *Five Views of Federalism: 'Converse-1983' in Context*, 47 VANDERBILT LAW REVIEW 1229 (1995)
—— *Foreword: Lord Camden Meets Federalism—Using State Constitutions to Counter Federal Abuses*, 27 RUTGERS LAW JOURNAL 845 (1996)
—— THE BILL OF RIGHTS (Yale University Press 1998)
—— *Intratextualism*, 112 HARVARD LAW REVIEW 747 (1999)

Benedict Anderson, Imagined Communities: Reflections on the Origin and Spread of Nationalism (Verso 1983)

David W. K. Anderson, References to the European Court (Sweet & Maxwell 1995)

Miguel Azpitarte Sánchez, *Las Relaciones entre el Derecho de la Unión y el Derecho del Estado a la Luz de la Constitución Europea*, 1 Revista Española de Derecho Constitucional Europeo 75 (2004)

Lynn A. Baker & Ernest A. Young, *Federalism and the Double Standard of Judicial Review*, 51 Duke Law Journal 75 (2001)

Zygmunt Bauman, Legislators and Interpreters. On Modernity, Post-Modernity and Intellectuals (Cornell University Press 1987)

Joxerramon Bengoetxea, The Legal Reasoning of the European Court of Justice. Towards a European Jurisprudence (Clarendon Press 1993)

Jonas Bering Liisberg, *Does the EU Charter of Fundamental Rights Threaten the Supremacy of Community Law? Article 53 of the Charter: A Fountain of Law or just an Inkblot?*, Jean Monnet Working Paper 4/01

Rudolf Bernhardt, *Reform of the Control Machinery under the European Convention on Human Rights: Protocol No. 11*, 89 American Journal of International Law 145 (1995)

Leonard F.M. Besselink, *Entrapped by the Maximum Standard: On Fundamental Rights, Pluralism and Subsidiarity in the European Union*, 35 Common Market Law Review 629 (1998)

—— The Member States, the National Constitutions and the Scope of the Charter, 8 Maastricht Journal of European and Comparative Law 68 (2001)

Alexander Bickel, The Least Dangerous Branch (Yale University Press 1986)

Robert Blackburn & Jorg Polakiewicz (eds.), Fundamental Rights in Europe. The European Convention on Human Rights and its Member States, 1950–2000 (Oxford University Press 2001)

Philip Bobbitt, Constitutional Fate (Oxford University Press 1982)

Daniel Bodansky, *The Legitimacy of International Governance: A Coming Challenge for International Environmental Law?*, 93 American Journal of International Law 596 (1999)

Armin Von Bogdandy, *The European Union as a Human Rights Organization? Human Rights and the Core of the European Union*, 37 Common Market Law Review 1307 (2000)

Robert Bork, *Neutral Principles and Some First Amendment Problems*, 47 INDIANA LAW JOURNAL 1 (1971)

ANNA BREDIMAS, METHODS OF INTERPRETATION AND COMMUNITY LAW (North-Holland Publishing Company 1978)

William J. Brennan, Jr., *State Constitutions and the Protection of Individual Rights*, 90 HARVARD LAW REVIEW 489 (1977)

—— *The Bill of Rights and the States: The Revival of Sate Constitutions as Guardians of Individual Rights*, 61 NEW YORK UNIVERSITY LAW REVIEW 536 (1986)

L. NEVILLE BROWN & FRANCIS G. JACOBS, THE COURT OF JUSTICE OF THE EUROPEAN COMMUNITIES (Sweet & Maxwell 1983)

Gráinne de Búrca, *The Language of Rights and European Integration*, in NEW LEGAL DYNAMICS OF EUROPEAN INTEGRATION 29 (Jo Shaw & Gillian More eds. 1995)

—— *The Principle of Subsidiarity and the Court of Justice as an Institutional Actor*, 36 JOURNAL OF COMMON MARKET STUDIES 217 (1998)

—— *The Drafting of the European Union Charter of Fundamental Rights*, 26 EUROPEAN LAW REVIEW 126 (2001)

—— *Convergence and Divergence in European Public Law: The Case of Human Rights*, in CONVERGENCE AND DIVERGENCE IN EUROPEAN PUBLIC LAW 131 (Paul Beaumont, Carole Lyons & Neil Walker eds. 2002)

Anne-Marie Burley & Walter Mattli, *Europe before the Court: A Political Theory of Legal Integration*, 47 INTERNATIONAL ORGANIZATION 41 (1993)

ALAN CAIRNS, CHARTER VERSUS FEDERALISM: THE DILEMMAS OF CONSTITU-TIONAL REFORM (McGill-Queens University Press 1992)

Evan H. Caminker, *'Appropriate' Means-Ends Constraints on Section 5 Powers*, 53 STANFORD LAW REVIEW 1127 (2001)

IRIS CANTOR, THE LIMITS OF JUDICIAL DISCRETION IN THE EUROPEAN COURT OF JUSTICE (Nomos Verlagsgesellschaft 1998)

—— *Primus Inter Pares. Who is the Ultimate Guardian of Fundamental Rights in Europe?*, 25 EUROPEAN LAW REVIEW 3 (2000)

—— *Harmonizing the European Community's Standard of Judicial Review?*, 8 EUROPEAN PUBLIC LAW 135 (2002)

MAURO CAPPELLETTI, MONICA SECOMBE & JOSEPH H. H. WEILER (eds.), I INTEGRATION THROUGH LAW. EUROPE AND THE AMERICAN FEDERAL EXPERIENCE (European University Institute 1986)

—— THE JUDICIAL PROCESS IN COMPARATIVE PERSPECTIVE (Clarendon Press 1989)

Paolo G. Carozza, *Uses and Misuses of Comparative Law in International Human Rights: Some Reflections on the Jurisprudence of the European Court of Human Rights*, 73 NOTRE DAME LAW REVIEW 1217 (1998)

Marc Carrillo, *El Diálogo entre Tribunales como Condición Necesaria para la Tutela de los Derechos Fundamentales*, in INTEGRACIÓN EUROPEA Y PODER JUDICIAL 313 (Alejandro Saiz Arnaiz & Maite Zelaia eds. 2006)

Marta Cartabia, *The Italian Constitutional Court and the Relationship Between the Italian Legal System and the European Union*, in THE EUROPEAN COURT AND NATIONAL COURTS, DOCTRINE AND JURISPRUDENCE. LEGAL CHANGE IN ITS SOCIAL CONTEXT 133 (Anne-Marie Slaughter, Alec Stone Sweet & Joseph H. H. Weiler eds. 1998)

Damian Chalmers, *Judicial Preferences and the Community Legal Order*, 60 THE MODERN LAW REVIEW 164 (1997)

Sujit Choudhry, *Globalization in Search of Justification: Toward a Theory of Comparative Constitutional Interpretation*, 74 INDIANA LAW JOURNAL 819 (1999)

ANDREW CLAPHAM, I HUMAN RIGHTS AND THE EUROPEAN COMMUNITY: A CRITICAL OVERVIEW (Nomos Verlagsgesellschaft 1991)

Jeffrey C. Cohen, *The European Preliminary Reference and U.S. Supreme Court Review of State Court Judgments: A Study in Comparative Judicial Federalism*, 44 AMERICAN JOURNAL OF COMPARATIVE LAW 421 (1996)

Jason Coppel & Aidan O'Neill, *The European Court of Justice: Taking Rights Seriously?*, 29 COMMON MARKET LAW REVIEW 669 (1992)

DRUCILLA CORNELL, THE PHILOSOPHY OF THE LIMIT (Routledge 1992)

—— *Two Lectures on the Normative Dimensions of Community in the Law*, 54 TENNESSEE LAW REVIEW 327 (1997)

COUNCIL OF EUROPE, COLLECTED EDITION OF THE TRAVAUX PRÉPARATOIRES (M. Nijhoff 1975)

Robert M. Cover & T. Alexander Aleinikoff, *Dialectical Federalism: Habeas Corpus and the Court*, 86 THE YALE LAW JOURNAL 1035 (1977)

—— *The Uses of Jurisdictional Redundancy: Interest, Ideology, and Innovation*, 22 WM. & MARY L. REV. 639 (1981)

Paul Craig, *Democracy and Rule-making Within the EC: An Empirical and Normative Assessment*, 3 EUROPEAN LAW JOURNAL 105 (1997)

—— *Report on the United Kingdom*, in THE EUROPEAN COURT AND NATIONAL COURTS, DOCTRINE AND JURISPRUDENCE. LEGAL CHANGE IN ITS SOCIAL CONTEXT 195 (Anne-Marie Slaughter, Alec Stone Sweet & Joseph H. H. Weiler eds. 1998)

Robert M. Cover & T. Alexander Aleinikoff, *Constitutions, Constitutionalism, and the European Union*, 7 EUROPEAN LAW JOURNAL 125 (2001)

—— & GRÁINNE DE BÚRCA (eds.), THE EVOLUTION OF THE EU LAW (Oxford University Press 1999)

DEIRDRE M. CURTIN, POSTNATIONAL DEMOCRACY. THE EUROPEAN UNION IN SEARCH OF A POLITICAL PHILOSOPHY (Kluwer 1997)

—— & Ronald van Ooik, *The Sting is Always in the Tail. The Personal Scope of Application of the EU Charter of Fundamental Rights*, 8 MAASTRICHT JOURNAL OF EUROPEAN AND COMPARATIVE LAW 102 (2001)

—— & Ige Dekker, *The Constitutional Structure of the European Union: Some Reflections on Vertical Unity-in-Diversity*, in CONVERGENCE AND DIVERGENCE IN EUROPEAN PUBLIC LAW 60 (Paul Beaumont, Carole Lyons & Neil Walker eds. 2002)

Jens C. Danmann, *The Role of Comparative Law in Statutory and Constitutional Interpretation*, 14 ST. THOMAS LAW REVIEW 513 (2002)

RENAUD DEHOUSSE, THE EUROPEAN COURT OF JUSTICE (St. Martin's Press 1998)

JACQUES DERRIDA, THE OTHER HEADING. REFLECTIONS ON TODAY'S EUROPE (Indiana University Press 1992)

Luís María Díez Picazo, *Europa: Las Insidias de la Soberanía*, 79 CLAVES DE LA RAZÓN PRÁCTICA (1988)

—— *¿Una Constitución sin Declaración de Derechos? (Reflexiones Constitucionales sobre los Derechos Fundamentales en la Comunidad Europea)*, 32 REVISTA ESPAÑOLA DE DERECHO CONSTITUCIONAL 135 (1991)

—— *Reflexiones sobre la Idea de Constitución Europea*, 20 REVISTA DE INSTITUCIONES EUROPEAS 533 (1993)

—— CONSTITUCIONALISMO DE LA UNIÓN EUROPEA (Civitas 2002)

Olivier Dord, *Systèmes Juridiques Nationaux et Cours Européennes: De l'Affrontement a la complémentarité?*, 96 POUVOIRS. REVUE FRANÇAISE D'ETUDES CONSTITUTIONNELLES ET POLITIQUES 5 (2000)

JOHN S. DRYZEK, DELIBERATIVE DEMOCRACY AND BEYOND. LIBERALS, CRITICS, CONTESTATIONS (Oxford University Press 2000)

Andrew Drzemczewski, *The European Human Rights Convention: Protocol No. 11—Entry into Force and First Year of Application*, 21 HUMAN RIGHTS LAW JOURNAL 1 (2000)

Pierre Drzemczewski, *The Council of Europe's Position with Respect to the EU Charter of Fundamental Rights*, 22 HUMAN RIGHTS LAW JOURNAL 14 (2001)

Ronald Dworkin, *The Model of Rules*, 35 University of Chicago Law Review 14 (1967)

—— A Matter of Principle (Harvard University Press 1985)

—— Law's Empire (Harvard University Press 1986)

Piet Eeckhout, *The EU Charter of Fundamental Rights and the Federal Question*, 39 Common Market Law Review 945 (2002)

Pavlos Eleftheriadis, *Aspects of European Constitutionalism*, 21 European Law Review 32 (1996)

Jon Elster, *Deliberation and Constitution Making*, in Deliberative Democracy 97 (Jon Elster ed. 1998)

Christoph Engel, *The European Charter of Fundamental Rights. A Changed Political Opportunity Structure and its Normative Consequences*, 7 European Law Journal 151 (2001)

Richard A. Epstein, *Exit Rights Under Federalism*, 55 Law and Contemporary Problems 147 (1992)

Ulrich Everling, *The Court of Justice as a Decisionmaking Authority*, 82 Michigan Law Review 1294 (1984)

—— *Will Europe Slip on Bananas? The Bananas Judgment of the Court of Justice and National Courts*, 33 Common Market Law Review 401 (1996)

Udo Di Fabio, *A European Charter: Towards a Constitution for the Union*, 7 Columbia Journal of European Law 159 (2001)

Richard Fallon, *A Constructivist Coherence Theory of Constitutional Interpretation*, 100 Harvard Law Review 1189 (1987)

James D. Fearon, *Deliberation as Discussion*, in Deliberative Democracy 44 (Jon Elster ed. 1998)

Natividad Fernández Sola, *À Quelle Nécessité Juridique Répond la Négociation d'une Charte des Droits Fondamentaux de l'Union Européenne?*, 442 Revue du Marché Commun et de l'Union Européenne 595 (2000)

Luigi Ferrajoli, Derechos y Garantías. La Ley del más Débil (Trotta 1999)

Víctor Ferreres Comella, Justicia Constitucional y Democracia (Centro de Estudios Políticos y Constitucionales 1997)

—— *Souveraineté Nationale et Intégration Européenne dans le Droit Constitutionnel Espagnol*, 9 Les Cahiers du Conseil Constitutionnel 106 (2000)

—— *Integración Europea y Crisis del Modelo Centralizado de Justicia Constitucional*, 65 Revista Vasca de Administración Publica 73 (2003)

—— *The European Model of Constitutional Review of Legislation: Toward Decentralization?*, 2 International Journal of Constitutional Law 461 (2004)

Víctor Ferreres Comella, *El Juez Nacional ante los Derechos Fundamentales Europeos. Algunas Reflexiones en torno a la idea de diálogo*, in Integración Europea y Poder Judicial 231 (Alejandro Saiz Arnaiz & Maite Zelaia eds. 2006)

—— Constitutional Courts and Democratic Values. A European Perspective (Yale University Press 2009)

Paul Finkelman, *James Madison and the Bill of Rights: A Reluctant Paternity*, 9 The Supreme Court Review 301 (1990)

Owen Fiss, *Objectivity and Interpretation*, 34 Stanford Law Review 739 (1982)

—— *Conventionalism*, 58 Southern California Law Review 177 (1985)

—— The Law As It Could Be (New York University Press 2003)

Peter Fitzpatrick, *New Europe and Old Stories: Mythology and Legality in the European Union*, in Europe's Other: European Law Between Modernity and Postmodernity 27 (Peter Fitzpatrick & James Henry Bergeron eds. 1998)

Lawrence Friedman, *The Constitutional Value of Dialogue and the New Judicial Federalism*, 28 Hastings Constitutional Law Quarterly 93 (2000)

Jennifer Friesen, *Adventures in Federalism: Some Observations on the Overlapping Spheres of State and Federal Constitutional Law*, 3 Widener Journal of Public Law 25 (1993)

Michael Gallagher & Pier Vincenzo Uleri (eds.), The Referendum Experience in Europe (Macmillan Press 1996)

Diego Gambetta, *'Claro!': An Essay on Discursive Machismo*, in Deliberative Democracy 19 (Jon Elster ed. 1998)

Stephen A. Gardbaum, *Law, Politics and the Claims of Community*, 90 Michigan Law Review 685 (1992)

James A. Gardner, *The Failed Discourse of State Constitutionalism*, 90 Michigan Law Review 761 (1992)

Geoffrey Garret, *The Politics of Legal Integration in the European Union*, 49 International Organization 171 (1995)

Conor A. Gearty (ed.), European Civil Liberties and the European Convention on Human Rights. A Comparative Study (Martinus Nijhoff 1997)

Steven Greer, *Constitutionalizing Adjudication under the European Convention on Human Rights*, 23 Oxford Journal of Legal Studies 405 (2003)

Constance Grewe, *Les Conflits de Normes entre Droit Communautaire et Droits Nationaux en Matière de Droit Fondamentaux*, in L'Union Européenne et les Droits Fondamentaux 57 (Stéphane Leclerc, Jean François Akandji-Kombé, and Marei-Joelle Redor, eds. 1999)

Dieter Grimm, *The Modern State: Continental Traditions*, in GUIDANCE, CONTROL AND EVALUATION IN THE PUBLIC SECTOR 89 (Franz-Xaver Kaufmann et al. eds. 1986)

—— *Does Europe Need a Constitution?*, 1 EUROPEAN LAW JOURNAL 282 (1995)

—— *The European Court of Justice and National Courts: The German Constitutional Perspective after the Maastricht Decision*, 3 COLUMBIA JOURNAL OF EUROPEAN LAW 229 (1997)

Annie Gruber, *La Charte des Droits Fondamentaux de l'Union Européenne: Un Message Clair Hautement Symbolique*, 15 PETITES AFFICHES. LA LOI 4 (2001)

Ernst B. Haas, *International Integration: The European and the Universal Process*, 15 INTERNATIONAL ORGANIZATION 366, 366 (1961)

—— BEYOND THE NATION-STATES. FUNCTIONALISM AND INTERNATIONAL ORGANIZATION (Stanford University Press 1964)

—— *Technocracy, Pluralism and the New Europe*, in INTERNATIONAL REGIONALISM 152 (Joseph Nye ed. 1968)

Peter Häberle, *Derecho Constitucional Común Europeo*, in DERECHOS HUMANOS Y CONSTITUCIONALISMO ANTE EL TERCER MILENIO 187 (Antonio-Enrique Pérez Luño ed. 1996)

—— *Elementos Teóricos de un Modelo General de Recepción Jurídica*, in DERECHOS HUMANOS Y CONSTITUCIONALISMO ANTE EL TERCER MILENIO 151 (Antonio-Enrique Pérez Luño ed. 1996)

—— *¿Existe un espacio público europeo?*, 3 REVISTA DE DERECHO COMUNITARIO EUROPEO 113 (1998)

JÜRGEN HABERMAS, MORAL CONSCIOUSNESS AND COMMUNICATIVE ACTION (MIT Press 1990)

—— *Comment on the Paper by Dieter Grimm: Does Europe need a Constitution?*, 1 EUROPEAN LAW JOURNAL 303 (1995)

—— BETWEEN FACTS AND NORMS (MIT Press 1998)

—— THE INCLUSION OF THE OTHER (MIT Press 1998)

—— THE POSTNATIONAL CONSTELLATION (MIT Press 2001)

ALEXANDER HAMILTON, JAMES MADISON & JOHN JAY, THE FEDERALIST PAPERS (Clinton Rossiter ed. 1999)

Robert Harmsen, *National Responsibility for European Community Acts Under the European Convention on Human Rights: Recasting the Accession Debate*, 7 EUROPEAN PUBLIC LAW 625 (2001)

H. L. A. HART, THE CONCEPT OF LAW (Oxford University Press 1997)

TREVOR C. HARTLEY, THE FOUNDATIONS OF EUROPEAN COMMUNITY LAW (Oxford University Press 1998)

Trevor C. Hartley, *The Constitutional Foundations of the European Union*, 117 Law Quarterly Review 225 (2001)

Laurence R. Helfer, *Consensus, Coherence and the European Convention on Human Rights*, 26 Cornell International Law Journal 133 (1993)

—— & Anne-Marie Slaughter, *Toward a Theory of Effective Supranational Adjudication*, 107 Yale Law Journal 273 (1997)

Claire L'Heureux-Dubé, *The Importance of Dialogue: Globalization and the International Impact of the Rehnquist Court*, 34 Tulsa Law Journal 15 (1998)

Lars Hoffmann, *The Convention on the Future of Europe—Thoughts on the Convention-Model*, Jean Monnet Working Paper 11/02, New York School of Law (2002)

Simon Hug, Voices of Europe. Citizens, Referendums, and European Integration (Rowman & Littlefield Publishers 2002)

Francis G. Jacobs, *The Uses of Comparative Law in the Law of the European Communities*, in Legal History and Comparative Law 99 (Richard Plender ed. 1990)

—— *Human Rights in the European Union: The Role of the Court of Justice*, 26 European Law Review 331 (2001)

Jean Paul Jacqué & Joseph H. H. Weiler, *On the Road to European Union—A New Judicial Architecture: An Agenda for the Intergovernmental Conference*, 27 Common Market Law Review 185 (1990)

Paul W. Kahn, *Community in Contemporary Constitutional Theory*, 99 Yale Law Journal 1 (1990)

—— *Interpretation and Authority in State Constitutionalism*, 106 Harvard Law Review 1147 (1993)

—— *The Question of Sovereignty*, 40 Stanford Journal of International Law 259 (2004)

C. N. Kakouris, *Use of the Comparative Method by the Court of Justice of the European Communities*, 6 Pace International Law Review 267 (1994)

Ellis Katz & G. Alan Tarr (eds.), Federalism and Rights (Rowman & Littlefield Publishers 1984)

Bruno Kaufmann & M. Dane Waters (eds.), Direct Democracy in Europe. A Comprehensive Reference Guide to the Initiative and Referendum Process in Europe (Carolina Academic Press 2004)

Markku Kiikeri, Comparative Legal Reasoning and European Law (Kluwer Academic Publishers 2001)

Claire Kilpatrick, *Community or Communities of Courts in European Integration? Sex Equality Dialogues Between UK Courts and the ECJ*, 4 European Law Journal 121 (1998)

Claire Kilpatrick, *Gender Equality: A Fundamental Dialogue*, in LABOUR LAW IN THE COURTS. NATIONAL JUDGES AND THE EUROPEAN COURT OF JUSTICE 31 (Silvana Sciarra ed. 2001)

Allard Knook, *The Court, the Charter, and the Vertical Division of Powers in the European Union*, 42 COMMON MARKET LAW REVIEW 367 (2005)

Juliane Kokott, *Report on Germany*, in THE EUROPEAN COURT AND NATIONAL COURTS, DOCTRINE AND JURISPRUDENCE. LEGAL CHANGE IN ITS SOCIAL CONTEXT 77 (Anne-Marie Slaughter, Alec Stone Sweet & Joseph H. H. Weiler eds. 1998)

Jan Komárek, *European Constitutionalism and the European Arrest Warrant: In Search of the Limits of 'Contrapunctual Principles'*, 44 COMMON MARKET LAW REVIEW 9 (2007)

NEIL K. KOMESAR, IMPERFECT ALTERNATIVES. CHOOSING INSTITUTIONS IN LAW, ECONOMICS, AND PUBLIC POLICY (The University of Chicago Press 1994)

Thijmen Koopmans, *Comparative Law and the Courts*, 45 INTERNATIONAL AND COMPARATIVE LAW QUARTERLY 545 (1996)

Lewis A. Kornhauser, *Adjudication by a Resource-Constrained Team: Hierarchy and Precedent in a Judicial System*, 68 SOUTHERN CALIFORNIA LAW REVIEW 1605 (1995)

Nico Krisch, *The Open Architecture of Human Rights Law*, 71 THE MODERN LAW REVIEW 183 (2008)

Hans Christian Krüger & Jörg Polakiewicz, *Proposals for a Coherent Human Rights Protection System in Europe*, 22 HUMAN RIGHTS LAW JOURNAL 1 (2001)

Mattias Kumm, *Who is the Final Arbiter of Constitutionality in Europe?: Three Conceptions of the Relationship between the German Federal Constitutional Court and the European Court of Justice*, 36 COMMON MARKET LAW REVIEW 351 (1999)

Nicholas Lavender, *The Problem of the Margin of Appreciation*, 4 EUROPEAN HUMAN RIGHTS LAW REVIEW 380 (1997)

Koen Lenaerts, *Constitutionalism and the Many Faces of Federalism*, 38 AMERICAN JOURNAL OF COMPARATIVE LAW 205 (1990)

—— *Fundamental Rights to be Included in a Community Catalogue*, 16 EUROPEAN LAW REVIEW 367 (1991)

—— *Fundamental Rights in the European Union*, 25 EUROPEAN LAW REVIEW 575 (2000)

—— *Bricks for a Constitutional Treaty of the European Union: Values, Objectives and Means*, 27 EUROPEAN LAW REVIEW 377 (2002)

George Letsas, A Theory of Interpretation of the European Convention on Human Rights (Oxford University Press 2007)

Hans Lindahl, *European Integration: Popular Sovereignty and a Politics of Boundaries,* 6 European Law Journal 239 (2000)

Peter L. Lindseth, *Democratic Legitimacy and the Administrative Character of Supranationalism: The Example of the European Community,* 99 Columbia Law Review 628 (1999)

Diego J. Liñán Nogueras & Javier Roldán Barbero, *The Judicial Application of Community Law in Spain,* 30 Common Market Law Review 1135 (1993)

Neil MacCormick, *Beyond the Sovereign State,* 56 The Modern Law Review 1 (1993)

—— *The Maastricht-Urteil: Sovereignty Now,* 1 European Law Journal 259 (1995)

—— *Risking Constitutional Collision in Europe?,* 18 Oxford Journal of Legal Studies 517 (1998)

—— Questioning Sovereignty. Law, State and Nation in the European Commonwealth (Oxford University Press 1999)

Michael McConnell, *Federalism: Evaluating the Founder's Design,* 54 University of Chicago Law Review 1848 (1987)

—— *Institutions and Interpretations: A Critique of City of Boerne v. Flores,* 111 Harvard Law Review 153 (1997)

—— *The Right to Die and the Jurisprudence of Tradition,* Utah Law Review 665 (1997)

Christopher McCrudden, *A Common Law of Human Rights?: Transnational Judicial Conversations on Constitutional Rights,* 20 Oxford Journal of Legal Studies 499 (2000)

Miguel Poiares Maduro, *Las Formas del Poder Constitucional de la Unión Europea,* 119 Revista de Estudios Políticos 11 (2003)

Paul Mahoney, *Judicial Activism and Judicial Self-Restraint in the European Court of Human Rights: Two Sides of the Same Coin,* 11 Human Rights Law Journal 57 (1990)

—— *Marvelous Richness of Diversity or Invidious Cultural Relativism?,* 19 Human Rights Law Journal 1 (1998)

G. Federico Mancini, *The Making of a Constitution for Europe,* 26 Common Market Law Review 595 (1989)

—— & David T. Keeling, *Democracy and the European Court of Justice,* 57 The Modern Law Review 175 (1995)

Thomas de la Mare, *Article 177 in Social and Political Context,* in The Evolution of EU Law 216 (Paul Craig & Gráinne de Búrca eds. 1999)

Walter Mattli & Anne-Marie Slaughter, *The Role of National Courts in the Process of European Integration: Accounting for Judicial Preference and Constraints*, in The European Court and National Courts, Doctrine and Jurisprudence. Legal Change in its Social Context 253 (Anne-Marie Slaughter, Alec Stone Sweet & Joseph H. H. Weiler eds. 1998)

Deborah Jones Merritt, *The Guarantee Clause and State Autonomy: Federalism for a Third Century*, 88 Columbia Law Review 1 (1988)

Frank I. Michelman, *Traces of Self-Government*, 100 Harvard Law Review 4 (1986)

Franck Moderne, *La Notion de Droit Fondamental dans les Traditions Constitutionnelles des Etats Membres de l'Union Européenne*, in Réalité et Perspectives du Droit Communautaire des Droits Fondamentaux 35 (Frédéric Sudre & Henri Labayle eds. 2000)

Michael S. Moore, *A Natural Law Theory of Interpretation*, 58 Southern California Law Review 277 (1985)

Kalypso Nicolaidis & Robert Howse (eds.), The Federal Vision: Legitimacy and Levels of Governance in the United States and the European Union (Oxford University Press 2001)

Nanette A. Neuwahl, *Article 173 Paragraph 4 EC: Past, Present and Possible Future*, 21 European Law Review 17 (1996)

Carlos Santiago Nino, The Ethics of Human Rights (Clarendon Press 1991)

—— The Constitution of Deliberative Democracy (Yale University Press 1996)

Thomas A. O'Donnell, *The Margin of Appreciation Doctrine: Standards in the Jurisprudence of the European Court of Human Rights*, 4 Human Rights Quarterly 474 (1982)

Siofra O'Leary, *Aspects of the Relationship between Community Law and National Law*, in The European Union and Human Rights 23 (Nanette A. Neuwahl & Allan Rosas eds. 1995)

Rodger A. Payne & Nayef H. Samhat, Democratizing Global Politics (State University of New York Press 2004)

Kathryn A. Perales, *It Works Fine in Europe, so Why not Here? Comparative Law and Constitutional Federalism*, 23 Vermont Law Review 885 (1999)

Ingolf Pernice, *Multilevel Constitutionalism and the Treaty of Amsterdam: European Constitution-Making Revisited?*, 36 Common Market Law Review 703 (1999)

—— *Integrating the Charter of Fundamental Rights into the Constitution of the European Union: Practical and Theoretical Propositions*, 10 Columbia Journal of European Law 5, 23–25 (2003–2004)

Michael J. Perry, *The Authority of Text, Tradition, and Reason: A Theory of Constitutional 'Interpretation'*, 58 SOUTHERN CALIFORNIA LAW REVIEW 551 (1985)

Pierre Pescatore, *The Protection of Human Rights in the European Communities*, 9 COMMON MARKET LAW REVIEW 73 (1979)

―― *Le Recours, dans la Jurisprudence de la Cour de Justice des Communautés Européennes, a des Normes Déduites de la Comparaison des Droits des Etats Membres*, 2 REVUE INTERNATIONALE DE DROIT COMPARÉ 337 (1980)

MONTSERRAT PI LLORENS, LOS DERECHOS FUNDAMENTALES EN EL ORDE-NAMIENTO COMUNITARIO (Ariel 1999)

―― LA CARTA DE LOS DERECHOS FUNDAMENTALES DE LA UNIÓN EUROPEA (CEI 2001)

Fabrice Picod, *Les Sources*, in RÉALITÉ ET PERSPECTIVES DU DROIT COMMUNAUTAIRE DES DROITS FONDAMENTAUX 125 (Frédéric Sudre & Henri Labayle eds. 2000)

Robert C. Post, *Justice Brennan and Federalism*, 7 CONSTITUTIONAL COM-MENTARY 236 (1990)

―― *Foreword: Fashioning the Legal Constitution: Culture, Courts and Law*, 117 HARVARD LAW REVIEW 4 (2003)

―― & Reva Siegel, *Equal Protection by Law: Federal Antidiscrimination Legislation After Morrison and Kimel*, 110 YALE LAW JOURNAL 441 (2000)

Ulrich K. Preuss, *Problems of a Concept of European Citizenship*, 1 EUROPEAN LAW JOURNAL 267 (1995)

Andrezej Rapaczynski, *From Sovereignty to Process: The Jurisprudence of Federalism after Garcia*, 8 THE SUPREME COURT REVIEW 341 (1985)

HJALTE RASMUSSEN, ON LAW AND POLICY IN THE EUROPEAN COURT OF JUSTICE (Martinus Nijhoff Publishers 1986)

―― *Between Self-Restraint and Activism: A Judicial Policy for the European Court*, 13 EUROPEAN LAW REVIEW 28 (1988)

JOHN RAWLS, POLITICAL LIBERALISM (Columbia University Press 1995)

―― *The Law of Peoples*, in ON HUMAN RIGHTS. THE OXFORD AMNESTY LECTURES 1993 41 (Stephen Shute & Susan Hurley eds. 1995).

Norbert Reich, *Judge-made 'Europe à la carte': Some Remarks on Recent Conflicts between European and German Constitutional Law Provoked by the Banana Litigation*, 7 EUROPEAN JOURNAL OF INTERNATIONAL LAW 103 (1996)

J. Rinze, *The Role of the European Court of Justice as a Federal Constitutional Court*, PUBLIC LAW 426 (1993)

Thomas Risse, *'Let's Argue!'; Communicative Action in World Politics*, 54 INTERNATIONAL ORGANIZATION 1 (2000)

Gil C. Rodríguez Iglesias & Alejandro Valle Gálvez, *El Derecho Comunitario y las Relaciones entre el Tribunal de Justicia de las Comunidades Europeas, el Tribunal Europeo de Derechos Humanos y los Tribunales Constitucionales*, 1 Revista de Derecho Comunitario Europeo 336 (2000)

Carlos F. Rosenkrantz, *Against Borrowings and Other Nonauthoritative Uses of Foreign Law*, 1 International Journal of Constitutional Law 269 (2003)

Jed Rubenfeld, *Legitimacy and Interpretation*, in Constitutionalism. Philosophical Foundations 194 (Larry Alexander ed. 1998)

—— *Unilateralism and Constitutionalism*, 79 New York University Law Review 1971 (2004)

Edward L. Rubin & Malcolm Feeley, *Federalism: Some Notes on a National Neurosis*, 41 UCLA Law Review 903 (1994)

—— *Puppy Federalism and the Blessings of America*, 574 Annals Am. Acad. Pol. & Soc. Sci. 37 (2001)

Francisco Rubio Llorente, *Mostrar los Derechos sin Destruir la Unión (Consideraciones sobre la Carta de Derechos Fundamentales de la Unión Europea)*, 64 Revista Española de Derecho Constitucional 13 (2002)

John G. Ruggie, *Territoriality and Beyond: Problematizing Modernity in International Relations*, 47 International Organization 139 (1993)

Wojciech Sadurski, *Charter and Enlargement*, 8 European Law Journal 340 (2002)

—— *Accession's Democracy Dividend: The Impact of the EU Enlargement upon Democracy in the New Member States of Central and Eastern Europe*, 10 European Law Journal 371 (2004)

Alejandro Saiz Arnaiz, La Apertura Constitucional al Derecho Internacional y Europeo de los Derechos Humanos. El Artículo 10.2 de la Constitución Española (Consejo General del Poder Judicial 1999)

—— *El Tribunal de Justicia, los Tribunales Constitucionales y la Tutela de los Derechos Fundamentales en la Unión Europea: entre el (potencial) Conflicto y la (deseable) Armonización. De los Principios no escritos al Catálogo Constitucional, de la Autoridad judicial a la Normativa*, in Constitución Europea y Constituciones Nacionales 531 (Marta Cartabia, Bruno de Witte & Pablo Pérez Tremps eds. 2005)

Michael J. Sandel, Liberalism and the Limits of Justice (Cambridge University Press 1982)

Daniel Sarmiento, *European Union: The European Arrest Warrant and the Quest for Constitutional Coherence*, International Journal of Constitutional Law 1 (2008)

HENRY G. SCHERMERS ET AL. (eds.), ARTICLE 177 EEC: EXPERIENCES AND PROBLEMS (Elsevier Science Publishers 1987)
—— *The European Communities Bound by Fundamental Human Rights*, 27 COMMON MARKET LAW REVIEW 249 (1990)
Ulrich Scheuner, *Fundamental Rights in European Community Law and in National Constitutional Law*, 12 COMMON MARKET LAW REVIEW 171 (1975)
Theodor Schilling, *The Autonomy of the Community Legal Order—An Analysis of Possible Foundations*, 37 HARVARD INTERNATIONAL LAW JOURNAL 389 (1996)
Christoph U. Schmid, *From Pont d'Avignon to Ponte Vecchio. The Resolution of Constitutional Conflicts between the European Union and the Member States through Principles of Public International Law*, European University Institute Working Paper No. 98/7 (1998)
—— *Correspondence: The Neglected Conciliation Approach to the 'Final Arbiter' Conflict: A Critical Comment on Kumm 'Who is the Final Arbiter of Constitutionality in Europe?'*, 36 COMMON MARKET LAW REVIEW 509 (1999)
—— *All Bark and No Bite: Notes on the Federal Constitutional Court's 'Banana Decision'*, 7 EUROPEAN LAW JOURNAL 95 (2001)
Jeoren Schokkenbroek, *The Basis, Nature and Application of the Margin-of-Appreciation Doctrine in the Case-Law of the European Court of Human Rights*, 19 HUMAN RIGHTS LAW JOURNAL 30 (1998)
SILVANA SCIARRA (ed.), LABOUR LAW IN THE COURTS. NATIONAL JUDGES AND THE EUROPEAN COURT OF JUSTICE (Hart Publishing 2001)
DAVID L. SHAPIRO, FEDERALISM. A DIALOGUE (Northwestern University Press 1995)
MARTIN SHAPIRO, FREEDOM OF SPEECH: THE SUPREME COURT AND JUDICIAL REVIEW (Prentice-Hall 1966)
—— & ALEC STONE SWEET, ON LAW, POLITICS AND JUDICIALIZATION (Oxford University Press 2002)
LARRY SIEDENTOP, DEMOCRACY IN EUROPE (Penguin Books 2001)
Spiros Simitis, *The Complexities of Living with an Interpretation Prerogative— Some Observations on an Imperfect Dialogue*, in LABOUR LAW IN THE COURTS. NATIONAL JUDGES AND THE EUROPEAN COURT OF JUSTICE 291 (Silvana Sciarra ed. 2001)
Anne-Marie Slaughter, *A Typology of Transjudicial Communication*, 29 UNIVERSITY OF RICHMOND LAW REVIEW 99 (1994)
—— *The Real New World Order*, 76 FOREIGN AFFAIRS 183 (1997)

Anne-Marie Slaughter, *Judicial Globalization*, 40 Virginia Journal Of International Law 1103 (2000)

—— *A Global Community of Courts*, 44 Harvard International Law Journal 191 (2003)

—— Alec Stone Sweet & Joseph H. H. Weiler (eds.), The European Court and National Courts, Doctrine and Jurisprudence. Legal Change in its Social Context (Oxford 2000)

Jens Steffek, *The Legitimation of International Governance: A Discourse Approach*, 9 European Journal of International Relations 249 (2003)

Eric Stein, *Lawyers, Judges, and the Making of a Transnational Constitution*, 75 American Journal of International Law 1 (1981)

—— *Uniformity and Diversity in a Divided-Power System: The United States' Experience*, 61 Washington Law Review 1081 (1986)

Alec Stone Sweet, *Constitutional Dialogues in the European Community*, in The European Court and National Courts, Doctrine and Jurisprudence. Legal Change in its Social Context 305 (Anne-Marie Slaughter, Alec Stone Sweet & Joseph H. H. Weiler eds. 1998)

—— *Judicialization and the Construction of Governance*, 32 Comparative Political Studies 147 (1999)

—— Governing with Judges. Constitutional Politics in Europe (Oxford University Press 2000)

—— & Thomas L. Brunnell, *The European Court, National Judges, and Legal Integration: A Researcher's Guide to the Data Set on Preliminary References in EC Law, 1958–98*, 6 European Law Journal 117 (2000)

—— & Helen Keller (eds.), A Europe of Rights: The Impact of the ECHR on National Legal Systems (Oxford University Press 2008)

Cass R. Sunstein, *Beyond the Republican Revival*, 97 Yale Law Journal 1539 (1988)

—— *Incompletely Theorized Agreements*, 108 Harvard Law Review 1733 (1995)

—— Legal Reasoning and Political Conflict (Oxford University Press 1996)

John Temple Lang, *The Sphere in which Member States are Obliged to Comply with the General Principles of Law and Community Fundamental Rights Principles*, 2 Legal Issues of European Integration 23 (1991)

James B. Thayer, *The Origin and Scope of the American Doctrine of Constitutional Law*, 7 Harvard Law Review 129 (1983)

Neus Torbisco Casals, Groups Rights as Human Rights (Springer 2006)

Aida Torres Pérez, *La Dimensión Estructural de la Carta de Derechos Fundamentales de la Unión Europea. Relaciones Verticales y Cláusulas Horizontales*, 67 Revista Vasca de Administración Pública 253 (2003)

Takis Tridimas, The General Principles of EC Law (Oxford University Press 1999)

Mark Tushnet, *The Possibilities of Comparative Constitutional Law*, 108 Yale Law Journal 1225 (1999)

Tom R. Tyler, Why People Obey the Law (Yale University Press 1990)

Juan Ignacio Ugartemendia Eceizabarrena, *Una Reflexión Acerca de la Influencia del Derecho Comunitario sobre la Concepción Estatal de los Derechos Fundamentales*, 58-II Revista Vasca de Administración Pública 65 (2000)

—— El Derecho Comunitario y el Legislador de los Derechos Fundamentales. Un Estudio de la Influencia Comunitaria sobre la Fundamentalidad de los Derechos Fundamentales (IVAP 2001)

Antonio Vitorino, *La Charte des Droits Fondamentaux de l'Union Européenne*, 3 Revue du Droit de l'Union Européenne 499 (2000)

Mary L. Volcansek, Judicial Politics in Europe (Peter Lang 1986)

Jeremy Waldron, *Vagueness in Law and Language: Some Philosophical Issues*, 82 California Law Review 509 (1994)

—— Law and Disagreement (Oxford University Press 1999)

Neil Walker, *Flexibility within a Metaconstitutional Frame: Reflections on the Future of Legal Authority in Europe*, in Constitutional Change in the EU. From Uniformity to Flexibility? 9 (Gráinne de Búrca & Joanne Scott eds. 2000)

—— *The Idea of Constitutional Pluralism*, 65 The Modern Law Review 317 (2002)

Christian Walter, *Constitutionalizing (Inter)national Governance—Possibilities for and Limits to the Development of an International Constitutional Law*, 44 German Yearbook of International Law 171 (2001)

Ian Ward, *Identity and Difference: The European Union and Postmodernism*, in New Legal Dynamics of European Union 15 (Jo Shaw & Gillian More eds. 1995)

—— The Margins of European Law (St. Martin's Press 1996)

Herbert Wechsler, *The Political Safeguards of Federalism*, 54 Columbia Law Review 543 (1954)

Joseph H. H. Weiler, *Eurocracy and Distrust: Some Questions Concerning the Role of the European Court of Justice in the Protection of Fundamental Rights within the Legal Order on the European Communities*, 61 Washington Law Review 1103 (1986)

Joseph H. H. Weiler, *The European Court at a Crossroads: Community Human Rights and Member State Action*, in Du Droit International au Droit de l'Intégration 821 (F. Capotorti et al. eds. 1987)

—— *The Transformation of Europe*, 100 Yale Law Journal 2403 (1991)

—— *Methods of Protection: Towards a Second and Third Generation of Protection*, in II Human Rights and the European Community: Methods of Protection 555 (Antonio Cassese, Andrew Clapham & Joseph H. H. Weiler eds. 1991)

—— *A Quiet Revolution. The European Court of Justice and its Interlocutors*, 26 Comparative Political Studies 510 (1994)

—— *Does Europe Need a Constitution? Reflections on Demos, Telos and the German Maastricht Decision*, 1 European Law Journal 219 (1995)

—— *The European Union Belongs to its Citizens: Three Immodest Proposals*, 33 European Law Review 150 (1997)

—— The Constitution of Europe (Cambridge University Press 1999)

—— *Editorial: Does the European Union Truly Need a Charter of Rights?*, 6 European Law Journal 95 (2000)

—— *Epilogue: The Judicial Après Nice*, in The European Court of Justice 215 (Gráinne de Búrca & Joseph H. H. Weiler eds. 2001)

—— *Federalism Without Constitutionalism: Europe's Sonderweg*, in The Federal Vision 54 (Kalypso Nicolaidis & Robert Howse eds. 2003)

—— & Nicolas J. S. Lockhart, *'Taking Rights Seriously' Seriously: The European Court of Justice and its Fundamental Rights Jurisprudence*, 32 Common Market Law Review 51 (1995)

—— & Ulrich R. Haltern, *The Autonomy of the Community Legal Order—Through the Looking Glass*, 37 Harvard International Law Journal 411 (1996)

Arthur E. Wilmarth, Jr., *The Original Purpose of the Bill of Rights: James Madison and the Founders' Search for a Workable Balance between Federal and State Power*, 26 American Criminal Law Review 1261 (1989)

Bruno de Witte, *Community Law and National Constitutional Values*, 2 Legal Issues of Economic Integration 1 (1991)

—— *Sovereignty and European Integration: The Weight of Legal Tradition*, in The European Court and National Courts, Doctrine and Jurisprudence. Legal Change in its Social Context 277 (Anne-Marie Slaughter, Alec Stone Sweet & Joseph H. H. Weiler eds. 1998)

—— *The Past and Future of the European Court of Justice in the Protection of Human Rights*, in The EU and Human Rights 859 (Philip Alston ed. 1999)

Bruno de Witte, *The Closest Thing to a Constitutional Conversation in Europe: The Semi-Permanente Treaty Revision Process*, in CONVERGENCE AND DIVERGENCE IN EUROPEAN PUBLIC LAW 39 (Paul Beaumont, Carole Lyons & Neil Walker eds. 2002)

Jan Wouters, *National Constitutions and the European Union*, 1 LEGAL ISSUES OF ECONOMIC INTEGRATION 25 (2000)

Ernest A. Young, *Protecting Member State Autonomy in the European Union: Some Cautionary Tales from American Federalism*, 77 NEW YORK UNIVERSITY LAW REVIEW 1612 (2002)

HOWARD CHARLES YOUROW, THE MARGIN OF APPRECIATION DOCTRINE IN THE DYNAMICS OF EUROPEAN HUMAN RIGHTS JURISPRUDENCE (Martinus Nijhoff Publishers 1996)

Manfred Zuleeg, *A Community of Law: Legal Cohesion in the European Union*, 40 FORDHAM INTERNATIONAL LAW JOURNAL 623 (1997)

INDEX